Urban Gardening FOR DUMMIES®

by Paul Simon, Charlie Nardozzi, and The Editors of the National Gardening Association

WILEY

John Wiley & Sons, Inc.

Urban Gardening For Dummies®

Published by
John Wiley & Sons, Inc.
111 River St.
Hoboken, NJ 07030-5774
www.wiley.com

WILEY

About the Authors

Paul Simon is a nationally recognized landscape architect, public artist, horticulturist, master gardener, and urban designer. With over 20 years of experience, Paul brings a wealth of knowledge, skills, and abilities from various fields in the gardening, horticulture, and design industries.

Paul holds a B.S. in Landscape Architecture from the University of Kentucky with a diverse curriculum in site design, urban design, community planning, geography, architecture, plant and soil sciences, forestry, and civil engineering. He is also an esteemed member of the American Society of Landscape Architects.

Paul is personally committed and driven toward solving developable solutions while maintaining professional integrity and respect for the environment.

Many of his projects specialize in urban design, parks and community gardens, public art, outdoor learning, and green design initiatives — some of which have been nationally published, recognized, and awarded. Paul is also driven to create human environments that are sustainable, socially relevant, economically feasible, and user functional.

In addition, Paul is involved as a horticultural editor for `www.kids gardening.org`. Kids Gardening is a leading national provider of K-12, plant-based educational materials, providing programs and initiatives for plant-based education in schools, communities, and backyards across the country. Paul continues to provide unique articles underscoring the importance of kids gardening and outdoor learning.

Charlie Nardozzi is a nationally recognized garden writer, speaker, and radio and television personality. He has worked for more than 20 years bringing expert gardening information to home gardeners through radio, television, talks, online, and the printed page. Charlie delights in making gardening information simple, easy, fun, and accessible to everyone. His energy, exuberance, and love of the natural world also make him an exciting public speaker and presenter. He has spoken at national venues such as the Philadelphia Flower Show, Master Gardener conferences, and trade shows.

Charlie is a garden coach and consultant teaching and inspiring home gardeners to grow the best vegetables, fruits, flowers, trees, and shrubs in their yards.

Charlie co-hosts *In The Garden*, tips on the local CBS affiliate television station (WCAX-Channel 3), a weekly, call-in radio show on WJOY-1230AM, and the *Vermont Garden Journal* on Vermont Public Radio.

Charlie is also known for his writing. He has written for national magazines such as *Organic Gardening* and contributed to many of the *For Dummies* gardening titles, authoring *Vegetable Gardening For Dummies* in 2009. He also authored the *Ultimate Gardener* (HCI Press, 2009) which highlights heart-warming stories about the trials and tribulations of gardening and *Northeast Fruit and Vegetable Gardening* in (Cool Springs Press, April, 2012). He also contributed to other book project such as *Vegetables from an Italian Garden* (Phaidon Press, 2011).

Charlie's skills as a garden communicator extend beyond the printed page. He's the former host of PBS's *Garden Smart*, reaching more than 60 million households. He has also been a gardening expert on many national syndicated television and radio shows such as HGTV's *Today at Home*, Discovery Channel's *Home Matters*, Sirius Radio's *Martha Stewart Living*, and *Garden Life Radio*

Charlie also works with companies/organizations to provide horticultural guidance on special adult and kids projects. He's worked with the Hilton Garden Inn on their "Grow a School Garden Project," Gardener's Supply Company and Stonyfield Yogurt on their "Eat a Rainbow Project," and farm-to-school programs with Shelburne Farms and Northeast Organic Farmers Association (NOFA).

He was the senior horticulturist and spokesperson for the National Gardening Association (NGA), where he wrote and edited articles for their magazine and online newsletters, conducted media interviews about gardening, and provided horticultural consultation to NGA programs.

Authors' Acknowledgments

From Paul: I'd like to take this opportunity to express my gratitude to the many people who have been instrumental over the years in developing my background as an urban designer, horticulturist, landscape architect, and public artist.

Thanks to my parents John and Kristine Simon and my uncle Albert Bremer who helped guide me many years ago into the horticulture and design professions. Thanks to former employers including Quansett Nurseries in South Dartmouth Massachusetts and Hillenmeyer Nurseries in Lexington Kentucky who have taught me so much about the planting, nursery, and landscaping industries.

Big thanks to the University of Kentucky College of Agriculture and the Landscape Architecture Department for their well-rounded teachings to design human environments that are sustainable, socially relevant, artful, and functional, especially professors Janice Cervelli, Thomas Nieman, Horst Schach, and Ned Crankshaw. Also thanks to the University of Vermont Extension Master Gardener program which does incredible work recruiting, training, and overseeing volunteer extension master gardeners and multiple gardening programs and opportunities.

Special thanks to the National Gardening Association for the opportunity to co-author a book with Charlie Nardozzi and provide an A to Z guide on Urban Gardening practices. And a super-special thanks to Susan Littlefield who has helped edit many of the chapters and continues to provide professional horticultural guidance and expertise in addition to her editorial support.

Thanks to Nancy Reinhardt for copyediting and Mike Pecen for his technical review of the chapter submissions and Kathryn Born for illustrations. Also thanks to Chrissy Guthrie and Erin Calligan Mooney for their consistent help in guiding chapter submissions and scheduling the timely management for the books completion.

Finally, thanks to my wife Rubi and my children Nathalie, Olivia, and Elena who together share the love and passion for gardening, and to my mother-in-law Norma who has helped our busy family keep it together.

From Charlie: I'd like to thank Chrissy Guthrie and Erin Mooney for their expertise in keeping the book on target. Thanks to the National Gardening Association for the opportunity to write another *For Dummies* book and to Paul Simon, my co-author, for being so easy to work with, offering his expertise in landscape architecture and gardening. I appreciate Kathryn Born for her illustrations, Nancy Reinhardt for her keen eye while copyediting, Mike Pecen for his horticultural review of the chapters, and Susan Littlefield for editing every chapter.

Dedications

From Paul: I would like to dedicate this book to all of you who are digging into the earth, greening our cities, and sharing your knowledge to support a sustainable future for all.

From Charlie: I dedicate this book to all those budding gardeners in urban areas who are transforming concrete jungles into thriving, vibrant, green communities, growing food for themselves and their neighbors, reversing crime and pollution, and generally creating a wholesome place to live.

Publisher's Acknowledgments

We're proud of this book; please send us your comments at http://dummies.custhelp.com. For other comments, please contact our Customer Care Department within the U.S. at 877-762-2974, outside the U.S. at 317-572-3993, or fax 317-572-4002.

Some of the people who helped bring this book to market include the following:

Acquisitions, Editorial, and Vertical Websites

Senior Project Editor: Christina Guthrie

Acquisitions Editor: Erin Calligan Mooney

Copy Editors: Amanda Langferman, Nancy Reinhardt, Jessica Smith

Assistant Editor: David Lutton

Editorial Program Coordinator: Joe Niesen

Technical Editor: Mike Pecen, ASLA

Editorial Manager: Christine Meloy Beck

Editorial Assistants: Rachelle Amick, Alexa Koschier

Art Coordinator: Alicia B. South

Cover Photos: FRONT: © Compassionate Eye Foundation/Steven Errico / Getty Images BACK: © Chuck Eckert / Alamy BACK: © jean gill / iStockphoto.com

Cartoons: Rich Tennant (www.the5thwave.com)

Composition Services

Project Coordinator: Sheree Montgomery

Layout and Graphics: Jennifer Creasey, Joyce Haughey, Christin Swinford

Proofreaders: John Greenough, Christine Sabooni

Indexer: Ty Koontz

Illustrators: Kathryn Born, Ron Hildebrand

Publishing and Editorial for Consumer Dummies

    Kathleen Nebenhaus, Vice President and Executive Publisher

    David Palmer, Associate Publisher

    Kristin Ferguson-Wagstaffe, Product Development Director

Publishing for Technology Dummies

    Andy Cummings, Vice President and Publisher

Composition Services

    Debbie Stailey, Director of Composition Services

Contents at a Glance

Table of Contents

Introduction

••

*U*rban gardening trends are undoubtedly on the rise, and the excitement to green our cities and develop edible landscapes is being shared across the world. City planning officials and municipalities are recognizing this healthy trend and taking appropriate measures to redraft regulations in support of many urban agricultural initiatives. Individuals and local organizations are forming grassroots alliances to make urban areas more livable and self-sustaining. Of course the urban environment certainly presents its own set of challenges, but with the right tools, know-how, and a little help, a dedicated urban gardener can succeed — and we hope this book can provide you some guidance along the way.

The ways to garden the city are as varied as our cities are. Your ambition may be to transform a vacant lot, an underutilized parking area, or your back deck or patio into a green oasis. Perhaps you wish to become involved in a community garden association, or build your own urban farm? Whatever level of gardening you choose, you are on the right path supporting the health of our environment and a renewal of our cities.

About This Book

This book provides a complete A–Z guide for the urban gardener. Topics include preparing urban soil conditions, how to plant, where you can plant, and the many types of plantings suitable for urban gardens. And, of course, urban edibles are especially covered.

You also discover some techniques for reducing air and water pollution and how gardens may reduce crime, increase property values, and contribute to healthier, improved neighborhoods.

From rooftops, balconies, patios, along walls and stairways, or growing indoors, we cover many urban gardening techniques and trends to help get you started right away!

Conventions Used in This Book

To help you navigate through this book, we included some conventions to follow:

- ✔ All references to temperature are in degrees Fahrenheit (F) and measurements in feet and inches.

- ✔ When we refer to plant hardiness, we are using the U.S. Department of Agriculture Plant Hardiness Zone Map, which you can find at `http://planthardiness.ars.usda.gov/PHZMWeb`.

- ✔ When we refer to the Extension Service, we're talking about the government- or university-sponsored service that offers helpful information on gardening. The Master Gardeners we refer to are volunteers trained by horticultural professionals in each state to also offer gardening advice. The Extension Service can be found through your local land-grant university, such as the University of Connecticut. The Master Gardeners for the United States and Canada can be found for each state on this website: `www.extension.org/pages/9925/state-and-provincial-master-gardener-programs:-extension-and-affiliated-program-listings`.

- ✔ Most plant types are listed first by common name and then by botanical name initials.

Following are a few other conventions to keep in mind:

- ✔ Whenever a new term is introduced in a chapter, it appears in *italic,* followed by a brief definition or cross-reference.

- ✔ Key words or phrases appear in **bold.**

- ✔ Numbered steps also appear in **bold.**

What You're Not to Read

Although we'd love it if you read every word we've written and kept *Urban Gardening For Dummies* by your bedside table for midnight inspirations, we realize urban gardeners (like everyone else) are busy people. So, if you want the meat and potatoes of the book, you can skip over the sidebars and any text marked with the Technical Stuff icon. Sidebars appear in gray boxes and feature interesting but nonessential information that's related to the main text. The Technical Stuff icon features information that is beyond need-to-know but that further enhances your understanding of a given topic.

Foolish Assumptions

Every book starts with a few assumptions about who will be reading it. While most don't state their assumptions, we're going to be right up front with ours:

- ✔ You live in a small to large city and are interested in growing plants safely.
- ✔ You know someone in a small to large city who you think is interested in growing plants safely.
- ✔ You know someone in a small to large city who you think should be interested in growing plants safely.
- ✔ You don't have much gardening experience.
- ✔ You want to improve your physical surroundings, adding greenery, healthy food plants, and wildlife habitat to your yard all while growing the plants organically.
- ✔ You're even willing to sacrifice precious deck and balcony space for a few pots filled with delicious herbs and greens.
- ✔ You want to share and impress your friends and family with the amount of garden beauty and food you can grow in the city on the ground, roof, wall, or public space.

How This Book Is Organized

Like most Dummies books, *Urban Gardening For Dummies* is broken into parts. Each part has chapters related to that theme. Here's an overview to get you started.

Part 1: Urban Gardening 101

In Part I, we give you an overview of urban gardening, including preparing your soil, planting, and where you can place the many types of plantings suitable for urban gardens, especially edibles! Chapter 1 covers city gardening and how you can best develop your urban green thumb. In Chapter 2, we show you how urban landscapes help reduce air and water pollution and how gardens may reduce crime, increase property values, and contribute to healthier, improved neighborhoods. In Chapter 3, we describe the urban microclimate, including the urban *Heat Island Effect,* local weather patterns, and how you can actually influence weather conditions at micro-level to benefit the health of your urban garden.

Part II: Gardening Basics

In Part II, the digging really begins — in the soil, that is. Chapter 4 discusses analyzing soil types, understanding soil pH, drainage, and poor and contaminated soil conditions. In Chapter 5, we give you the scoop on how you can build good soil for your garden with manure, organic fertilizers, and compost. In Chapter 6, you'll discover when to seed, when to transplant, and how to select the right plants for your garden. We even show you some tricks of the trade for planting annuals, veggies, perennials, roses, trees, and shrubs.

Part III: Places and Ways to Garden

So where can you garden in the city? Head over to Part III for answers to this question from the ground up. Chapter 7 shows you ways to create a beautiful and artful outdoor room with arbors, recycled materials, and water features. In Chapter 8, we get funky with container gardening and show you creative ways to plant pots of every possible shape and size. Apartment dwellers need not feel left out — Chapters 9, 10, and 11 take on building rooftop and balcony gardens and demonstrate some vertical growing strategies. Chapter 12 helps you find ways to green up city buildings and transform vacant lots into unique urban green spaces.

Part IV: Growing Plants in the City

Whether you're gardening in a container on an apartment balcony or in a community garden, or even in your own backyard, you need to know the basics of growing all your favorite plants. Part IV gives you the *how-to* information on growing edibles, flowers, trees, shrubs, and lawns. In Chapter 13, we get into the nitty-gritty of how to plant your own vegetable garden. Flowers are up next in Chapters 14 and 15, where we discuss annual and perennial flower gardens. In Chapter 16, you see how to select and plant the right tree or shrub for your yard. Chapter 17 covers (ahem) how to keep your urban lawn and ground covers growing strong.

Part V: Growing to Perfection

All your gardens are planted and your flowers and veggies are starting to bloom; it's time to find out how to care for your new green babies. Chapter 18 describes how to weed your gardens and the advantages of using various mulches to keep weeds at bay and retain soil moisture. Water is a critical element to any garden, so in Chapter 19 we show you the best ways to water your plants, as well as save money and time. Even the best garden can have trouble with insects, diseases, and animals. Chapter 20 identifies some of the worst offenders and gives you organic solutions for stopping them in their tracks.

Part VI: The Part of Tens

No *For Dummies* book is complete without a "Part of Tens," and this one includes some great gardening tips. From the top ten essential garden tools to ten kid-friendly ways to garden in the city, Part VI offers an assortment of helpful and creative urban gardening solutions. We even include a chapter on ten ways to develop a *sustainable* urban garden, including how to involve your community and collaborate with others.

Icons Used in This Book

Like all *For Dummies* books, this one has icons that highlight tips, warnings, technical stuff, and things to remember. Here are the ones we use in this book.

This icon highlights important information that makes you a better gardener. It's stuff you don't want to forget.

This stuff is for the gardener that wants to understand more and go a little deeper. It's not essential, but it's certainly cool information.

This icon highlights tips that help you save time, money, and resources. Everyone can use those kinds of tips!

This icon keeps you alert to possible problems that may arise, even in the garden. We try to help you avoid mistakes by pointing out possible gardening pitfalls.

Where to Go from Here

You are one of a growing herd of people gardening in the city. Feel proud. Not only are you creating beauty and food for yourself and your family, you're helping make cities more livable places and reducing your urban area's dependence on outside resources for energy and food.

Use this book as a starting place to inspire and inform you on how to get started greening your city. Skip to the chapters that interest you most to get the information you need to grow plants and create gardens. But don't stop here. Check with local resources, organizations, and other gardeners you meet to share information and ideas so that you can grow a green and prosperous city for all to enjoy.

And if you're looking for more detailed information about growing specific plants or specific growing methods, check out some of the other *For Dummies* gardening books, such as *Organic Gardening For Dummies,* 2nd Edition, by Ann Whitman, Suzanne DeJohn, and the National Gardening Association; *Herb Gardening For Dummies,* 2nd Edition, by Karan Davis Cutler, Kathleen Fisher, Suzanne DeJohn, and the National Gardening Association; *Container Gardening For Dummies,* 2nd Edition, by Bill Marken, Suzanne DeJohn, and the Editors of the National Gardening Association; *Vegetable Gardening For Dummies,* 2nd Edition, by Charlie Nardozzi; *Lawn Care For Dummies,* by Lance Walheim and the National Gardening Association; and *Roses For Dummies,* 2nd Edition, by Lance Walheim and the Editors of the National Gardening Association.

Part I
Urban Gardening 101

The 5th Wave   By Rich Tennant

"It's my husband's idea of a drip irrigation system."

In this part...

In this part, we provide an overview of urban gardening, from preparing healthy soil conditions to how to plant, from where you can plant to the many types of plantings suitable for urban gardens, especially edibles! We also discuss how urban landscapes help reduce air and water pollution and how gardens may reduce crime, increase property values, and contribute to healthier, improved neighborhoods. Finally, we describe the urban microclimate, including the urban *Heat Island Effect,* local weather patterns, and how you can actually influence weather conditions at a micro-level to benefit the health of your urban garden.

Chapter 1

Gardening in the City

● ●

In This Chapter

▶ Understanding this urban gardening movement

▶ Getting the basics on building healthy soil

▶ Seeing the many creative ways to garden in a city

▶ Discovering what plants you can grow in urban environments

▶ Growing your plants well in the city

● ●

*A*s more and more people move to cities from rural areas, they bring their love and knowledge of gardens with them. We're seeing a renaissance of urban gardening in cities around the world. City dwellers are realizing that they can't just rely on rural farms and transportation to supply them with food, fuel, and the energy they need. Cities need to be inhabitable, and having clean air and water are top priorities for maintaining the quality of life in cities. Not only does a cleaner environment and fresher food make for a more livable city, it makes for healthier residents with fewer medical issues.

In this chapter, we give you an overview of all the ways you can garden in the city. We cover the basics of growing healthy soil, the many places to have a city garden, the types of plants that grow well in urban environments, and ways to keep them healthy.

Knowing the Basics of Soil Prep

Most people think of soil as nothing more than the dirt that's beneath their feet. They couldn't be more wrong. Soil is a living entity, and healthy soil is more than just the dirt you see in vacant lots or around construction sites. Plants need healthy soil to grow, and in the city, that becomes even more imperative. Cities stress plants with their heat, cold, wind, air and water pollution, vandalism, and soils lacking in nutrients. Healthy soils to the rescue! A healthy soil can keep your plants vibrant, and just like the human body, when plants are healthy they can better withstand all types of environmental stresses.

Here are some of the ways to nurture and build a healthy soil in the city. More details on soils are available in Chapter 4.

- ✔ **The living soil.** Soil is loaded with living organisms. These microbes help make nutrients, water, and minerals available to plants. Unhealthy soil is devoid of organic matter (the food of microbes), microbes, and any life-giving capacities. Your job as a gardener is to build up your soil so your plants will thrive. This can mean amending your existing soil with compost and other forms of organic matter or replacing your existing soil with something better.

- ✔ **Start with organic matter:** We wax poetic about the value and role organic matter plays in a healthy soil in Chapter 5. Street merchants don't peddle organic matter, but someday it may be considered that valuable. Right now though, many kinds of organic matter are available for free. Organic matter comes in many forms; hay, straw, untreated grass clippings, leaves, compost, manure, and pine needles. Knowing how to use it to feed your soil is important for a healthy garden.

- ✔ **A soil checkup:** Our bodies need a checkup every so often to make sure they are healthy, so why shouldn't your soil? It's important to figuratively take your soil's temperature by doing a soil test and other tests. Check the pH (measure of acidity and alkalinity). Check the water drainage to be sure your plants don't sit in wet soils too long. Wet soils can harm many types of plants. Analyze your soil for potential contaminants that may be in your patch of urban heaven. Knowing what you've got for soil helps you know what to do to improve it.

- ✔ **Feed your soil.** We all know that the foods we put in our bodies affect how we feel. Well, plants aren't any different. What you feed your trees, shrubs, and garden plants influences their health and growth rate. Knowing your plants and your soil helps you determine what fertilizers and amendments to add to make for healthier plants.

Finding the Many Places to Garden the City

Most people think of gardens as beautiful places in pastoral settings. Even in botanical gardens that grace most cities around the globe, the greenery and gardens there create a sanctuary that is fenced in and often hidden from view.

But cities have many places to garden beyond the botanical garden. Many city residents have a yard where they can tuck in gardens. In some communities, rules may be in place restricting where on your property you can garden and what you can plant. But city residents in many areas are challenging the notion they can't grow food gardens in their own front yard. Pulling up the traditional lawn and planting tomatoes, zinnias, and apples is just one way urbanities are gardening in the city. Here are some other obvious and not so obvious ways they also are growing greenery amidst the concrete and steel. We talk more about the many places and ways to garden in Part III.

- ✔ **Vacant lots.** Many cities are taking vacant lots and transforming them into small parks, green oases, and community gardens. These "community" gardens often take on the flavor of the residents and become meeting places for the neighborhood. Often the garden is a harbinger of change in the neighborhood. Once a garden springs up in a vacant lot, trash and litter may be picked up, graffiti replaced with murals, and decorative art work installed in the neighborhood. All this creates an identity reflecting the various cultural and ethnic backgrounds of the residents in the neighborhood.

- ✔ **Grow it in a pot.** Container gardening has revolutionized the ways people can grow plants in small spaces. Container growing helps avoid many soil issues because you are using soil specifically adapted to pot growing. Plus, if you don't have the spacc or proper conditions in the ground where you live, it's pots to the rescue. Containers not only fit in unusual places, like fire escapes, but they are mobile and can be moved with the sun and season.

- ✔ **Growing on the roof.** Rooftop gardens can produce food for a hungry city, reduce the urban Heat Island Effect (we talk about that in Chapter 3), and reduce storm water runoff. If the roof won't work, try the walls. Green wall gardens are springing up in many cities that not only have many of the same benefits as green roofs, but also visually soften the look and feel of a city block. We talk about green walls in Chapter 10. Trellises, pergolas, fences, and arbors are all ways to make use of the vertical space gardeners may have in their otherwise space-limited yard. Growing vines upward is a way to maximize what you have growing in the city.

- ✔ **Inside gardening.** You're probably getting the idea we believe you can garden anywhere outdoors in the city, but some folks have only a balcony or patio or live many stories up. The solution for these land-deprived residents is apartment gardens. Using grow lights and maximizing the light through windows, you can grow houseplants that clean your air and edible plants to provide food. Windowsill herb gardens and salad gardens under lights are just some of the ways apartment dwellers can jump on the green bandwagon. We'll talk more about apartment gardening in Chapter 11.

Growing All Kinds of Plants in The City

Now that you're convinced you really have more gardening opportunities than you thought in the city, naturally the next question is, "What should I grow?" Well, the simple answer is grow what you like. But that answer isn't enough for most city dwellers. There are soil, space, pollution, and other issues facing urban gardens. So it's important to grow the right plants for your area and, ideally, ones adapted to city culture. Take a look at some of the options.

Trees and shrubs

Trees and shrubs do more than dress up a yard. They provide shade, wildlife habitat, beauty, and potentially, food. It all starts with the right tree or shrub for your space. There may be utility lines above and below ground that workers need to access. The last thing you want is to buy and plant a tree and have it grow well for years, only to have the utility company come and cut it down when it begins to interfere with their lines. Planting a tree or shrub whose mature size is to big for the space available leads to drastic, harmful, and unattractive pruning.

You'll also need to find the right tree or shrub for the existing sun/shade conditions, climate, soil conditions, water availability, and wind conditions. It may sound daunting, but in Chapter 16, we highlight those trees and shrubs that can handle city life and keep performing for you.

If you're like many city dwellers, food gardening is becoming more of a priority, and growing berries and fruit trees fits perfectly with that vision. Dwarf varieties of fruit trees are well suited to small spaces, and self-pollinating fruit trees and berries allow you to enjoy a harvest from just one plant. Even a small city yard usually allows space for a delicious harvest of home-grown fruit!

Edibles

Speaking of edible gardening, vegetables and herbs also fit beautifully in city yards and containers. Whether in a community garden, front or back yard, or a large container, you can grow a whole host of vegetables in most cities. While the ultimate size of the plants isn't as big an issue with vegetables as it is with trees and shrubs (melons, winter squash ,and corn being the exceptions), it's still important to grow varieties adapted to your climate and space. Dwarf varieties of tomatoes and cucumbers, for example, make growing these popular veggies easier in containers.

The city has many potential problems the budding veggie gardener must deal with, but one thing is does help you with is the length of the growing season. Because cities tend to absorb heat during the day and radiate it out at night, the overall environment stays warmer than the surrounding countryside.

This means when your cousin upstate is getting frost, you may still have a few weeks of growing left. You can really push the envelope with devices that protect plants from frost such as cold frames and floating row covers.

 If you really want to grow edibles easily, try growing perennial herbs. Some perennial herbs can actually be called weeds, they're that tough to kill. Try a container filled with mint, lovage, or chives as a good way to start your edible garden. Once you see how easy it is to grow these, get going with annual herbs such as basil, parsley, and cilantro.

Annual flowers

Annual flowers are perhaps the easiest city plants to grow. They are bred to bloom their heads off all season long. Many annuals are small plants that easily fit in containers and small spaces. There is such a range of plant types and flower colors that you can become the van Gogh of the neighborhood just by arranging your annual flower varieties in beds or pots.

Probably the most important part of annual flower gardening is choosing the right plant for your location. (Does this advice sound like a broken record yet?) Some annuals like full sun and heat, while others like part shade and cool temperatures. Many people redesign the interior of their home periodically, picking up seasonal themes. You can do the same in the annual flower garden, changing your annual flower garden by the season. For example, grow cool weather-loving annuals in spring and fall and heat lovers in summer.

 The deadhead is dead. It used to be that deadheading annual flowers (clipping or pinching off the faded flowers) was the norm. Many new annual flower varieties drop their spent blossoms naturally and don't require deadheading. So all you have to do is keep the plants alive and they will thrive.

Perennial flowers and roses

If you like flowers but get tired of replanting each spring (after all, that's what annual flowers are, one and done), then go for perennial flowers. Most people think of perennial flowers in terms of broad borders filled with multicolored flowers of various colors and textures, like on an English country estate. Well, perennial flowers can be arranged like that, or they can also be used in many other ways in the garden.

Perennial flowers come back consistently each year, and some get larger and spread as well. While the flowers of some perennials, such as peonies and iris, may seem delicate, the plants themselves are long lived and tough as nails. I've seen perennial flowers, such as daylilies and bee balm, surviving in pavement cracks and abandoned lots in the city. As with annuals, you'll have to chose between sun and shade lovers.

Some perennials can be invasive, taking over an area if you don't watch out. Bee balm, lily of the valley, ajuga, and English ivy are just some of the aggressive perennials that may be great in a contained area but can wreak havoc in a garden by running rampant over less aggressive plants.

Roses are pure delight. They fit beautifully in an urban garden because many rose varieties are small in stature but big in the size and number of flowers. Some are even small enough to fit in containers. Hybrid roses need more attention compared to species and landscape varieties. Climbers are perfect for arbors and walkways. In Chapter 15, we talk all about variety selection, fertilizing, and pruning these shrubs so they stay healthy in your yard.

Lawns and groundcovers

It's tiring having concrete, asphalt, and gravel beneath your feet. If for no other reason, lawns are good for the spirit just because they give us something soft and comfortable to step on.

Lawns soften the urban environment in other ways. Grass quiets a yard, reduces storm water runoff, and provides habitat for microbes and wildlife. Although we've been known to trash the American lawn as a wasteful landscape feature, in the city, green is good. If lawns fit your landscape needs, then grow grass. Choose warm or cool season grass types, depending on where you live. Grow lawns in areas around your yard where you'll entertain, play games, or just hang out.

If your yard doesn't have enough sun for lawn grass, consider planting ground covers instead. Ones like vinca and sweet woodruff grow best in shady conditions — just what you find in many cities. The right groundcover grown on healthy soil will spread to fill areas under trees and around shrubs. They create the green lawn effect, except you can't walk on them very frequently. But even this idea is being tested by new ground covers that can be stepped on occasionally. We give you ideas on growing lawns and groundcovers in Chapter 17.

Exploring the Down and Dirty of Growing

Planting the right plant for your yard and needs is the first step to a successful garden. Keeping it healthy is the clincher. Watering, weeding, mulching, and pest control are all important pieces of a healthy garden. That's why we devoted a whole section to growing plants. Here's what to expect.

Weeding and mulching

We're all about reducing the amount of labor and time spent working in the garden and increasing the amount of time we spend enjoying and eating from the garden. Reducing competition from weeds will lead to a healthy garden. Weeding early and often, reducing perennial weeds, and not letting weeds go to seed are all ways to reduce the weed pressure.

One of the other ways to reduce weed woes is to use mulch. Laying organic or inorganic materials such as black plastic, straw, or old leaves on the soil will stop weeds from germinating and growing in your garden. Plus, some mulch materials, such as the bark mulches, are decorative and beautiful to look at too. We talk all about weeding and mulching in Chapter 18.

Watering

Water is a precious resource and will only get more precious in time. That's why we devoted all of Chapter 19 to the most efficient and best ways to water your trees, shrubs, vegetables, flowers, and lawns.

The best ways to water are generally the most efficient. Drip irrigation and soaker hoses apply water right around the base of plants so little is wasted on pathways or to evaporation into the air. Watering in the morning helps roots absorb water better while it's cool and reduces the amount of disease on plant leaves since they can dry before evening. Collecting water from roofs after natural rainfalls and storing it for future use reduces the amount you need to buy from the water company or municipality.

Dry conditions in cities can kill plants as fast as any pest. That's why it's important to look for drought-tolerant trees, shrubs, flowers, herbs, and vegetables to grow if drought is common where you live. Check with your County Extension office or Master Gardener program for a list of drought-tolerant plants adapted to your area, then look for them at your local garden center.

Pest patrol

We couldn't talk about gardening without talking about insects, animal pests, and diseases. If you follow all the guidelines we mention in the chapters on soil building, plant selection, site preparation, and growing advice, you shouldn't have many pests to control. But even the best gardeners have to deal occasionally with pests like rabbits, dogs, or caterpillars or contend with an outbreak of mildew on their garden plants. It just can't be avoided. That's why it's important to follow these steps for the safest and most effective pest controls:

- ✔ **Identify.** Make sure you know what's causing the problem. Sometimes it's weather, pollution, or even people that are affecting your plants, not animals, insects, or diseases.

- ✔ **Decide.** Once you know what the cause of the problem is, then you'll need to decide if it's worth controlling. Sometimes it's late in the season and you're ready to wrap up the growing season anyway. Other times a plant may have finished producing and can be pulled up to be replanted with something else. Some plants, such as potatoes, can take lots of leaf damage and still produce a good crop.

- ✔ **Prevent.** If you know it's likely that certain animals, insects, or diseases may attack your garden, then it's often a good idea to plan ahead for them. Using preventive measures such as growing resistant varieties, creating fences or barriers, and planting when the pests are less likely to attack are ways to reduce any need to control pests.

- ✔ **Trap.** Before reaching for the sprayer, consider traps as a control strategy. Insect and animal traps can remove enough of the pests to reduce the pressure on plants and save your harvest. They may not control all your pests but will bring the population down to acceptable levels.

- ✔ **Organic sprays.** As a last resort, use targeted organic sprays, such as *Bacillus thuringiensis* (Bt), to control the pests. Sometimes a few well-timed applications of a spray is all you need for the season.

Go to Chapter 20 for more details on specific plant pests.

Chapter 2

Reaping the Benefits of Urban Gardening

*T*he popularity of urban gardening is increasing at just the right time As the world population grows from 7 billion to an estimated 9 billion people by 2050, cities will continue to grow and get larger. With population growth and concentrations changing, a new approach is evolving, focused on making cities more self-sufficient. Cities around the world are taking steps to grow more of their own food, reduce energy consumption, and purify their water and air, all within the city limits.

Urban gardens are an ideal solution to many city woes. Urban gardens produce fresh, healthy food that helps improve nutrition and makes for a better diet. Urban gardens provide greenery that can purify air, reduce water runoff, and decrease pollution. Gardens provide a rallying point for community revitalization. Community gardens and parks provide places for neighbors to meet and form stronger community bonds. Gardens contribute to safer, more beautiful neighborhoods. Properly planted trees and shrubs help reduce heat in cities in summer and help maximize solar gain in winter to reduce energy consumption. Urban gardens are a grassroots solution to these and many other urban issues, empowering city residents to make changes in their lives that will affect their whole neighborhood, one block at a time.

Enjoying Local Produce from Urban Food Gardens

With stagnant economic activity and concerns about the quality of our food supply, many people have gone back to the vegetable garden. It's not a new trend. Back in the 1940s, the United States had "victory gardens" to support the World War II effort. We grew 40 percent of all the produce we needed in those backyard gardens. Today it's estimated that more than 40 million households in the U.S. have an edible garden. They spent almost 3 billion dollars in 2010 on those gardens. This growth in edible gardening has hit the city, too.

Urban food gardens are as varied as the cities they reside in. While they all strive to achieve the basics of producing fresh, healthy food for their gardeners, many of these gardens have become conduits for other projects that empower people and build stronger communities. We cover the basics on growing your own food in the city in Chapter 13, but here we'd like to highlight where you can grow food in the city and some great programs around the country that are using urban food gardens to transform their cities.

Looking at places to grow food

At first glance, growing food in the city seems like an impossible task. Acres of concrete, air and water pollution, little open land, and vandalism all would appear to thwart any effort to grow a garden. But despite all the odds, city dwellers are growing more and more food in some likely (and unlikely) places. Gardeners are getting creative about where and how they grow food, especially if they don't have a backyard. Here are some examples:

- **Community gardens.** Community gardens are popping up all around cities wherever there are vacant lots for people to form a garden and rent out the plots. Cities such as San Francisco, Detroit, New York, and Chicago have long histories of active community garden programs. We cover community gardening in depth in Chapter 12.

- **Rooftop gardens.** One thing cities have lots of is roofs. In Chapter 9, we talk about the details of growing gardens on your roof to produce food and flowers.

- **Container gardens.** No land, no problem. Grow your urban garden in a container. City residents are creative about popping containers almost anywhere there's enough light for plants to grow. Fire escapes, alleyways, balconies, and rooftops are just some places you'll spot a container garden. We'll go into details on container gardening in Chapter 8.

✔ **Shared gardens.** This is a relatively new concept in gardening. Garden sharing matches people with some land in the city but little desire to garden with people without land and a great desire to garden. The gardeners come in, till and grow crops on their neighbors' land, and share the harvest with the owners. It's a win-win for both groups.

✔ **Public land.** Cities have parks and lots of public land in odd places. Some towns are transforming those parks and public spaces into edible landscapes for all to enjoy. Gardeners can be found cultivating road medians, traffic islands, pocket parks, and other unused, public land in the city. There are even cities looking at transforming old bridges into parks with greenery and food garden plots.

Checking out urban food gardening projects

Certainly this book is all about growing your own garden in the city. In the remaining chapters, we hope to give you the skills and resources to do just that. But you won't be alone as an urban gardener. There are thousands of gardeners in cities across the country creating amazing urban gardens and farms right now. To inspire you, here are just a few examples of the public and private groups that are creating a new urban fresh food scene.

SLUG

The San Francisco League of Urban Gardens (SLUG) has been supporting people growing food since 1983. Starting as a volunteer organization providing seeds for city residents, the organization has grown into a thriving nonprofit coordinating 100 community gardens and providing education, resources, and tools to urban gardeners. While they still support the mission of providing garden space for San Franciscans, SLUG now also focuses on social and economic issues, using gardens as a way to uplift neighbors. They created Urban Herbals, an organic food line, that is supported by food produced at housing projects in the city. This project employs local workers and provides internships to youth to learn how to make a living growing food in the city. They have created landscape crews that work with the city to revitalize urban parks and natural areas. These activities have helped SLUG grow to an organization that employs 150 to 200 city people each year, all involved in urban gardens and greenery.

GreenNet

Chicago may be known as the Windy City, but it's also gaining a reputation as a green city as well. GreenNet is a coalition of nonprofit organizations and public agencies committed to improving the quality, amount, use, and wide geographic distribution of sustainable, green open space in the city. One of their main focuses is the community garden system. GreenNet helps coordinate more than 600 community gardens spread over 50 wards throughout the city. They provide how-to information on starting and maintaining a community garden. GreenNet also helps gardens find grant funding for projects and coordinates resources with the City of Chicago to identify and create more neighborhood gardens throughout the city.

Philadelphia Green

Most people know Philadelphia for its rich history as the birthplace of America. Fewer know that Philadelphia has one of the largest urban gardening programs in the country. For more than 30 years, the Pennsylvania Horticultural Society, working with local community groups and the city, has been turning Philadelphia into a green city. They have shown that gardening can be integrated into the entire fabric of city life. Their program, Philadelphia Green, helps support 400 community gardens, 80 neighborhood parks, rooftop gardens, greenery in vacant lots, gardens on public lands, and even gardens around public institutions. They sponsor gardens around the Philadelphia Museum of Art and Penns Landing along the Delaware River. Philadelphia Green is a great example of a public/private partnership that provides residents with the support they need to grow gardens in their neighborhoods.

Beacon Food Forest

Seattle is a cutting-edge city in many ways. Now it has become one of the first cities in the world to create a new city park specifically to grow fruit and food for city residents. The Beacon Food Forest is a 7-acre park in the Beacon Hill district that is being planted with hundreds of different types of edibles, including walnuts, chestnuts, blueberries, raspberries, apples, pears, pineapples, citrus, guavas, persimmons, honeyberries, lingonberries, and herbs. The other novel aspect of this park is that all the food will be available to the public to pluck anytime they like for free. The park highlights a trend in cities to grow more permanent food gardens featuring berry bushes and fruit trees.

Gleaning The Harvest

While growing a whole park of fruit is a novel idea, many cities have begun to better utilize the permanent food plantings residents already have in their landscapes. *Gleaning* is rescuing and redistributing food that would normally go to waste. While this is popular on farms as a way to gather leftover crops for food shelves, even cities are discovering gleaning opportunities to alleviate urban hunger.

Many gleaning groups work with local volunteers and food banks to harvest and redistribute the food wealth. While most of this food is gleaned from rural farms, a growing number of gleaning programs across the country are looking at urban community gardens, urban farms, and residential fruit plantings as places to glean food. One group in Toronto, *Not Far From The Tree*, has been gleaning for three years in that city. They identified many city residents who don't know what to do with the extra fruit from the fruit trees growing in their yards. The gleaners come in, pick, and redistribute the fruit for them. In 2010, hundreds of volunteers harvested more than 20,000 pounds of fruit from 228 trees. A group in Los Angeles, *Fallen Fruit*, combines urban gleaning with performance art. They hold events such as the *Public Fruit Jam*, a community-wide event designed to teach citizens how to can jams and jellies, and the *Nocturnal Fruit Forage*, a nighttime ramble through neighborhoods searching for fruit, as ways to teach the community about the bounty that already exists in their neighborhoods and how to use it for the greater good.

Food on the Roof

Space to garden is hard enough to find in New York City, but farming? Some groups have found ways to grow food in the city without the use of land. Located three flights up in the air, the Eagle Street Rooftop Farm in Brooklyn is a 6,000-square-foot vegetable operation. They have an on-site farmer's market, the first rooftop CSA (Community Supported Agriculture program), bicycle-delivered produce to area restaurants, and a range of farm-based and educational programs throughout the growing season. Since 2009, they have grown a wide variety of vegetables and herbs, ranging from tomatoes to cilantro, cut flowers, and hops for beer brewing. They even have beehives for making honey. The most successful crops so far have been hot peppers (they plan on starting a line of hot sauces), cherry tomatoes, and sage.

The Brooklyn Grange is another similar operation located in the same city. They have been growing more than 1 acre of produce ten stories in the air on rooftops in Brooklyn and Queens since 2010. They provide fresh produce to residents, restaurants, and shops for nine months of the year.

From Motown to growtown

Detroit used to be known as a music, culture, and manufacturing hub. But years of urban decay and decline have left Detroit with one-quarter fewer people now than in its heyday and many vacant lots. However, something new is happening in Detroit these days. and much of the change is being spurred on by grassroots groups using gardens to promote economic activity and development. Instead of seeing those vacant lots and empty buildings as a blight, many residents are taking matters into their own hands and growing a new Detroit. Since 2000, more than 800 gardens have been registered with the Detroit Agricultural Network. Some urban farms are popping up to provide local residents with healthy, affordable food. Since there are more than 44,000 empty lots in Detroit, representing about 5,000 acres, the potential is great for the city to feed itself. The city council is changing laws to make farming in the city limits easier.

And it's not just fresh food that is being produced. New restaurants using this local food are opening and new food-related businesses are creating an uptick in economic activity. Many of these activities are happening in downtrodden neighborhoods. Although Detroit still has a way to go, the city is showing that gardens can be a building block of a new economic life in urban areas.

The Brooklyn Grange and Eagle Street projects highlight the growing trend of urban rooftop gardening around the world. We talk more about that trend in Chapter 9.

Growing Power

Will Allen is a former business executive and professional basketball player. He looked at his wife's hometown of Milwaukee and saw the need for safe, affordable food for people living in the city. Her family happened to own a farm on the outskirts of Milwaukee, so Will started Growing Power as a way to produce healthy food. He later purchased a 3-acre, old garden center in town to grow more food and start his educational activities. While growing food is the means, Will's primary concern is to educate people and youth about the importance of a healthful diet. What started as a way to give urban youth some skills for growing their own food has become a nationwide movement. Growing Power creates Community Food Centers where people can learn the skills needed to grow, process, market, and distribute food sustainably in their city. On his original 3-acre farm in Milwaukee, Will grows 20,000 plants and raises thousands of fish and a livestock inventory of chickens, goats, ducks, rabbits, and bees. The program has now blossomed into branches that provide technical assistance to urban farming programs in states such as Georgia, North Carolina, Ohio, and Minnesota.

Growing Power uses food and the skills associated with growing it to help educate and create economic opportunities for people living in inner cities. The simple act of growing food empowers city dwellers to take the opportunity to create a better life. Over the years Will and his group have taught hundreds of kids and inspired thousands more to begin growing their own food and growing a better life as well.

Creating Healthy Cities

Urban food gardening is certainly taking off across the country, but gardens can do more than just provide city residents with food. Thoughtfully placed trees, shrubs, and other landscape features can help reduce air, water, and noise pollution and decrease summer heat and winter cold in the city. Gardens not only brighten up a neighborhood, but research has shown they increase property values, reduce crime, and foster a sense of pride in the community.

Reducing pollution

Some cities, such as Los Angeles and Beijing, are almost as famous for their smog as for their culture and vibrancy. Air pollution has a harmful effect on the quality of life in cities, leading to increased illness among the residents. However, there is a simple solution everyone can take part in. Plant trees and shrubs!

Trees and shrubs are great air filters. They help purify city air polluted from car traffic and industrial factories while providing shade and habitat for wildlife. Cities are notorious for having bad air pollution. Here are some of the worst chemical culprits that contribute to that pollution and their sources.

✔ **Carbon dioxide.** This greenhouse gas comes in large part from the burning of oil, coal, and natural gas for energy. Trees have the unique ability to absorb carbon as they grow and create a carbon "*sink.*" A sink locks carbon dioxide up within the tissues of the tree, preventing it from going into the atmosphere as a heat-trapping "greenhouse gas." In fact, 1 acre of trees absorbs enough carbon dioxide per year to match that emitted by driving a car 26,000 miles.

✔ **Sulfur dioxide.** Often found in cities where coal-fired electricity generating plants are found, this pollutant travels by air and affects other areas downwind in the form of acid rain.

✔ **Ozone.** This pollutant forms from a chemical reaction of sunlight and automobile exhaust gases. Ozone is the major pollutant in smog.

✔ **Methane.** This is another pollutant that's emitted from burning of fossil fuels. It also is released from landfills and by livestock.

✔ **Nitrous oxide.** Formed from the burning of fossil fuels and automotive exhausts, nitrous oxide is another chemical ingredient in acid rain.

✔ **Chlorofluorocarbon.** This pollutant leaks from old air conditioners, refrigerators, and industrial foam and damages Earth's protective ozone layer in the atmosphere.

Trees remove the gaseous forms of these pollutants by absorbing them through their pores. Air pollution particulates are trapped and filtered by the leaves, stems, and twigs and washed to the ground by rainfall so we don't inhale them into our lungs.

Not only do trees and shrubs filter these pollutants out of the atmosphere, but in exchange they provide oxygen for wildlife and us. A mature tree produces as much oxygen in a growing season as ten people inhale in a year.

We talk a lot about greening the outdoors, but indoor plants are valuable, too. Houseplants can filter the air we breathe. Strategically placed houseplants such as areca palm, rubber trees, and pothos can filter air pollutants from a room, providing better quality indoor air, especially during the winter when homes are more sealed up. Place two to three houseplants in 12-inch-diameter pots per 150 square feet of room to keep your air clean.

Cleaning the water

Trees, shrubs, and gardens also are important water purifiers in the city. Cities have so much impervious material like asphalt, concrete, and hard-packed soil that storm water often runs off into water sewage systems, overwhelming them during rainy periods and washing pollutants from buildings and streets into waterways. This leads to untreated effluent entering our lakes, streams, and rivers. Trees, shrubs, and gardens can absorb storm water, reducing the amount entering the sewage system. In the process, these plants filter out toxins in the water as well. Tree canopies also reduce the impact of rain beating on green surfaces, allowing more rain to be absorbed into the city soils and less to run off. In Chapter 19, we talk more about creating a special type of perennial garden, called a *rain garden*, as another way to reduce storm water runoff.

Reduced storm water runoff is also seen when roofs are topped with greenery. Cities such as Chicago, Washington, DC, and Baltimore are leading the way in creating more green roofs. These city roofs grow plants that absorb rainwater, reducing the amount that ends up on the street. In one Maryland study, green roofs reduced the amount of water runoff from storms by 74 percent.

Cutting back on noise pollution

Cities are echo chambers of noise. Noise from cars, trucks, people, and sirens bounces off city buildings, creating a chaotic sound environment. All that noise creates a lot of stress among people living in cities. It's no wonder city dwellers seek out parks and green spaces as a way to relax. Trees and shrubs help absorb city sounds, making for a quieter existence. To test this out, go into a city park and gauge the noise levels. Then walk to the edge of the park and listen to the difference. Even planting a few trees and shrubs around your yard will help alleviate noise pollution in your neighborhood.

Filtering out air and noise pollution with green walls

Green walls are another way to make cities more livable. The technology of vertical gardening (we talk more about this in Chapter 10) has advanced so that growing plants on a vertical wall is not only possible, it's being done in cities around the globe from France to California. The benefits of growing plants on walls in the city are similar to those of growing trees and shrubs. They reduce air pollution and lower cooling costs in summer and heating costs in winter in adjacent buildings. Green walls also buffer sounds in urban canyons and increase biodiversity by creating wildlife habitat for birds, butterflies, bats, bees, and other insects. Indoors, green walls are being used to filter out air pollutants in public spaces such as schools.

Making cities more livable

Green plants also make cities more livable in other ways. The primary one is by moderating the air temperature. As global warming continues around the Earth, weather patterns are turning more erratic. Many cities are experiencing hotter summers and some are having colder winters. While it may appear much of this is out of our control due to global climate conditions, there are things we can do to mitigate the effects of the changing climate at home. Planting more trees and shrubs is certainly the easiest and has the most impact. And those same trees, shrubs, and gardens can increase the value of where we live at the same time.

Here are some of the ways planting a garden with trees and shrubs can help make living in the city a little easier.

- ✔ **Reduce the Heat Island Effect.** The Heat Island Effect is the increase in summertime temperatures in cities due to all their surfaces, like buildings and asphalt streets, that absorb heat and radiate it back into the atmosphere. Trees and shrubs can reduce that effect. Urban neighborhoods with mature trees can be up to 11 degrees cooler in summer than neighborhoods without trees. We talk more about the Heat Island Effect in Chapter 3.

- ✔ **Keep winters warmer.** The opposite of the Heat Island Effect happens in winter in cities. Because of all the concrete, glass, and construction material, winds whipping through cities create a colder environment. Trees and shrubs slow the speed of wind in cities, while at the same time, deciduous trees allow the sun's winter rays to warm homes and offices.

- ✔ **Reduce energy use.** In both the previous cases, you use less electricity to cool your house or apartment in summer and less heat to warm it in winter. You save money and help the environment by keeping additional fossil fuels from being burned to produce energy and emitting their pollutants into the atmosphere. Now that's something everyone can be on board with.

- ✔ **Increase property values.** Although this may not directly impact your quality of life in the city, it sure makes you feel better knowing your property is valuable. Residential properties located close to community gardens have increased property values compared to those not located close to a garden. In a New York City study, residences within 1,000 square feet of a community garden had higher property values than comparable properties located outside that area.

Improving the neighborhood

Gardens, trees, and shrubs contribute to a better quality of life in cities in very tangible ways. They produce food, reduce pollution and energy use, and increase property values. And there are other factors they bring to bear that make for a healthier lifestyle.

- **Reduced crime.** Intuitively you might think that more gardens and greenery in your neighborhood would mean more crime because criminals would have more places to hide. However, research tells another story. Researchers at the University of Illinois compared crime rates at 98 apartments in public housing developments in Chicago. They categorized apartments by the level of greenery around them. They found buildings with high levels of greenery had one-half as many crimes compared to buildings with low levels of greenery. If you want to clear your neighborhood of crime, start by building gardens and green spaces.

- **Less graffiti and trash.** Neighborhoods with community gardens and more greenery, in general, have less trash and graffiti on the walls and buildings. People take pride in the beauty they've created, and others seem to notice and appreciate it as well.

- **Better health.** Denver Urban Gardens found that more than 50 percent of community gardeners meet national guidelines for fruit and vegetable intake, compared to 25 percent of non-gardeners. If you grow your own food, you're more likely to eat better. And you're likely to share what you grow with your neighbors. The same study showed 95 percent of community gardeners gave away some of the produce they grew to friends, family, and people in need; 60 percent specifically donate to food assistance programs.

- **More beauty.** Gardens are just plain beautiful. That's an obvious statement, but often urban areas are filled with decay and unattractive buildings. Gardens bring natural beauty to places that may be lacking it. How can you measure the impact a beautiful sunflower or a maple tree will have on the quality of life of city dwellers living there?

- **More community spirit.** Gardens foster community spirit. Numerous studies have shown that community and urban gardens bring people together. Neighborhoods have a renewed sense of pride, satisfaction, and community involvement. This is often illustrated by neighborhood festivals and parties springing up, anchored by the gardens.

Chapter 3

The Urban Microclimate

*T*hroughout the year, the urban environment is directly affected by regional climate conditions, such as hot and cold temperatures, direct sunlight, shade, forceful winds, and gentle breezes. The climate conditions in the immediate area surrounding your urban dwelling make up your *urban microclimate.*

A variety of factors, including solar radiation, surrounding air temperatures, air movement, sun orientation, humidity, topographical location, proximity to lakes or waterfront exposure, paved surfaces like roads and parking lots, buildings, and rooftop conditions, influence your urban microclimate.

Although you don't have any control over regional weather patterns, temperatures, and annual precipitation rates, which together make up the *macroclimate,* you can influence your surrounding microclimate. This chapter explains the different micro- and macroclimatic conditions that impact gardens in general and provides some tips on selecting appropriate plant materials and green initiatives to help you influence the climate surrounding your urban garden setting.

The Sunny City: Working with the Sun and Warmer Urban Temperatures

Urban environments typically experience higher temperatures than suburban areas because urban areas have vast amounts of paved surfaces, which lead to a lot more sunlight penetration. In essence, the urban setting is like a "heat sink," where the roofs, buildings, and paved surfaces heat up and reradiate the penetrated sunlight, causing temperatures to increase. Wooded lots in the suburbs absorb and filter some of this direct sunlight exposure, allowing temperatures to stay cooler there.

Of course, sunlight is essential for the development of your garden and landscape plantings; you just have to know how to use it. By choosing the right plant materials and putting them in the right places, you can lower your cooling costs significantly, reducing the need for air-conditioning systems and, in turn, reducing carbon dioxide emissions. (See why reducing carbon emissions is so important later in "Minimizing the Heat Island Effect.")

Taking advantage of seasonal solar angles

In the continental United States, the sun travels east to west along a southern exposure. The solar angle changes from summer to winter, but the sun continues to always travel east to west and the duration of sun exposure changes season to season.

The summer solar path (see Figure 3-1a) for the continental United States travels east to west along a high southern angle, resulting in a longer period of daylight and decreased shadow lengths.

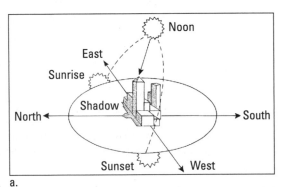

a.

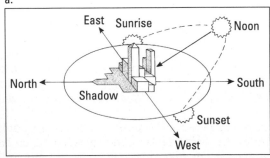

Figure 3-1:
Summer and
winter solar
paths.

b.

Illustration by Kathryn Born.

The winter solar path (see Figure 3-1b) for the continental U.S. travels east to west along a lower southern angle, resulting in a shorter period of daylight and increased shadow lengths.

Understanding the difference between summer and winter solar angles can help you employ strategies to either increase or reduce solar impacts to your urban garden and thus help improve your landscape's overall microclimate. In cold or temperate climates, the goal is often to capture as much sun as possible during the winter season and to provide shade from the heat of the summer sun. Placing *deciduous trees* (trees that drop their leaves in winter) along the path of sunlight, for example, helps accomplish both strategies by maximizing a cooling effect in the summer while providing needed solar exposure for more heat gain in the winter season.

Dealing with solar glare

Another sunny aspect urban gardeners may have to contend with is solar glare. *Solar glare* is the indirect sunlight that's reflected from surfaces such as pavement, water, building facades, signs, billboards, and other reflective surfaces. Solar glare can occur more in urban environments, where these reflective surfaces, such as buildings, are more prevalent.

Many urban buildings are now constructed with antireflective coatings and specialty glass to help reduce and diffuse solar glare. However, even with some diffusion, reflection can still occur. For instance, solar panels designed to absorb sunlight can still reflect one-third of the sun's rays.

The additional gain of indirect lighting may help or hinder your garden plantings, so you need to keep solar glare in mind when developing your urban garden and selecting your plantings. For example, urban gardeners with gardens in the shadows of surrounding buildings may welcome any reflective indirect sunlight from solar glare. In other cases, where urban gardens are exposed to normal direct sunlight throughout the day, gardeners may want to minimize as much indirect/additional exposure due to solar glare as possible.

Minimizing the Heat Island Effect

Cities naturally (or should we say *unnaturally*) have higher temperatures than their surrounding suburbs. This phenomenon is known as the *urban heat island effect,* and it's due to the fact that urban environments include so many heat-absorbing surfaces, such as roofs, concrete, and asphalt-paved surfaces.

One of the main causes of the Heat Island Effect is the changing of land surfaces to other materials that retain heat, like concrete and asphalt. A secondary contributor is waste heat from human sources such as cars, air conditioners, and factories.

Figure 3-2 illustrates the increased temperatures within urban areas as compared to the lower temperatures in surrounding suburban communities.

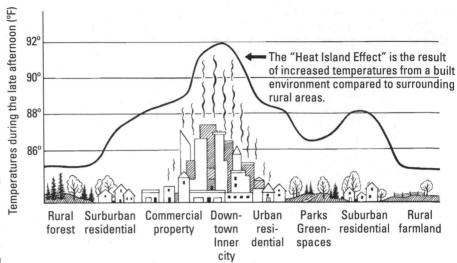

Figure 3-2:
The urban
Heat Island
Effect.

Illustration by Kathryn Born.

The Environmental Protection Agency (EPA) recognizes that while some Heat Island Effects can be positive, like extending the plant-growing season, many of them have more negative impacts, such as increased energy consumption, elevated amounts of pollutants, compromised health and comfort, and impaired water quality.

So what can you, as an urban gardener, do to help reduce this Heat Island Effect? Check out the following sections for some ideas.

Adding some green wherever you can

One way to reduce the Heat Island Effect in urban areas is to reduce the number of heat-retaining surfaces by adding a little green wherever you can. Here are a couple of examples for how to do so:

✔ **Develop urban green spaces and plant trees and shrubs.** Planting trees and shrubs and developing green spaces, such as gardens, within the urban environment helps decrease the Heat Island Effect and reduce temperatures. These planting surfaces help retain and absorb sunlight rather than reflect the sun's rays, helping to decrease urban temperatures increased by other solid surfaces like roads, rooftops, and expansive parking lots.

✔ **Use green roof systems.** Green roof systems provide many benefits. When used on a community-wide scale, they help reduce the Heat Island Effect by decreasing areas where reflected heat gain from solid roof surfaces can occur. Green roofs also provide a useable and aesthetic urban amenity by retaining rainwater, reducing the amount of storm water runoff and retaining and returning water to the atmosphere through transpiration and evaporation.

The added vegetation on a green roof can create a small microclimate of cooler air in the summer months, decreasing your need to air-condition your home. Not to mention, increased vegetation in cities helps lower dust and particulate matter, in turn, cleaning the air and reducing smog. For more on rooftop gardening, see Chapter 9.

Reducing carbon emissions

In addition to heat-retaining surfaces, carbon emissions from human sources like cars, lawn mowers, and waste heat from air conditioners contribute to the urban Heat Island Effect. Following is a list of tips you can use to help reduce this environmental impact:

✔ Avoid synthetic fertilizers and pesticides.

✔ Use people-powered equipment rather than gasoline-powered.

✔ Use electric-powered equipment rather than gasoline-powered.

✔ Install energy-efficient lighting.

✔ Minimize the use of soil amendments such as mined minerals, peat, and bagged organic fertilizers, whose harvesting, mining, manufacturing, and transporting use energy, release carbon, or disrupt the environment.

✔ Plant trees and shrubs that are well-adapted to your region and that will sequester and store carbon.

✔ Choose landscaping materials with a low carbon footprint. For the most part, this means buy your materials locally, save gas, and therefore decrease carbon emissions.

✔ Use salvaged wood and repurposed materials when possible.

✔ Generate your own energy through solar power, wind power, or hydro power if your municipality and zoning ordinances allow you to do so.

✔ Grow your own fruits, vegetables, and herbs (our personal favorite).

✔ Use cover crops and mulch to cover bare soil to prevent carbon loss and soil erosion.

✔ Minimize your use of garden plastics (in mulch, pots, and so on), and when you do use them, be sure to recycle them when you're done.

✔ Minimize lawn areas and use sustainable lawn care practices to decrease your "mowable area."

It is important to note some realities here on carbon reduction. While efforts to individually decrease our carbon footprint will not have any significant impacts to reduce urban temperatures, a greater community-wide effort here can decrease the urban Heat Island Effect.

The Windy City: Working with Seasonal Urban Wind Patterns

Wind flow is created by the sun heating the air. Of course the direction of winds varies quite a bit. Wind patterns change seasonally due to the angles and changes of our sun. Understanding wind flow and how it affects your urban garden and landscape may be useful to you. Perhaps you would like to screen against harsh winter winds or channel in a cool summer breeze?

The direction of wind is determined from where it originates. For example, a southerly wind will blow from the south to the north and a northerly wind will blow from the north to the south. For the majority of the U.S., many summer breezes come from the south or southwest. During the winter, wind patterns usually come from the northwest or northerly direction, but again this can vary greatly depending on where you live. This section helps you understand techniques on how to analyze your wind patterns and develop your urban landscape with wind in mind.

Because wind patterns vary greatly across the country, the best way to find out the general direction of summer breezes and prevailing winter winds in your area is to contact your local national weather service contact office. To find out who your local contact is, start your search at www.weather.gov.

We also found a wind map at hint.fm/wind that compiles data from weather.gov and their national digital forecast database on an hourly basis into a living portrait of wind flow for the continental U.S. Here, you can zoom in and analyze the directional wind patterns for your area in real time.

Another popular site to visit is www.weather.com, where their new interactive map allows you to view past, current, and future weather projections locally. You can also customize the map to review wind speeds in your region.

Of course there are special circumstances you can also keep in mind when it comes to wind direction and flow. For instance, if your urban residence is fronting near a large body of water or along the coastline, the wind pattern here would likely flow much differently than that of an inland property. Within our inner cities, tall buildings that project above other structures could channel air downward along the windward face of the building; also known as wind tunnels, these added winds can certainly affect our comfort levels.

With an understanding of urban wind patterns, how can you effectively design your urban gardens with wind in mind? While canopies at the base of buildings and other structures may help shelter against strong downward gusts of air, adding landscape features, trees, and plantings can help channel or protect against horizontal wind flows. Here are some additional tips you can consider to effectively approach wind flow in the urban landscape:

✔ In urban climates with hot summers, your goal may be to block the summer sun while channeling a summer southerly breeze. One way to do so is to place a semicircular row of deciduous trees and shrubs from southeast to southwest with a break in the middle (south). The trees can help channel these southerly gusts of wind into your urban garden while providing you some additional shade against the direct sunlight. This can help cool down an area of your urban landscape at a microclimate level.

✔ In urban climates with cold winters, the goal is to block against the strong, cold winter winds with a row of trees and shrubs while continuing to capture the winter sun and maximize solar exposure. A dense row of evergreens placed appropriately (usually north and northwest) can be a very effective screen against cold winter winds.

When you put in a garden in the spring, you may need to put up a temporary wind screen to help protect tender new transplants and seedlings from the drying effects of the cold and harsh late winter winds.

In temperate urban climates, which include the majority of U.S. cities, city planners have to employ both of these strategies to protect against winter winds while channeling summer breezes.

What's the weather got to do with it?

Before humans invented central heating and air conditioning, people actually paid much more attention to their local climate conditions. If they wanted to keep their homes cool, they would build the homes appropriately amid a canopy of trees or design buildings with overhanging eaves to shade the windows and help protect them from the warming rays of the sun.

Creating a successful urban garden is very similar to building a comfortable home before the modern conveniences of central heat and air. You have to consider your local climate conditions before placing and developing your garden. Native plants that have been properly selected for the existing conditions are often the most suitable choice, even in urban settings. If they're well-adapted to their site, they may take less care and maintenance than nonnative species because they're already conditioned to accept local conditions, such as soils, rainfall, humidity, and regional temperatures.

Taking Macroclimate and Microclimate Conditions into Account in Your Garden

In this chapter, we cover some of the various aspects of the urban microclimate and introduce some of the challenges urban gardeners face when it comes to sun, wind, and urban weather patterns. Although you have no control over the *macroclimate* conditions, including regional weather patterns, temperatures, and annual precipitation rates, urban gardeners can influence their surrounding environment on a smaller microclimate level.

A great place to start is understanding your specific hardiness zone and the general climate conditions for your local region. Knowing your zone will also help you select appropriate plantings suitable for your climate conditions.

Knowing your hardiness zone

What is a plant hardiness zone and why is it important to know for urban gardening? Basically, the hardiness zones measure a plant's ability to withstand cold temperatures. The new hardiness zone map divides the U.S. into 13 zones with an analysis of the average minimum winter temperatures across the continent. The zones are further subdivided into *a* and *b* categories. Each zone represents a temperature range of 10 degrees; each *a* or *b* subdivision represents 5 degrees. The lower the number, the colder the zone; and the *a* category is colder than the *b* category. The colder the weather, the lower the zone number. Zone 3 is pretty cold; zone 8 is less cold.

While a few areas moved to slightly cooler zones, the majority of the changes on the new map reflect a shift to warmer zones, with the zone boundary generally moving up by half a zone, or 5 degrees. Although many of these changes are due to changes in climate patterns, some are a result of the increased regional accuracy of the map to better reflect the influence of local geography — like changes in elevation, nearness to a body of water, or nearness to an urban area — on temperature extremes.

In 2012, the U.S. Department of Agriculture (USDA) released an updated version of its Plant Hardiness Zone Map. The new map is based on temperature data collected during the 30-year period from 1976 to 2005, so its zone listings now incorporate more recent temperature trends. It's also based on data from even more weather stations than the previous map, enhancing its accuracy. Because of all this extra data, some areas of the country now have new zone designations compared to the old zone map.

Most trees, shrubs, and perennials are rated according to zone, so gardeners may select plants suited to the intensity of their local winter climate. Very handy! A plant considered hardy to zone 3 will grow in a zone 3 location or warmer. If rated hardy to zone 6, then it will grow in zone 6 or warmer. Many reliable plants are adapted to a wide range of zones (e.g., zones 3 through 8). These tend to be amenable to many growing situations.

On the USDA Map website, you can download and print the countrywide USDA Hardiness Zone Map or select your particular region of the country. One of the handiest aspects of the new map is its interactive feature that lets you find your zone by typing in your zip code on the map website. You can also zoom in on the map of your state to see the zone boundaries in detail and download and print maps of various sizes and resolutions. Go to `www.planthardiness.ars.usda.gov` to try out all the map's new features.

Considering your own microclimatic conditions

Although you can't change your regional weather or macroclimatic conditions, we learned that you can figure out how to effectively analyze your own city gardens and landscapes at a microclimatic level and make important adjustments to improve your urban gardening success. Understanding your urban microclimate can help you save money and (literally) create your own "cool place" within your urban garden space. Check out "The Windy City: Working with Seasonal Urban Wind Patterns" to see how it it's possible to channel a cool summer breeze into your urban garden.

Analyzing your site

One of the first things you can do when analyzing your site is determine how much sunlight your urban garden receives. Watch your site carefully to see just how much sun it gets throughout the day. If the site is sunny, is it intense afternoon sun or gentle morning sun? If it's shady, is the shade dense enough to keep anything except woodland plants from growing, or is it dappled shade with some sunlight filtering through that will allow for a wider variety of plants?

No matter what hardiness zone you live in, keep in mind different parts of your urban garden will likely have a few climatic variations of their own. By noting these different microclimates, you can determine how to locate plants in the most suitable spots and even how to broaden the array of plants you grow. Do a good analysis of your specific site to understand the urban challenges you need to take into consideration when it comes to plant hardiness zones because of solar glare, warmer temperatures, winds, shade, and the Heat Island Effect.

Putting the right plants in the right sites

There are basic *sun versus shade* considerations everyone understands. Some plants that need shade will simply burn up if you plant them in full sun. A plant that thrives on full sun will stretch and languish if you plant it in a densely shaded area. For the urban gardener, consider all factors when matching the right plant to the right site, especially when you're working with a variety of microclimate conditions that can affect your plants growth.

For example, a portion of an urban garden sheltered from the effects of winter winds may be a half zone warmer than the rest. Often, an exposed windy spot runs cold, whereas the heat radiating from buildings and pavement in a city can up-zone an urban location.

A garden in zone 6 may successfully over-winter zone 7 plants because of microclimate variations. Conversely, you may be able to develop your zone 6 garden that shivers through temperatures worthy of zone 4! Would this be gardener's luck or the result of your careful analysis of microclimate conditions?

Extending bloom time

Did you know that a large rock, a fence, a stone wall, a patio, large tree, or an adjacent building can create a unique microclimate within your urban garden? You can take advantage of these different microclimates to have a longer flowering season. For example, if you plant daffodils on the south side of your garden, they'll likely begin peeking out of the soil earlier than those that you plant in other areas. Then when the flowers on the south side start fading, the ones that are partially shaded in another part of your garden will begin to open up. And just like that, you get a bloom time that's twice as long!

Pushing the zones

You can do more than just increase bloom time when you take advantage of the different microclimates in your urban garden. You can also grow plants that are borderline hardy in your region. For example, a stone walkway or patio absorbs heat and may allow you to grow plants nearby that are usually only hardy in areas that are one zone warmer than yours. As an added bonus, the urban environment's increased temperatures and protection from harsh winter winds may allow you even more flexibility when selecting plantings. For example, some cites in the northern U.S. have successfully planted magnolia trees in areas where the additional protection against harsh winter winds and slightly warmer temperatures can sustain these plants in urban settings.

Overcoming the impacts of wind

Wind also influences the microclimates in your urban garden, both by lowering air temperatures and by increasing water loss through the foliage (transpiration). For instance, winter winds can easily damage some plants, such as rhododendrons and other broad-leaved evergreens, because they don't go completely dormant. As a result, they lose some water all winter long through their leaves and cannot adequately replace that water from the frozen soil. Strong winter winds can exacerbate this problem; therefore, protecting non-dormant plantings (like rhododendrons) from chill winds caused by an urban wind tunnel or exposed northerly exposure may be helpful to your plants' survival.

Part II
Gardening Basics

The 5th Wave   By Rich Tennant

©RICHTENNANT

The pH level in the soil seems a bit high.

In this part. . .

This part is where we really dig into citified gardening. From analyzing soil types to understanding soil pH, drainage, and poor and contaminated soil conditions. We discuss ways to improve your soil with organic fertilizers and composting, and even show you how you can build good soil for your garden. You will find out when to seed, when to transplant, and how to select the right plants for your garden. Finally, we offer some how-to procedures for planting annuals, veggies, perennials, roses, trees, and shrubs.

Chapter 4

Getting to Know Your Soil

Soil is the heart and soul of your garden. So how you treat it goes a long way in determining how well your plants grow. Healthy soil not only feeds the plants growing in it, but it also plays home to countless soil microorganisms that help your plants to better take up nutrients and water.

Soil is made up of many different elements, including the following:

✔ **Air spaces:** These spaces allow roots and water to travel through the soil. Water drainage is critical to a healthy soil.

✔ **Organic matter:** This stuff is the glue that holds soil particles together and creates a rich material called *humus*. (We talk more about humus in Chapter 5.) Organic matter is essential for soil life. Literally millions of microbes live in your soil, including fungi, bacteria, earthworms, and other microorganisms. This biological life is essential for soil health, and organic matter helps feed this life.

✔ **Soil particles:** These particles come in different sizes and help you determine the type of soil you have. While scientists study soils under microscopes to determine their types and qualities, you can determine a lot about your soil through some simple tests and observations. Knowing the type of soil you have helps you make a plan to turn it into the rich soil that can feed your plants — and, in turn, you, your family, and your friends.

In this chapter, we talk about the different types of soil, how to test it to find out what type you may have in your yard, and possible contaminants to watch out for in any urban environment.

Determining Your Type of Soil

When talking soil, a little knowledge goes a long way. And most important is recognizing your soil type and its health. Some soils are naturally fertile and need little altering, but others need an overhaul. Knowing where you stand with your soil helps you determine what fertilizers and amendments you need to add before you get started. We talk more about these amendments in detail in Chapter 5.

Urban soils have special considerations you need to know about. Certain contaminants like lead and other hazardous substances are potential pollutants in some city soils. Gardening in the city sounds ominous, but don't be discouraged. Testing can tell you whether you have any cause for concern. And, luckily, if your soil has elevated toxic levels, many tips and techniques can help fix the contaminated soil and build it back to optimum health.

The following sections give you a rundown of the soil types and how to figure out which one you have in your yard.

Understanding the different soil types

All soil is not created equal. Just like plants and people, soils have different characteristics that make them unique. Knowing the kind of soil you have helps you determine its strengths and weaknesses. While soil is composed of many elements (discussed earlier in the chapter), the place to begin is with your soil type. And you'll be glad to know that finding out is easier than asking your cute neighbor, "What's your type?" You just have to observe the composition of the soil's particles.

The following three types of particles can make up your soil:

✔ **Clay:** Clay is essential to your soil. Clay soil is naturally high in nutrients and holds moisture well, keeping your plants hydrated. However, clay soil often gets a bad rap because of some of its characteristics. Wet clay soils stick to your shoes when you walk on them. And because the individual soil particles are so small, clay has smaller air spaces. As a result, it drains water slowly and is slow to warm up in spring. When dry, clay soil cracks and makes your garden look like the Mojave Desert.

✔ **Sand:** Sand is the opposite of clay in many ways. Because of the large particle size, sand has lots of air spaces, so it drains water quickly and warms up fast (think of a kid's sandbox or the beach). These characteristics make it ready to plant in spring sooner than clay. However, it's also the first type of soil to dry out in summer and doesn't hold nutrients as well as clay.

> ✔ **Silt:** Silt is like the right bed in *Goldilocks and the Three Bears.* It has medium-sized particles, so it holds some water, but not too much. It holds some nutrients, but not as many as clay. It warms up fast in spring, but not as quickly as sand. A soil dominated by silt is a gardener's friend.

Most soils are a combination of these three particles, but the particle type that dominates dictates many of the properties of your soil.

The ideal soil is 40 percent sand, 40 percent silt, and 20 percent clay. You'll hear this mixture referred to as *loam.* It takes the best from each soil particle type. It has good water drainage and allows air to infiltrate the soil like sand, but it also holds moisture well and is fertile like silt and clay. Loam is the ideal, but if your soil falls a little short, don't worry. Through the addition of organic matter, you can create a loamier soil that has all the attributes you desire. (See Chapter 5 for details.)

Figuring out what you have

After you know the different particles of soil (see the preceding section), you can determine what combination or soil type you have. You can try a few tests (from simple to more complex) to get a general idea of your soil type. We describe each in the following sections. Choose one or two tests to help you get an idea of your soil type.

The squeeze test

To do this test, be sure your soil is damp, but not soaking wet. Grab a small handful of the soil in your hand. Rub some of the soil between your fingers. If it feels gritty, it's mostly sand. If it feels slick and slimy, it's mostly clay.

The ribbon test

Take a handful of damp soil and make a ribbon by rolling the soil between your hands. If you can form a ribbon and hold it vertically without it breaking, you have mostly clay soil. If you can make a ribbon, but it breaks off when you try to hold it up, you probably have somewhere between 25 and 50 percent clay in your soil. If you can't make a ribbon at all, chances are your soil is more than half sand.

The jar test

The jar test is for the scientists in the crowd. It's a bit more precise than the other tests. To do this test, take soil from a number of places in your garden and mix the samples together in a bucket. Scoop up a cup of your soil and follow these steps:

1. **Let the soil dry out on a flat surface until it becomes crumbly.**

2. **Remove any roots, stones, or debris and crush it into a powder with a mortar.**

3. **Place a 1-inch-thick layer in the bottom of a quart-sized clear glass jar.**

4. **Fill the jar two-thirds full with water and add a pinch of salt (or 1 teaspoon of liquid dish detergent) to help the soil particles separate. Shake vigorously.**

5. **Let the solution settle into different layers.**

   The sand will settle quickly (within a few minutes) to form the bottom layer. A few hours later, the silt will settle. You should be able to see a visual difference between the large sand particles and the smaller silt particles. The clay may take days to settle out.

6. **Measure the total amount of soil, and then measure each layer.**

   To determine the percentage of each soil type, you need to do a little math. If, for example, the total amount of soil is 1 inch deep and you had a ½-inch-thick layer of sand, your soil is 50 percent sand. If the next layer (silt) is ¼ inch deep, you have 25 percent silt. The remaining 25 percent, then, is clay.

Checking Your Soil's Drainage

The soil particle size we discuss in the earlier section, "Understanding the different soil types," determines how well your soil drains water. The microbes and plant roots need a balance of air and water in the soil to thrive, which is why proper soil water drainage is essential. While some plants, such as cactuses, can survive on dry soil that drains water fast, and other plants, such as willows, can survive in temporary standing water, most plants need a well-drained soil to grow their best.

You don't have to be a rocket scientist to see where in your yard the soil drains too well or poorly. Brown patches on your lawn in midsummer while the rest of the lawn is green may be a sign that the soil under the grass is predominantly sand. If, after a rain, you have puddles of water in certain spots in your yard that last longer than in other sections of the yard, the soil in those spots is likely to be mostly clay.

If you want to be a little more exact about how well your soil drains, particularly where you want to place your garden, you can conduct a percolation test or a metal rod test. Read on for more.

Performing a percolation test

To find out whether the spot where you plan to grow a garden or plant a tree is adequately drained, you can do a *percolation test.* Here are the steps to follow:

1. **Dig 1-foot by 1-foot holes in several places on your planting site.**

2. **Let the soil dry out for a few days.**

   Cover the holes to keep water out (and to make sure no one — human or beast — falls in).

3. **After the holes dry out, fill them with water and determine how long the holes take to drain completely.**

   Use a timer so you don't forget what time you started. Then use the following list to determine you soil's likely drainage pattern:

   - If the water drains out within 10 minutes of filling it, the soil drains too well. It will probably dry out too fast for most plants.

   - If the water drains out within 30 minutes of filling it, the soil is still draining fast, but it's probably okay for plants that like well-drained soils.

   - If the water drains within 30 minutes to 4 hours of filling it, you have ideal drainage. Most plants thrive in this type of drainage situation.

   - If the water takes longer than 4 hours to drain, the soil is poorly drained and probably won't be good for most plants. It's best suited to plants that are adapted to wet soils, such as cattails and certain irises.

You can improve whatever drainage conditions you have by adding organic matter. Adding organic matter to the soil helps fast-draining soils retain more water and poorly drained ones to dry out faster. Organic matter really is the miracle additive for soil. And, of course, selecting plants that are adapted to your existing drainage conditions makes it more likely that they will grow and thrive. You can read about what organic matter is appropriate for your situation in Chapter 5.

Mastering the metal rod test

The *metal-rod test,* which helps you determine how well your soil drains, is particularly important in urban areas because you never know what's been buried under the soil you're trying to grow in. Some garden areas have an impervious layer of soil called a *hardpan,* which is made of solid materials like asphalt, packed clay, or concrete. This layer can prevent soil water from draining, creating a wet environment for plants to grow in.

Knowing whether you have these materials under your garden and how deep down they are can help you decide whether to move your garden to a different spot or build raised beds on top of the soil instead.

The metal rod test couldn't be simpler. Just take a ½-inch-diameter metal rod and push it into the soil in different places around your garden. If you can push the rod down 6 to 8 inches without meeting any firm resistance, your soil doesn't have an impervious layer and it's okay to garden or plant in. If you do find an impervious layer, you can dig down to see what it is, or you can simply build your garden up. Raised beds and vertical gardening are tackled in Chapters 6 and 10.

Discovering Your Soil's pH Level

The sweetness (alkalinity) or sourness (acidity) of your soil is measured by a term called *pH.* This term is used a lot in gardening circles. It's not necessary to understand the chemistry behind this "measure of hydrogen ion concentration" (sorry; we just had to throw that in). What you really need to know is the pH number of your soil. The pH scale runs from 1 to 14, with 1 being the most acidic and 14 the most alkaline. You'll likely never see soils at the extremes of this range. Most soils lie between 5 and 9, and most plants grow best with a pH between 6 and 7.

Knowing your pH is important. Plants can't absorb certain nutrients if the soil's pH isn't in the proper range for them. For example, blueberries love a highly acidic soil in the pH range of 4 to 5. If the pH is higher than that, the plants can't take up nutrients well, the leaves turn yellow, and the plant becomes stunted.

You can raise the pH by adding lime, and you can lower it by adding sulfur. In general, areas of the country that have high rainfall amounts, such as the East and Pacific Northwest, tend to have acidic soils, and drier areas, such as the Southwest, tend to have more alkaline soils. Clay soils and soils high in organic matter tend to buffer the pH, keeping it around neutral (a pH of 7). Sandy soil and soils low in organic matter, on the other hand, are more susceptible to swings in the pH level.

A soil test tells you the pH level of your soil so you know how much lime or sulfur (if any) you need to add. You can conduct a home test or you can hire a professional to do it for you. Just keep in mind that a home test is inexpensive but not as detailed or reliable as a professional test.

Taking a proper sample for your soil test

The key to getting a useful soil test result from a laboratory or a home kit is to take a proper soil sample. Follow these steps:

1. **Remove the sod or top vegetation and dig down 4 to 6 inches into the soil to get a soil sample.**

2. **Take six to eight soil samples from various locations in your garden.**

   Do separate tests from various crops. For example, collect samples for your vegetable garden in one test and samples for a lawn in another test.

3. **Mix all the soil samples for a single test in a clean bucket and take a sample of the sample.**

   Place two cups of the soil sample in a plastic bag to send to the laboratory, or use the sample for your home kit testing.

After you know how much lime or sulfur you need to apply, you're ready to spread it. In the small gardens often found in urban areas, spreading these materials by hand is the easiest. Spread the lime or sulfur at least a few months before planting; the minerals need time to take effect. To hasten the effects, work the lime or sulfur into the top 6 inches of the soil after spreading.

Lime and sulfur come in two forms: powder and pellet. Powdered lime and sulfur react quickly with the soil to change the pH. However, they're dusty and can irritate your lungs. Avoid spreading these materials on windy days, and wear gloves and a mask when spreading. People with respiratory issues should avoid using powdered forms of these amendments. Pelleted lime and sulfur are easier to use, but they can be more expensive and harder to find.

In urban areas especially, salts from de-icers used on snow and ice can build up in the soils and become toxic to plants. A simple solution if you're concerned about salt build-up in your soil or if a soil test indicates you have high salt levels, is to flush your soils in spring with water to remove the salt from the upper layers.

Finding Out What Lies Beneath the Soil

City soils are unique. After centuries of development, building, and moving of earth, it's hard to find soil in its natural state in the city. Often what's below the surface of your urban garden is a lot more than soil. Old building debris, parts of roads, power lines, buried treasures, and ancient civilizations can all be found beneath your garden! You can literally dig down through city soils and mark the changing centuries and see the lives people lived by the debris they left behind. The soil can tell a city's story.

But we digress. What you really want to know is what's below your soil and whether you should be concerned about it. You need to be aware of two types of materials in city soils: solid objects and chemical contaminants. Each can make gardening in the city a chore and potentially hazardous, so you need to think about them before you plant that first seed. We show you how to prepare in the following sections.

Doing a little digging (literally and figuratively)

When you're looking around the yard at your house, apartment, or community garden to find the right spot to plant, take a little time to understand the history of your site. Do some research in the local library or municipal offices to find out the former uses for your yard. Old maps and history books may give you a clue as to what used to be on your site and what hazards you should potentially be looking for.

Perhaps your site was an old junkyard, metal-finisher factory, or body shop, or maybe it had railroad tracks going through it. And don't forget that sometimes roads were rerouted, leaving concrete and asphalt buried beneath your lot. Any clues as to what used to be on or under your site may give you an idea of the safest location to place your garden or plant your shrub or tree.

The old materials we talk of may be lying not too far below the soil surface, where they can affect soil water drainage and the ability of tree roots to penetrate into the soil and get a good hold. So do a little experimental digging of a few holes here and there before locating your garden to be sure there aren't any large objects buried beneath the soil.

Before you begin digging in your yard, you need to be sure you don't have any buried power, gas, or water lines under the soil. Chances are you won't be digging deeply enough to hit utility lines, but if the utility company ever has to come in and make repairs in the future, they have the right to dig up everything above their lines, including your prized garden. Check out www.call811.com, which is the website for the national "call before you dig" program. At the site, you can find contact information for your local one-call center.

Protecting yourself from soil contaminants

A larger concern with your garden site than the buried materials that physically make it difficult for plants to grow (see the preceding section) is the contamination from past use of your site. Old industrial cities, in particular, may have soils contaminated with a variety of chemicals. Lead, benzene, and cadmium are just some of the chemicals that could be present in your soil (and hazardous to your health).

Contaminated soil is an especially important issue if you're growing edible crops or have young children or grandchildren who may ingest the soil. Many of the chemicals enter the body through ingestion, but some risk of exposure through breathing in chemical dust is possible as well. Also, some people have skin sensitivity to chemicals simply by touching them.

Common contaminants to be aware of

Table 4-1 shows some of the potential chemicals you need to be aware of.

Table 4-1	Common Sources of Urban Soil Contamination	
Source	*Previous Site Usage*	*Specific Contaminants*
Paint (before 1978)	Old residual buildings; mining, leather, tanning, landfill operations; aircraft component making	Lead
High-traffic areas	Next to heavily trafficked highways and roadways; near roadways built before leaded fuel was phased out	Lead, zinc, polycyclic aromatic hydrocarbons (PAH)
Treated lumber	Lumber treatment facilities	Arsenic, copper, chromium
Burning waste	Landfill operations	PAHs, dioxins
Contaminated manure	Agriculture	Copper, zinc (from copper and zinc salts added to animal feed)
Coal ash	Coal-fired power plants; landfills	Molybdenum, sulfur
Sewage sludge	Sewage treatment plants; agriculture	Cadmium, copper, zinc, lead, persistent bioaccumulative toxins (PBTs)
Petroleum spills	Gas stations; residential/ commercial/industrial uses (anywhere an above-ground or underground storage tank has been located)	PAHs, benzene, toluene, xylene, ethyl benzene
Pesticides	Widespread pesticide use, such as in orchards; pesticide formulation, packaging, and shipping	Lead, arsenic, mercury chlordane, and chlorinated pesticides

(continued)

Table 4-1 *(continued)*

Source	Previous Site Usage	Specific Contaminants
Commercial/ industrial site usage	Factories manufacturing building supplies, chemicals, and other potentially hazardous materials	PAHs, petroleum products, solvents, lead, other heavy metals (such as arsenic, chromium, cadmium, mercury, zinc)
Dry cleaners	Service businesses using chemicals for clothes cleaning	Stoddard solvents, tetrachloroethene
Metal-finishing operations	Factories using hazardous chemicals during painting and finishing work	Metals and cyanides

*Adapted from the EPA

The chemical lists in Table 4-1 look scary, but don't let them deter you from growing food and flowers in the city. The reality is that even though most urban soils have some detectable contaminants, the levels in most cases may not be high enough to warrant action on your part. However, if the levels are high, you can take some steps to remediate the soil, or you can apply some garden techniques that allow you to grow your bounty in the city.

To determine whether the toxin levels are high enough to warrant action, you simply have to hire a professional to do a soil test to check for heavy metals or other pollutants. You can work with the cooperative extension service in your state or a private soil lab. These tests can get pricey if you're testing for a number of possible contaminants, so narrowing the list to the most likely culprits is a good idea (check out the earlier section "Doing a little digging (literally and figuratively))" for some information on researching your site. Doing a soil test on healthy soil every three to four years is fine.

You may be able to find city, state, or federal programs to help offset the cost of these tests. Check online or with your local health department.

The soil test results give you the soil's contaminant levels and the safe standard for each contaminant. You can use this information to determine what action (if any) that you take. For example, the safe standard for lead in soils is 300 milligrams (this amount may vary depending on where you live). Some gardeners may not be comfortable with any detectable lead levels and may consider gardening elsewhere or bringing in new soil if any contamination is detected. Others may feel okay about gardening around a small amount of contamination. Only you can make that decision.

Tips to avoid contamination in your soon-to-be garden

Creating a little green patch in the city can be tough when you're worried about contamination from chemicals and other toxins. However, don't let it stop you from trying. Here are some tips to avoid contamination:

- **Locate your garden away from building foundations.** Lead-based paint chips are most likely found close to buildings where painting occurred. This advice is especially important if the building is old enough to have had lead-based paint used on it. (Lead was banned as a paint additive in 1978.)

- **Build raised beds, lay a sheet of landscape fabric on the bottom, and bring in fresh soil and compost to fill them.** However, don't use chemically treated lumber in your raised bed construction; otherwise you risk introducing new toxins to your soil. We talk more about building a raised bed in Chapter 6.

- **Build a fence or plant a hedge as a barrier to block dust from potential sources of contamination, such as highways or railroad tracks.** After all, it's not only old chemicals and pollutants that are a concern. Present-day vehicle and industrial exhaust can also drift into your yard and contaminate the soil.

- **Mulch thickly (roughly 4 inches) around your plants to minimize their contact with the soil.** We talk more about mulch in Chapter 18.

- **Teach young children not to eat dirt or unwashed vegetables.** Most contaminants get into the body through ingestion. As a result, all produce should be cleaned thoroughly before storing or eating. And, of course, mud pies are a no-no.

- **Wear gloves in the garden and wash your hands thoroughly after working in the garden.** Even though most contaminants are introduced through the mouth, some folks can also have skin reactions to chemicals in the soil. So gloves are important. Also, if you don't wear gloves and wash after gardening, you risk putting the chemicals into your mouth when eating, coughing, or otherwise touching your face.

- **If you're growing vegetables, grow fruiting crops, such as tomatoes, peppers, beans, and okra, rather than root crops, leafy vegetables, or herbs.** Fruiting crops are held above the soil and are less likely to have contaminants on them compared to these other crops. If you do grow leafy vegetables, be sure to remove the outer and bottom leaves before eating. These parts of the plant are in closest contact with the soil and have the most potential to be contaminated. And if you grow root veggies, peel them to remove the skins where contaminants may reside.

- **Add organic matter to the soil through compost or cover crops.** Organic matter makes metals less mobile in the soil and lessens the amount taken up by the plants. We talk more about the miracle of organic matter in Chapter 5.

✔ **Maintain a pH of 6.5 or more.** The higher pH makes metals less mobile in the soil and lessens the amount taken up by the plants. You can read more about pH in the earlier section "Discovering Your Soil's pH Level."

✔ **Replace contaminated soil.** You can physically dig out contaminated soil and send it to a toxic waste site. Then bring in new soil that you know isn't contaminated.

Scientists have done ongoing research in the field of phytoremediation to remove toxins from soil. *Phytoremediation* is the practice of growing plants that are good at accumulating certain toxins. For example, at the University of Southern Maine in Portland, Maine, researchers reduced the lead levels in urban soils by 100 milligrams by growing leafy mustard greens and spinach on contaminated soil. Of course, the plants used must be properly discarded, but the practice raises the idea that contaminated soils in cities can be brought back to a safe and productive life. However, keep in mind that using phytoremediation shouldn't be your only method of reducing exposure to contaminated soils.

Chapter 5

Feeding and Fertilizing Your Soil

*H*ealthy soil and healthy plants start with good soil structure, which consists of a good balance of nutrients in the soil and a balance of soil microbes to make those nutrients available. This balance of microbes and soil nutrients is perhaps one of the most important qualities of healthy soil, but unfortunately, many new gardeners often overlook it.

Like all living creatures, microorganisms need food to survive. The food of choice for soil microbes is *organic matter* (any dead plant or animal material that was once alive).

Organic matter comes in many forms. The most basic is old plants, such as grass clippings, weeds, and hay, but animal manure and compost are also valuable options. Regardless of what form it comes in, though, it creates a better environment for microbes to live, more physical spaces in the soil for air and water, and room for plant roots to grow.

Although plant matter, animal manure, and compost all help build healthy soil, sometimes your garden needs a little extra nutrient boost. That's where organic fertilizers come in. They can correct a nutrient deficiency or imbalance without harming critical soil microbial life in the process.

In this chapter, we give you the ins and outs of feeding your soil with various types of organic matter, and we show you how to use fertilizer to give your plants and soil a nutrient boost when they need it.

Organics 101: Plant Matter

The soil is the heart of your garden, and organic matter is the soul of your soil. We simply can't overemphasize this point. Organic matter in the soil is miraculous stuff. It can take a sandy, lifeless soil and make it teem with vitality again. It can take a rock-hard, clay soil and open it up into a loose, easy-to-work, fertile material.

Although it's a great addition to any soil, organic matter is a particularly important addition to soils that you till or turn over a lot, such as the soil in a vegetable or annual flower garden. As oxygen is introduced into the soil during the tilling process, the soil microbes go wild on the organic matter, eating it up fast. As those microbes die off, the soil gets a temporary boost in nutrients; however, the overall organic matter content of the soil decreases over the long term. So adding organic matter is especially critical in these heavily used soils.

Organic matter double duty

We like to use organic matter in vegetable and flower gardens for multiple purposes. For instance, we lay down a 3-inch-thick layer of untreated grass clippings, hay, and straw between our rows of annual crops. This organic layer does two jobs:

✔ It serves as a dry walkway in the garden.

✔ It feeds the soil as it decomposes.

In addition to this dual-purpose organic layer, we like to add dried leaves to the garden in the fall and till them under in the spring, providing more fodder for our microbial friends.

For perennial flowers, trees, and shrubs, bark mulch and pine needles make great mulch that also serves two purposes:

✔ Preserves soil water

✔ Stops weeds from growing

We talk more about mulching in Chapter 18, but here's the short story: Although these materials decompose slowly, especially in colder climates, bark mulch, wood chips, and sawdust do add organic matter to the soil over time, feeding your plants along the way. If you think simply mulching isn't enough to help a tree grow strong, look at the forest. Countless huge redwoods, oaks, and maple trees tower in forests with little more than an annual mulch of decomposing leaves to feed the tree roots each year.

Organic matter comes in many forms, and each form has its own ideal uses. Some are more readily available to the urban gardener than others. Here are some of the more common types of plant-based organic matter you can use in your garden:

- ✔ **Leaves:** This form of organic matter is the one that most city gardeners have easy access to. Adding green leaves to your garden gives plants a rich source of nitrogen, but adding primarily dried leaves is best because they are widely available in fall for the raking. Try to gather leaves that are not close to busy streets, where particulate air pollution may be accumulating on them.

- ✔ **Grass clippings:** Although many urban gardeners don't have large lawns, any amount of grass clippings can be helpful to your soil. Just make sure you use only grass clippings from lawns that haven't been treated with chemical herbicides; the residues from the chemicals may adversely affect your plants. If you don't have much grass of your own, contact a lawn service in your neighborhood to see what it does with its grass clippings. If they're untreated, you may be able to get more than you need to mulch your garden and build you soil.

- ✔ **Pine needles:** Pine needles may be available for the taking in your urban area. Keep in mind, however, that they're naturally acidic, so use them only on plants such as blueberries and rhododendrons that like an acidic soil pH.

- ✔ **Wood chips:** Wood chips, sawdust, and bark mulch are great materials to use around trees, shrubs, and perennial plants. They take a long time to break down and feed the soil and provide an insulating layer for these long-lived plants. Contact a city arborist or local tree surgeon to see whether they have wood chips you can have. Be sure to ask before you get the chips whether the trees they came from had any insect or disease problems so you don't introduce a pest problem into your garden.

- ✔ **Hay and straw:** Most urban areas don't have ready access to hay and straw, and they can be expensive to purchase. But if you can afford them (or if you have a farm connection), they can be great additions to your garden. Both of these dried grasses take a growing season to break down, so they make for good mulches around annual plants and in pathways. One thing to keep in mind is that hay (although much widely available and cheaper than straw) tends to have weed seeds in it, while straw doesn't.

Adding a Little Something Extra to Build Soil Fertility: Animal Manure

Raw organic matter, like the grasses and wood chips we describe in the preceding section, is a good soil additive that feeds the microbes in it. However, it takes time to decompose into a form your plants can benefit from. Animal manure is better in this regard. Think of animals as composting factories: In goes the raw materials in the form of hay, straw, grass, and kitchen scraps, and out comes the fertilizer in the form of manure. Like organic matter, animal manure feeds the microbes in your soil, but it also contains nutrients that can directly feed your plants.

For annual vegetable and flower gardens, apply a 1- to 2-inch-thick layer of completely decomposed manure annually before the growing season to build and maintain the soil's fertility.

Each type of manure has its own advantages and disadvantages. Generally speaking, using decomposed or aged manures is best for two reasons:

- Composted manures are less smelly (a concern in urban areas when your neighbors are so close).
- Any volatile compounds in the manure that may harm your plants have been broken down.

Even though animals, such as cows, digest their food into a very decomposed form, other animals, such as horses, aren't as efficient, so their manure needs more time to decompose. If you happen to produce your own manure (your animals, that is!), then you need to let it compost or age for at least six months before you use it in your garden.

Don't use dog and cat manures in your garden. Although these manures are plentiful in city areas (just check out the park trash barrels loaded with plastic bags of dog poop), they contain pathogens that can infect humans. So be sure to toss your pets' poop in the trash and look for the manures we list in the table instead.

The manure most urban dwellers find at the local garden center or home center comes in bags. The best part about bagged manure is that it has been composted and sometimes sterilized and is ready to use in your garden. Bulk manure (manure not sold in bags) isn't the norm in most urban areas, but that may be changing in some municipalities. Buying manure in bulk is cheaper if you have a big garden.

Whether the animal manure is in bags or fresh off the farm, you need to know what type of manure you have so you can know how it best can be used in your garden or yard. Table 5-1 lists the most common types of animal manures, along with their advantages and disadvantages.

Table 5-1   The Scoop on Poop: Animal Manure Pros and Cons

Manure Type	Pros	Cons
Cow	Good nutrient-balanced manure with few weed seeds Mild smell	May have high salt levels
Horse	Dry and loaded with unde-composed organic matter Mild smell	May contain weed seeds
Chicken	High in nitrogen and good for plants that need an abundance of this nutrient	The high nitrogen content can burn tender plant roots if used fresh. Strong smell
Sheep and goat	Dry and well decomposed Mild smell	Fresh sheep manure can burn tender seedling roots because of the nitrogen content
Rabbit	Rich in nutrients	Strong smell
Worm	Rich in nutrients Can be used fresh or composted No smell Easy to raise in urban areas	It takes a lotta worms to make much compost. Best used as a compost tea (see "Liquid fertilizers" later in this chapter).

Manures of a different color: Green manures

When you say *manure,* most people automatically think of animal poop. But if you're not into animal manure, you do have another option. *Green manures* are plants that you grow in your garden specifically to till into the soil while they're still green as a fertilizer.

Green manures can work well in the city environment because all you need to get growing with green manures are the seeds. The main downside is that green manures take up space in your garden, so if you have a small plot or only a container garden, you may be limited to what you can grow.

On the plus side, besides feeding the microbes in the soil with organic matter as they decompose, legume green manures, such as peas, beans, and clover, fix nitrogen from the air and add it to the soil. Many legumes, including buckwheat, hairy vetch, and fava beans, also have flowers that attract beneficial insects and bees and look beautiful in your yard.

Making Compost and Growing Soil

Using organic matter and manures to build your soil fertility is important, but both materials have some drawbacks. For instance, raw organic materials like leaves and grass clippings are bulky; animal manures are hard to find unless you buy them in bags in stores, which tend to be pricey; and green manures (see the nearby sidebar, "Manures of a different color: Green manures") take up precious space. So what can urban gardeners do to get the proper fertility in their small-space gardens? The answer is compost.

You can buy bags of compost that are finished and ready to go and not have to deal with other organic materials. However, you save money and use materials right in your kitchen and yard by making your own compost. The beauty about making your own compost is that you can use materials you would normally throw away, and in a matter of months, produce rich, dark-colored compost that will enliven your soil and feed your plants.

Composting safely in the city

If you're interested in making your own compost, don't run out and buy or build a compost bin just yet. First, you need to figure out what you should and shouldn't compost.

What to compost

In general, you can compost anything that was once alive, within reason. Here's a short list of materials that you can safely compost:

- Hay, straw, pine needles, and hedge clippings
- Fresh and dried leaves
- Vegetables and fruit leftovers, peels, pulp from a blender, and scraps
- Egg shells, old bread, coffee grounds, and old tea bags
- Animal manures (except dog, cat, pig, and human)
- Sawdust, wood chips, shredded black-and-white newspaper (should be used sparingly because they break down slowly)
- Weeds (as long as they haven't gone to seed or are invasive)
- Old vegetable plants and flowers (as long as the plants aren't heavily diseased or insect ridden)
- Sod and soil

What not to compost

Avoid putting any of the following organic materials into your compost pile:

- ✔ Herbicide-treated grass clippings

- ✔ Kitchen scraps with meats, oils, fish, dairy products, and bones, which can all attract animals, such as rats and raccoons, to the pile

- ✔ Dog or cat feces, which can harbor diseases that infect humans even after being composted

Choosing a container

After you've decided what to compost, you have to figure out how to contain your pile. You can find many different compost bins on the market today, or you can make one yourself. Frankly, in an urban environment, the store-bought bin may be the best way to make compost without upsetting your neighbors. We're not saying that compost stinks (done properly, it's odor-free) or looks bad (it eventually looks like rich soil), but it's a process and some people just don't like the idea of seeing decomposing organic matter in their neighbor's yard. A commercial bin, such as the one in Figure 5-1, is made from high-quality plastic, wood, or metal and is covered so only you know the magic of what's happening inside. For very small gardens, try the commercial compost tumbler that mixes the compost ingredients each time you give is a whirl.

The ideal dimensions of your urban compost bin are 3-feet wide by 4-feet high. This is large enough to heat up and decompose quickly, yet not so large that it'll be hard to manage. Most commercial bins are about this size.

If you decide to make your own compost bin, you can do so by using wire cages, wood pallets, or wooden planks. Homemade bins tend to be more open and exposed to the environment, and the ingredients are more visible to you and your neighbors. Thus, they're good to use if you have a larger yard, more space, and lots of material to compost.

Whichever bin you choose, the way to build the pile is the same.

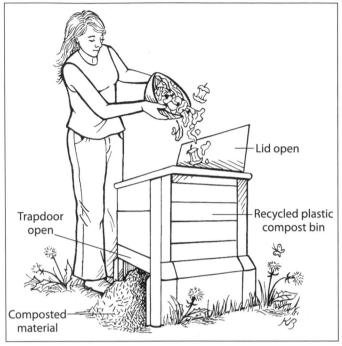

Lid open

Trapdoor
open

Recycled plastic
compost bin

Figure 5-1:
A
commercial
compost
bin.

Composted
material

Illustration by Kathryn Born.

Building your pile

Compostable materials basically come in two types:

- ✔ *Brown materials* are high in carbon and provide the long-term fuel to decompose all the materials in the pile. They include old hay, straw, dried leaves, sawdust, wood chips, and old grass clippings.

- ✔ *Green materials* are high in nitrogen and break down quickly. They jump-start the decomposition process in your pile and include fresh grass clippings, green weeds, kitchen scraps, fertilizer, and soil.

Having the right combination of brown and green materials is essential to creating a quickly decomposing pile. You just have to figure out the science behind making a compost pile. Fortunately, it's a simple technique to master:

1. **Find an out-of-the-way spot to place your bin.**

   Place your bin on soil, if possible, in part shade, but don't hide it so well that you forget about it. Keeping it close to the kitchen is ideal because you'll more easily remember to add the kitchen scraps.

2. **Add a 6-inch-thick layer of brown materials to the bottom of the bin.**

3. **Add a 2- to 3-inch-thick layer of green materials on top of the brown materials.**

4. **Repeat Steps 2 and 3 until you reach the top of the bin.**

5. **Water well.**

   Moisten each layer as you add it so that it's moist but not too wet.

6. **Cover, wait, and turn.**

   Cover the pile to prevent it from drying out or getting soggy due to rains. After a few weeks, it'll heat up and be noticeably warm. After it cools, turn the ingredients together, water, and let it heat up again. You may need to go through this cycle a few times until the pile no longer heats up. After a few months, when you can't recognize most of the original ingredients and the pile is a crumbly brown texture, your compost is ready to use.

Troubleshooting common composting problems

How fast your compost finishes depends on the ingredients, the weather, and the amount of turning you do. You'll get finished compost faster if you use shredded materials and the weather is warm than if you use bulky materials in the wintertime. If you prefer, you can simply build the pile and leave it alone without turning it. It will eventually decompose, but it'll take longer and the final product won't be as uniform. You'll likely still see undecomposed materials in the pile.

As with any new venture, you're bound to run into a few snags along the way to finished compost. The pile may smell, never heat up, or not break down all the way. Here are a few troubleshooting tips to keep in mind if you run into problems:

✔ **Experiment with the moisture.** If the pile is too wet or dry, it won't break down properly.

✔ **Watch your brown and green ratios.** If your pile has too much brown material, it won't heat up properly. If the pile has too much green material, it may have a foul smell or get slimy.

✔ **Make it the right size.** A pile that's too small may not have the mass to heat up properly. A pile that's too large is unwieldy.

Maintaining the right mix of brown and green materials is essential to making a good pile. Many urban dwellers accumulate little bits of kitchen scraps, grass clippings, and old plants periodically throughout the growing season. Instead of just tossing them in the compost pile as you would throw them in the garbage, keep them in a separate container. When you have enough to build a compost pile, add the right proportion of brown and green materials. As that pile is cooking, so to speak, you can start accumulating materials for the next pile. A pile that continually has materials added to the top won't ever decompose properly.

Composting with worms

Worms are amazing decomposers. They're voracious vegetarians, eating materials such as vegetable kitchen scraps, fruit peels, shredded black and white paper, pulverized eggshells, and coffee grounds. In fact, they eat their weight in kitchen scraps every day! Okay, so they aren't exactly chubby, but that's still impressive.

You can raise worms in bins in a closet, under the kitchen sink, in a basement — really anywhere they won't freeze and you can keep an eye on them. The payoff of raising worms is rich compost that's perfect for young seedlings, vegetables, houseplants, herbs, and just about any other plant. It's odorless and has a good balance of nutrients, and soil microbes love to eat it.

Worm composting is perfect for the urban dweller with limited space and lots of kitchen scraps and curiosity. Plus, kids love raising worms in the house. Don't worry! They won't escape and end up in the bedroom. They'll stay in the bin where the food is.

If you want to give worm composting a try, follow these steps to set up your worm bin:

1. **Get a bin**.

   You can raise worms in almost any sealed container, including an empty plastic soda bottle or a store-bought plastic or rubber storage box. But the easiest way is to purchase a commercial worm bin (see Figure 5-2). Commercial bins are the right size to fit under sinks and in small spaces, have the proper drainage holes, and include a lid to keep the worms' environment dark. If you make your own bin, drill 8 to 15 holes in the bottom for proper water drainage and place a tray to catch the water underneath it.

2. **Fill the bin three-quarters full with bedding material.**

   Moistened and shredded black-and-white newspaper is best. Add a handful of potting soil to help the worms digest the food scraps you'll hide in the newspaper. Fluff up the bedding so it's not matted.

3. **Get some worms**.

   Indoor worm bins need special worms. Don't go digging up night crawlers from your yard and expect them to work. The worm of choice for bins is the red wiggler. Red wigglers are adapted to indoor temperatures and environments. One pound of worms (approximately 1,000 worms!) can process 3 to 4 pounds of food scraps per week. Most kitchens can get started by purchasing 2 pounds of worms for their bin.

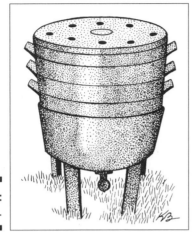

Illustration by Kathryn Born.

4. **Feed your worms by tucking food scraps in the bedding in different sections of the bin.**

   Worms like it dark and will go about finding the food and digesting it. They eat a variety of vegetarian specialties, including vegetable and fruit scraps, pulverized eggshells, coffee grounds, and tea bags. Avoid feeding them meats, dairy products, and oily foods, which can create foul odors or attract flies or rodents. Don't overfeed them; use 3 to 4 pounds of food scraps per week for a normal-sized bin (roughly 2 feet square and 8 inches deep).

After about 2 to 3 months, when the bin is mostly worm poop (called *castings*), it's time to harvest the compost. The easiest way is to push all the castings to one side of the bin and put fresh bedding in the other side. Give the worms a few days to migrate to the new food and then scoop out the finished worm manure.

For more information on raising worms indoors, check out *Worms Eat My Garbage* by Mary Appelhof (Flower Press).

Although using the worm castings straight from the worm bin is fine for plants, you can make the rich compost go farther by making *worm tea*. Simply place two cups of worm castings in cheesecloth or old pantyhose. Suspend the worm castings in a bucket of water for 24 hours, stirring occasionally. The water will turn brown from all the nutrients and microbes that leach into the water from the worm castings. Use the nutrient-rich water on plants within a few days and dump the worm castings in the garden.

Giving Your Plants and Soil a Boost with Fertilizers

In most situations, adding raw organic matter, compost, and manures to your soil will be enough to grow healthy flower and vegetable gardens, trees, shrubs, and lawns. But sometimes, you have to give your plants an added boost. That's where commercial fertilizers come in.

Commercial fertilizers apply the nutrients that plants need directly to the plants. Some are *complete,* meaning they contain relatively equal quantities of the three main plant nutrients — nitrogen, phosphorous, and potassium. Others have higher levels of one or more of these nutrients to offset a deficiency in your soil. You can determine when and how much fertilizer to apply based on your soil test (see Chapter 4 for details).

Getting to know the "big three" in commercial fertilizers

Often you see three numbers on your fertilizer bag or container indicating the levels of nitrogen, phosphorous, and potassium in the fertilizer. These nutrients are called the "big three" or *macronutrients* because plants need them the most.

- ✔ **Nitrogen (N):** This nutrient plays a key role in building proteins and *chlorophyll* (the pigment responsible for photosynthesis) in plants. It helps keep plant leaves green and healthy. Nitrogen leaches out of the soil quickly, so many urban gardeners have to add it on a regular basis to have a steady supply all season long.

- ✔ **Phosphorous (P):** Phosphorus helps promote good root growth and bulb formation. It's also important in fruit and seed formation and increased disease resistance. Phosphorous accumulates in soils and doesn't move about in the soil easily, so you may need to add it only occasionally. Phosphorous isn't readily available to plants if soils are cold or if the pH is below 5 or above 7. So before you add a fertilizer high in phosphorous, check these conditions to see whether you really need to add it.

- ✔ **Potassium (K):** This nutrient promotes plant vigor, fruit and vegetable flavor, disease resistance, and general cellular functioning in plants. Like phosphorous, potassium doesn't move easily in the soil, so you may have to add it only occasionally.

The best fertilizers are ones that contain these three nutrients in varying amounts (2-12-4, for example), otherwise known as complete fertilizers.

Balanced fertilizers contain the same amount of the three nutrients, such as 5-5-5. These are called complete fertilizers. Single-element fertilizers contain only one of these three nutrients, such as nitrogen (46-0-0). There are fertilizers that feature a certain nutrient over another such as 2-12-4. This is a fertilizer high in any one nutrient phosphorous and should be used if a soil test indicates a deficiency of that nutrient.

Plants need other nutrients, such as magnesium, calcium, and sulfur, in smaller quantities. These are called *secondary nutrients.* Plants also need minerals or *micronutrients,* such as boron, copper, and iron, in even smaller quantities. However, in most cases, if you have a nutrient problem in your soil, the deficiency is in one of the three macronutrients. Plus, if you're regularly adding organic matter, compost, and/or manures, you're probably adding enough of the micronutrients and minerals to keep the soil healthy.

Wet versus dry fertilizers

Fertilizer products come in two forms: liquid or granular. Each one has its own advantages and disadvantages.

Liquid fertilizers

Liquid fertilizers give plants a quick boost of nutrients because plant roots and leaves readily absorb them. When you apply liquid fertilizers to leaves, the process is often called *foliar feeding.* Liquid fertilizers are a great way to remedy a nutrient deficiency quickly or add highly soluble nutrients, such as nitrogen, to a plant. Some examples of liquid fertilizers include

- ✔ **Fish emulsion:** Fish emulsion, also called *fish fertilizer,* is made from the by-products of the fish industry. It can be a smelly product, but plants love it. It has a good balance of nutrients (5-2-2) that help young seedlings, in particular, grow strong. It often comes as a concentrate that's diluted in water.

- ✔ **Worm tea:** Although you can make your own worm tea (see the earlier section "Composting with worms"), you can also buy a liquid worm food already made for you. Worm tea offers many of the advantages of fish emulsion, but it doesn't have the bad smell.

- ✔ **Manure tea:** This fertilizing technique takes your use of manure to a whole new level. You can use the same process you use for making worm tea to make manure tea (see the earlier section "Composting with worms"), or you can buy it already made. Either way, it adds many of the nutrients you'd get from straight manure compost without all the bulk and bother.

Granular fertilizers

Granular fertilizers are probably the most common and easiest to use. They come in bags or boxes in quantities ranging from 1 to 50 pounds. They're easy to apply by hand and aren't messy to work with. However, they're not as quickly available to plants as liquid fertilizers; many of them need a few weeks to break down before plants can absorb their nutrients.

Granular fertilizers are processed and made from a blend of different products. They're often derived from materials such as soybeans or chicken manure (for nitrogen), bones or rock phosphate (for phosphorous), and greensand and wood ash (for potassium). Some varieties have special formations for specific plants like roses, citrus plants, and rhododendrons.

Although most granular fertilizers are complete fertilizers with a mix of ingredients, you can purchase some that feature specific nutrients. Here are a few examples of these types of granular fertilizers:

- **Alfalfa meal:** Made from alfalfa plants and pressed into pellet form, alfalfa meal is a good form of nitrogen and potassium fertilizer that stimulates plant growth. Roses are particularly fond of alfalfa meal fertilizer. Soybean meal is a similar plant-based granular fertilizer.

- **Corn gluten meal:** Mostly sold as an organic herbicide for crabgrass and dandelion control, corn gluten meal has about 10 percent nitrogen.

- **Bone meal:** This product is derived from animal and fish bones and is a good source of phosphorous (11 percent) and calcium (22 percent). It's good for bulbs and root crops, but it may attract animals such as dogs and raccoons.

- **Greensand:** Greensand is a mineral mined from old ocean deposits. It has a good amount of potassium (3 percent) and is slow to decompose, supplying this needed nutrient to your soil for years after you apply it.

- **Rock phosphate:** This phosphorous-rich mineral comes in a hard form (20 percent phosphate) and a soft form (16 percent phosphate). The hard form breaks down slowly in the soil, so it takes months to have an effect. Soft rock phosphate breaks down a little faster.

- **Limestone:** Although lime is commonly used to raise the pH of soil for better plant growth, depending on the type of lime you use, it also adds calcium (46 percent) and magnesium (38 percent). Choose *dolomitic lime* if you need more calcium and magnesium in your soil (based on a soil test) and *calcitic lime* if you need just calcium. (See Chapter 4 for details on how to do a soil test.)

Why use organic fertilizers rather than chemical ones?

We favor organic fertilizers over chemical ones for several reasons. Although organic fertilizers may be slower to release their nutrients, they offer you and your garden many advantages:

✓ Organic fertilizers feed the soil by supplying nutrients to microbes that help keep a healthy, balanced soil ecosystem. These microbes help fight disease organisms, supply secondary nutrients and micronutrients, and create humus that helps with water and nutrient uptake.

✓ Most organic fertilizers supply a slow, steady release of nutrients to the plants. They feed plants over time and don't give them just a quick shot of nutrients.

✓ Organic fertilizers are more widely available than ever before.

✓ Organic fertilizers can be free — if you make your own teas and compost (see the section "Making Compost and Growing Soil" for details).

The biggest benefits of chemical fertilizers are that they come in granular and liquid forms, they're widely available, and they tend to be less expensive than manufactured organic fertilizer. However, we avoid using them for the following reasons:

✓ Chemical fertilizers don't add organic matter or feed the soil's microorganisms. Chemical fertilizers are like taking a vitamin pill, while organic fertilizers are like eating a good meal.

✓ Most chemical fertilizers act quickly and don't have any staying power to feed plants over time. The exception is the time-release fertilizer that releases chemicals slowly into the soil over time. You add these small pellets around plants and in containers, and as you water them or as rain falls, the pellets release chemicals. But they still don't provide organic matter.

Applying a side dressing of fertilizer

You usually add manures, compost, organic matter, and/or manufactured organic fertilizers before planting to build the fertility of the soil in anticipation of the new garden season. But you can use fertilizers in another way, too, with a technique called *side dressing*. Side dressing means adding organic fertilizers while the plants are actively growing to ensure a steady supply of nutrients. The most common use for side dressing is with fast-growing annual flowers and vegetables because these plants use up and need more quickly available nutrients than trees, shrubs, and perennial flowers. You'll know your plants may need a side dressing of fertilizer if they are growing slowly or the leaves are small or yellowing.

To put side dressing to work for you, simply add a few tablespoons of a granular fertilizer per plant or a few pounds per 25-foot row of vegetables monthly during the growing season (see Figure 5-3). Or use liquid fertilizers by adding them to your watering can and applying them every few weeks. Follow the directions on the fertilizer container for the frequency.

Figure 5-3:
Applying
a side
dressing of
fertilizer.

Illustration by Kathryn Born.

Urban gardeners often take advantage of growing plants in containers, hanging baskets, and window boxes. These containers have a relatively small amount of soil that doesn't contain many nutrients naturally, not to mention watering and rain tend to leach the nutrients out of the soil. The result is often struggling, starving plants. But you can do something to help improve your container gardening success. Apply regular doses of fertilizer to the flowers, fruits, and vegetables you grow in containers throughout the growing season to help them survive. Generally, fertilizing with a liquid product every few weeks helps keep these plants growing strong. Follow the recommendations on the fertilizer's packaging for proper dosage amounts. (We talk more about container gardening in Chapter 8.)

Don't be overzealous when side dressing plants. Adding too much fertilizer, especially to containers, can cause fertilizer salts to build up in the soil, which can harm the roots of your plants. Also, adding fertilizer during dry spells or cold weather is a waste of time and money because the plants don't readily take up the nutrients under these conditions.

Chapter 6

Getting Your Hands Dirty: Planting How-To

. . . .

In This Chapter

▶ Considering your options when planting veggies and annual flowers

▶ Planting trees and shrubs in your yard

▶ Getting your perennial flowers and roses off to a good start

. . . .

*A*fter your soil is ready and the weather has warmed, you may be tempted to jump right into your garden and start planting. We're all for unbridled enthusiasm, but before you start digging up your yard, make sure you know what you're doing (and why).

Whether you start with seeds or transplants, annual flowers and vegetables are fast-growing plants that need to get off to a strong start. You can start perennial flowers from seed, but they usually work best as transplants. Trees and shrubs can be purchased *bare root* in spring without any soil on their roots, and roses come as either bare root plants or container plants.

Each of these plants requires different techniques for planting. Lucky for you, we cover them all in this chapter. (If don't have room to plant in the ground, consider container gardening. Find out more in Chapter 8.)

Planting Annual Flowers and Veggies

Annual flowers and vegetables are the perfect plants for an urban gardener to add to his garden. They're quick growing and versatile, they fit in small spaces and containers, and they offer food and flowers soon after planting. There are two ways to purchase your annual flowers and vegetables: as seeds or transplants. Your choice is more than a matter of preference. Some annual flowers and vegetables are easier to grow as transplants while others are a snap grown from seed. Then, some vegetables can *only* be grown from seeds.

In the following sections, we tell you how to prepare a place for your annuals and veggie plants, give you guidelines for choosing transplants or starting from seed, and then dig into planting. For tips on planning your garden and deciding what to grow, see Chapter 13 and 14.

Starting with a raised bed

The key to success in any annual flower or veggie garden is a properly prepared soil bed, and in an urban environment, the best way to prepare a soil bed is to use a *raised bed*. Generally speaking, raised beds are filled with 8 to 10 inches of soil and are no wider than 4 feet so you never have to step in the bed (and compact the soil) to reach your plants.

Reaping the benefits of raised beds

Perhaps the biggest benefit to using raised beds is that they help seeds germinate faster and transplants grow stronger with fewer problems. But they offer many other advantages as well:

- **The soil is ready faster.** Soil in raised beds warms up quicker and dries out faster in spring, allowing you to plant sooner.

- **The soil stays loose.** Because raised beds are no more than 3 or 4 feet wide, you should be able to reach into the center of your bed from either side. You don't have to walk or kneel on the soil, reducing soil compaction and making it easier for root crops in particular to grow.

- **You can concentrate your watering, fertilizing, and weeding.** Because you're growing in a compact space, watering, fertilizing, and weeding are much easier to do than if you were working in a big yard plot.

- **A raised bed defines your garden.** Urban yards are often home to many competing activities, such as kids playing, dogs running, and visitors walking around. A raised bed clearly shows where your garden begins and ends.

- **A raised bed is easier to work.** Because raised beds are elevated, you don't have to bend down as much. You can make them taller than 10 inches if you really don't want to stoop, and you can make the edges wide enough to sit on while you work.

Preparing your own raised bed

Raised beds can be permanent or temporary.

- **Permanent raised beds:** These beds are constructed of a long-lasting, rot-resistant material, such as cedar or hemlock wood, composite plastic wood, concrete blocks, bricks, or stones. Avoid using any chemically treated woods because their chemicals can leach into the soil.

To build a permanent raised bed, build a frame of the wood or material of choice making it no wider than 3 feet so you can reach the center of the bed without stepping on it and 10 inches tall. Keep the bottom open. If you're placing the raised bed over a grassy area, mow the grass low, then add the compost and topsoil to fill the bed to the top. The compost and topsoil will kill the grass so there's no need to remove it.

✔ **Temporary raised beds:** You construct these beds each spring without permanent borders (hence their name!). The beauty of temporary raised beds is that they allow your artistic side to come out. You can make them in almost any shape you want, including circles, squares, rectangles, and hearts.

To create a temporary raised bed, simply mound up the soil from pathways onto the bed area or bring in fresh soil until the bed is about 12 inches tall. Turn the soil in the bed and rake the top of the bed flat and smooth.

Figure 6-1 shows you what each of these beds looks like.

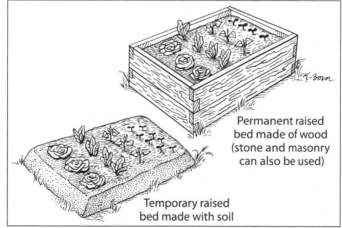

Permanent raised bed made of wood (stone and masonry can also be used)

Temporary raised bed made with soil

K. Born

Figure 6-1: Permanent versus temporary raised beds.

Illustration by Kathryn Born.

Soil is sometimes at a premium in city yards, so you may need to bring in some soil to fill your entire bed. The best soil to use is a combination of topsoil and compost. A 60/40 mix of topsoil to compost provides the nutrients your plants need without overfeeding. Each spring, you need to top your raised bed with 1 to 2 inches of compost for the season.

If you're building your raised bed on an impervious surface, such as asphalt or cement, you need to build the bed a little taller (2 to 4 inches) and place landscape fabric under it. Although the landscape fabric is a woven material that lets water penetrate, it prevents the soil from eroding away during rainstorms and prevents the movement of any harmful chemicals from the asphalt or cement into your soil.

Deciding whether to buy seeds or transplants

When you're planning an annual flower or vegetable garden, you need to decide whether you want to start with seeds or transplants. Growing annual plants from seeds offers the following advantages:

- ✔ **Variety:** Buying seeds enables you to select from a wider range of plant varieties than what you typically find at a local garden center.

- ✔ **Price:** Buying seeds is more cost effective and can save you money. For example, you can grow 20 to 30 tomato plants from a single packet of seed that costs only a few dollars. Buying that many tomato transplants could cost you ten times as much money. The same is true for many annual flowers.

- ✔ **Availability:** Sometimes buying seeds is the only way to go. Not only are some vegetables best grown from seed, but others are available only in that form. Root crops, such as carrots, beets, parsnips, and radishes, for example, never come as transplants, so you must use seeds to grow them.

- ✔ **History:** Growing your own plants from seeds is a satisfying experience. Plus, you know exactly what fertilizers and pesticides have been used to grow them.

On the other hand, buying transplants offers some unique advantages that a small-space, time-crunched urban gardener can really appreciate:

- ✔ **Growing season:** Some plants, like tomatoes and petunias, don't have enough time to produce flowers or fruits when grown from seeds planted directly in the garden in most parts of the country. As a result, you have to start their seeds early indoors before the weather is warm enough to plant outside. Many urban gardeners don't have the space, time, or suitable conditions to start plants early in their homes. So purchasing transplants that have been grown in ideal greenhouse conditions is often the most practical way to go with these kinds of plants.

- ✔ **Convenience:** Transplants are easy and immediate. When you purchase a ready-to-plant transplant, you can put it in the ground that day — no waiting, no fussing. Many times they've already been hardened off and are ready to grow when you buy them.

- **Quantity:** Transplants are good for small gardens. If you're growing only a few tomatoes, six basil plants, and a few marigolds, buying a few transplants is much easier than buying a whole packet of each plant, especially since you'll use only a few seeds.

- **Survival:** Transplants are more likely to survive. A well-grown transplant with a healthy root system that has been professionally grown is often more likely to survive the vagaries of weather and pests than a tender young seedling just starting out in the world.

If you decide to grow your annual flower and vegetable garden from seeds, you have to decide whether the plants you're planting are best sown directly into the garden or are better started from seeds indoors a number of weeks before planting outdoors. Here are some of the easiest direct sown vegetables and annual flowers:

- **Direct sown vegetables:** Squash, pumpkins, cucumbers, lettuce, spinach, beans, peas, kale, Swiss chard, beets, and carrots

- **Direct sown annual flowers:** Nasturtiums, poppies, morning glory, sunflowers, zinnias, cosmos, sweet peas, cleome, and forget-me-nots

When you start seeds indoors before planting them outdoors, you're basically growing your own transplants. During their time indoors, they grow large enough and mature enough to produce after you transplant them outdoors (just like transplants you buy at the store). The following plants are much simpler to grow from transplants:

- **Transplant vegetables:** Tomatoes, peppers, eggplant, broccoli, cabbage, cauliflower, onions, leeks, and Brussels sprouts

- **Transplant annual flowers:** Marigolds, geraniums, impatiens, begonias, petunias, pansies, and salvia

Many vegetables and annual flowers can be planted directly as seeds or as transplants. For example, you often find lettuce, cucumbers, squash, nasturtium, sunflower, zinnia, cosmos, and basil for sale as transplants, and broccoli, cabbage, onions, impatiens, petunias, and marigolds are usually available as seeds, too. Which type you use depends on the length of your growing season and your patience with growing plants from seeds indoors and nursing them along.

Making a seed-starting schedule based on frost dates

Before you get started sowing seeds or planting transplants, it's good to understand about frost dates and how they affect when you plant your seeds or seedlings indoors or outside. To keep track of the process, create a seed-starting schedule. You can begin planning your seed-starting schedule in the winter months or early spring season. Though this may seem early to be thinking about starting seeds, planning ahead is essential if you want to grow plants that need quite a bit of time under lights or a head start before being transplanted into the garden.

To plan your schedule for starting seeds early indoors or planting other seeds directly into your urban garden, start by making a list of everything you want to plant. Then follow these steps:

1. **Determine your region's frost-free date.**

   Find the average frost-free date for your area. If you haven't been keeping your own records, contact your county extension office or go to www.geocities.com/mastergardener2k/frost.html.

2. **Plant after any chance of frost.**

   Planting after the chance of frost (any temperature below 32 degrees F) is the main goal, but if you're looking to plant early, you can use different techniques to temporarily cover plants, retain additional heat, and keep out the cold to extend the planting season.

3. **Develop a planting schedule for each transplant; in other words, determine the set-out dates.**

   Check the seed packet or catalog for this information, or check out a gardening book or the Internet. These sources usually list each vegetable along with the number of weeks before or after the last frost the plant can be set out.

4. **Develop a seeding schedule.**

   After you know the set-out dates for the plants you want to grow, you need to figure out how far ahead of this date you should start your seeds if that's appropriate for that type of vegetable. You can usually find this information on the seed packet, but if it's not there, check the Web.

   The packet may tell you how many weeks from seeding to set-out, or it may tell you how many weeks from germination to set-out. If the latter is the case, you also have to look at the seed packet to find out how long the seeds take to germinate and figure this time period into your schedule. Some are quick, while others, like parsley, may take two weeks or more just to germinate. Make sure you plan for this extra time when figuring out your schedule.

5. **Record dates on your planting calendar.**

   Write the set-out date for each vegetable on a calendar. Then move backward through the weeks and record the seeding date. After you have all the set-out and seeding dates listed, go through the vegetables that you'll seed directly outdoors and do the same thing. Hang your new planting calendar somewhere prominent where you'll see it every day.

Your planting calendar is a very useful tool year to year because it helps provide a record of all your gardening activities, including when to start seeds indoors, when your frost-free dates were in the past, and when to transplant various plants outdoors. It gives you a recorded time line of what you did the year before so you can easily make adjustments the following year if you need to.

Growing your own seedlings

Growing your own annual flower or vegetable transplants isn't difficult; you just have to have the right equipment, time, and dedication. Here are some simple steps you can take to get your seeds started indoors:

1. **Find a few good containers to use.**

   You can use many different types of containers, including clean yogurt cups, peat pots, peat pellets, plastic pots, and plastic trays. Whatever type you use, make sure it has drainage holes and can hold at least a depth of 3 to 4 inches of seed-starting soil.

2. **Add 3 to 4 inches of seed-starting soil to each container.**

   Seed-starting soil is specially formulated to help young seeds grow easily. Avoid heavy potting soil mixes and garden soil; they can compact, making it hard for young roots to grow, and garden soil may contain harmful diseases that could attack the plants. Moisten the seed-starting mix before putting it into the containers.

3. **Sow your seeds into each container.**

   Follow the directions on the seed packet for how many seeds to sow per container and for how deep to sow the seeds in the soil.

4. **Mark your seeds.**

   For each container, use a permanent marker to write the name of your seedlings and the sowing date on a plastic or wooden plant marker and stick it in the soil.

5. **Cover your containers with a plastic sheet and place them in a warm location out of direct sunlight.**

   Check for germination every few days.

6. **After the seeds start to germinate, give your seeds some light.**

   Remove the plastic cover and place the containers under artificial lights (see Figure 6-2). Commercial full-spectrum grow lights are best, but if you don't have them, you can use a simple fluorescent shop light with one cool white bulb and one warm white bulb. Place the lights only a few inches from the top of the seedlings and move them up as the seedlings grow. Use a timer to keep the lights on for 14 hours a day.

7. **Thin, water, and feed.**

   After the second set of leaves has formed, thin your seedlings to one per small container by snipping out the extras with scissors. Keep the soil moist but not soggy, or your seedlings may get diseased and die. Fertilize with an organic liquid fertilizer, such as fish emulsion, as directed on the bottle, starting after the second set of leaves form.

8. **Keep them growing.**

   Keep the plants growing strong until one week before you plan to transplant them outdoors. Before transplanting the seedlings outdoors, harden off the seedlings (see the later section "Planting annual flower and vegetable seedlings" for details).

   If you're growing large plants, such as tomatoes, and you started with small containers like yogurt cups, you may need to transplant the seedlings into larger pots before transplanting them outdoors. After the height of the seedlings is three times the diameter of the pot, transplant them into a pot one size larger.

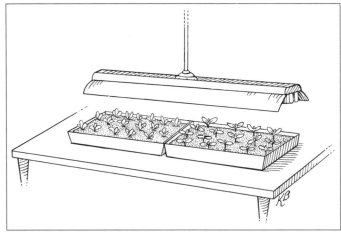

Figure 6-2:
An indoor seed-starting setup.

Illustration by Kathryn Born.

Picking out transplants

If you're not yet ready to go the grow-your-own-seedling route, head to your local garden center to buy your annual flowers and vegetables as transplants. Here are some things to keep in mind as you hunt around for the best plants:

✔ **Check the tops.** Healthy transplants have dark green leaves all the way to the soil line. Yellow leaves may be a sign of stressed or underfed plants.

✔ **Check the roots.** Take a peek at the root systems of some of the transplants. The roots should be white in color and fill the soil root ball; they shouldn't be growing out the drainage holes of the pot. Don't buy a plant whose roots are winding around in circles; that plant is _root bound,_ meaning the roots will take extra time to grow into the native soil, slowing the growth of your plant.

✔ **Avoid flowering plants.** Although seeing flowers on your new transplants is exciting, it's best to pick vegetables that aren't flowering at all or annual flowers with few flowers. Flowers take a lot of energy from plants, and at this stage, you want your veggie plants to spend that energy growing better roots, not flowers. For annual flowers, you may want to see the actual color of the flowers, so finding transplants with a few flowers is perfectly fine. But with both vegetables and annual flower transplants, we recommend that you snip off the flowers when you get your plants home so they can grow healthier and eventually form more flowers.

✔ **Small is beautiful.** Small transplants with healthy root systems are generally a better buy than large transplants. Small transplants go through less shock when you plant them in your garden because they have less foliage demanding nutrients and water from the roots. Large transplants, on the other hand, may take longer to get established in your garden. In fact, smaller transplants often catch up or even pass the larger ones because they transplant without skipping a beat.

Planting your annual or vegetable garden

Now that you have your transplants or have purchased your seed, it's time to plant into the soil. Plant your transplants or sow the seeds at the correct time for your area based on information on the seed packets or from your local Extension Service office or Master Gardeners. See Chapter 13 for more on the timing of transplanting.

Planting annual flower and vegetable seedlings

Whether you're ready to plant your homegrown seedlings or the ones you bought at a local garden center, the basic steps are the same:

1. **In the days leading up to planting, let your seedlings spend some time outside so they can harden off.**

   Hardening off means getting your seedlings accustomed to the outdoors before transplanting them into the garden or container. They'll experience less transplant shock and will be more likely to survive. To harden off plants, place your seedlings outdoors in a protected location for one to two hours on the first day; then bring them indoors. Each day thereafter, place them outside for longer periods of time each day. After seven days, you can leave them outdoors overnight. Always protect them from frost if the nights get chilly.

2. **Dig a hole twice as wide as the pot and as deep as the transplant is in the pot.**

3. **Carefully remove the plant from the pot.**

   Turn the pot upside down, holding your hand over the soil surface and around the seedling. Gently tap the bottom of the pot so the root ball slides out into your palm. You may have to gently squeeze the pot or run a knife around the inside edge if the seedling doesn't pop out easily. *Note:* If you're using biodegradable peat or cow pots, you don't have to remove the plant; you can plant the pot in the soil, too.

4. **Place the transplant deep enough in the soil that it's at the same depth as it was in the pot.**

   Some plants, such as tomatoes, are exceptions to this rule. You can plant them deeper in the soil because they form roots along their stems.

5. **Refill the space around the plant with soil.**

   Use the soil you removed from the hole to fill back in around the roots of the transplant, pressing gently to firm the soil. Double-check that the planting depth is correct (see the preceding step).

6. **Water well.**

   Water the soil around the transplant to saturate the soil. If the water runs off before soaking into the soil around the roots, build a small berm (or shelf) of soil around the transplant to contain the water in the plant's root zone.

Sowing annual flower and vegetable seeds

For those annual flowers and vegetables that you want to sow directly in the garden from seeds, follow these steps:

1. **Determine the right time to sow the seeds in your area.**

   Use your seed-starting schedule, look at each seed packet for information on the best sowing time for your region, or contact the Master Gardener Program in your area to determine the right time to plant (www. extension.org/pages/9925/state-and-provincial-master-gardener-programs:-extension-and-affiliated-program-listings).

2. **Prepare the soil.**

   Prepare your raised bed or garden soil the day before seeding. Remove large rocks, sticks, and other debris and amend the soil with a 1- to

2-inch-thick layer of compost (see Chapter 4 for more on soil quality and Chapter 5 for details on compost).

3. **Sow your seeds in patterns.**

Sow your seeds in straight rows or broadcast them in wide rows. Straight rows are more orderly and easier to weed, while broadcasting seeds allows you to fit more plants in the bed. Broadcast sowing works best on raised beds. Sow at the proper depth and spacing for each seed, based on the seed packet information. Press the soil over the seeds with your hands or a hoe after sowing.

4. **Gently water the seed bed.**

You want the water to soak into the soil and not wash away the seeds. Use a soaker hose or a watering can with small holes in the head so only a gentle spray falls on the seed bed.

5. **Weed your garden regularly.**

Watch for weeds in your bed and pull them as soon as you see them. If you become familiar with what your young seedlings look like (check out pictures online or in gardening books), it will be easier to figure out which seedlings are weeds to pull and which are plants to keep.

6. **Thin your seedlings.**

After the second set of leaves (called *true leaves*) forms, thin your seedlings to the proper spacing based on the recommendation on the seed packet. Unthinned seedlings will be overcrowded, resulting in poor root formation (for root crop vegetables like carrots) or poor flowering (for annual flowers).

Protecting young plants from frost

Cold frames may be the best solution for your urban garden. *Cold frames* are basically little houses where plants can get a head start at growing in the spring and extra growing time in the fall and early winter. These frame-type structures are good for starting seedlings early in the season for later transplanting or for growing some lettuce, spinach, and radishes to eat early.

Probably the simplest cold frame to make consists of just six bales of hay and a storm window. Arrange the hay bales in a rectangle on the southern side of your house and top them with a storm window. Start your seeds early in a flat and then place it in the center of the bales underneath the glass.

If you're growing only a few tender basil plants or a prized hot pepper and you need to protect them from the frost, recycle some plastic milk jugs with the bottoms cut out to use as temporary covers. For long rows of lettuce or greens, plastic row covers or floating row covers work well.

Planting Trees and Shrubs

While most urban gardeners focus on planting flowers, vegetables, and herbs, some may have the inclination and room to plant a tree or shrub. Trees and shrubs add both beauty and functionality to your landscape. For example, *deciduous* trees, which drop their leaves in winter, can reduce your cooling costs by shading your house in summer while allowing the sun to shine through in winter to warm your house. As an added bonus, trees and shrubs provide wildlife habitat for birds, bees, and other critters, and some even provide food.

In this section, we help you choose a healthy tree or shrub in the form you want, give some planting guidelines, and get you started on care. Check out Chapter 16 for more on the benefits of growing trees and shrubs in the city as well as for tips on what and where to plant.

Buying a tree or shrub

Regardless of what tree or shrub you want to grow, the planting process is the same. If you don't know which type of tree or shrub you want to add to your garden, consider your three options:

- **Bare root:** These deciduous trees and shrubs are dug from nurseries in the late winter, before the leaves emerge in spring, and shipped to you, usually via the mail. (You can also buy bare root roses in the spring directly from garden centers; we cover roses a little later in this chapter.) Bare root plants have had all the soil removed from around their roots, making them fairly lightweight, but because they have no soil to sustain them, you need to plant them soon after you get them. Bare root plants tend to be less expensive than container or balled and burlapped plants.

- **Container:** These trees and shrubs are grown in plastic containers in a nursery and then sold at garden and home centers. Generally, only small- and medium-sized trees and shrubs are sold as container plants. They're usually more expensive than bare root plants, but they also tend to be more mature plants whose roots haven't been disturbed, making them less likely to suffer from transplant shock.

- **Balled and burlapped:** Balled and burlapped trees and shrubs tend to be larger than the other two types. They're grown in a nursery and are dug up in spring, at which time their *root balls* (the soil masses around the roots) are wrapped in burlap to keep them together and moist. Balled and burlapped trees and shrubs are heavy, hard to move around, and expensive, but you get a mature plant without having to wait for it to grow.

While you can't know what a bare root plant looks like until it arrives on your doorstep, you have more control over what you get when shopping for container or balled and burlapped trees and shrubs. Before you purchase either of these plants, look for the following signs to make sure you choose a healthy specimen:

- **Healthy trunks and branches:** Beware of trunks and branches with dents or broken limbs.

- **Green, healthy leaves:** Stay away from trees or shrubs with signs of disease or insect damage.

- **Healthy roots:** A container tree or shrub with roots sticking out of the top of the root ball or with roots winding around inside the container and sticking out of the drainage holes is *root bound* and should be avoided.

- **Solid root balls on balled and burlap trees and shrubs:** Don't buy a tree or shrub that rocks independently of the root ball.

If you find the exact tree or shrub you want, but it's root bound, don't despair. You can still buy it and work to get it to grow strong in your yard. Simply remove the plant from the container and use a sharp knife to slice down vertically 1 to 2 inches deep through the outer roots on two to four sides of the root ball. Tease the roots with your hand so they aren't winding in a circle and then plant (see the next section for details).

Digging the hole and planting

Digging a hole big enough for a tree or shrub in urban soils can be challenging. Many urban soils are compacted or made up of gravel, fill, and concrete (and, therefore, not really soil at all!). Often what looks like a nice green lawn is really only a few inches of topsoil on top of old construction debris and fill. But after you have the hole, the planting process is similar to the way you plant many other plants. Here's a quick look at how to plant a tree or shrub, from digging the hole to laying the mulch:

1. **Dig a hole.**

   Regardless of what kind of soil you have, follow these tips to dig a good hole:

   - **Dig it wide.** Dig the hole three times as wide as the root ball. For bare root plants, just dig the hole wider than the extent of the roots when you spread them out horizontally. Most tree and shrub roots grow in the top foot of the soil, so they need room to expand as the tree grows. By loosening the soil around the root ball, you give those young roots a place to take hold. If the soil is rock hard, the roots won't penetrate it and they'll just stay around the root ball.

- **Don't dig too deep.** Dig the hole just deep enough so that the top of the root ball is level with the native soil. When you set the root ball on undisturbed soil, it's less likely to settle later and end up planted too deep.

2. **Place the plant in the hole.**

   For container plants, remove the pot. If you can't get the root ball out of the container, run a sharp knife around the inside edge of the pot and cut off any roots that protrude from the drainage holes. You may have to tease out the root ball if it's heavily root bound.

   For balled and burlapped plants, rock the root ball to one side and then the other to remove any burlap, twine, and wire. Just be sure to push on the root ball, not the trunk, or you may break off roots inside the ball. Although it's biodegradable, the burlap may take years to break down and it's best to remove as much non-plant material as possible without causing the root ball to fall apart. If you notice any roots that are kinked or encircling the root ball, trim them away.

   For bare root plants, make a small, volcano-like mound in the center of the planting hole and drape the roots evenly over the mound.

3. **Check the height of your plant.**

   Stand back and take a look at your work. Rotate the tree or shrub so that it looks the way you like. Double-check the height of the plant in the hole to make sure it's not too shallow or too deep.

4. **Backfill the hole to the soil line.**

   In most cases, you should backfill your hole with the native soil that you dug out. The tree or shrub needs to get used to growing in the native soil, so it's best to use it from the beginning. However, because many urban soils lack fertility and even real soil, sometimes you have to amend your native soil with a combination of compost and topsoil (see Chapter 4 for more on soil and Chapter 5 for more on compost).

Don't make the soil in the hole too fertile. If the soil around the roots is too different from the native soil, the roots will stay only in the planting hole and not venture out into the native soil. As the roots grow in the confines of the planting hole, they can encircle the trunk and eventually strangle the tree. Also, during a strong wind storm, a large urban tree may blow down if the roots haven't anchored themselves well into the native soil.

As you backfill the planting hole with soil, run a hose on a trickle or add water from a watering can in the hole at the same time. The water helps remove any air pockets from the soil, making for less settling later, and keeps the roots moist.

5. **Make a basin.**

   Make a low berm of soil around the outer circumference of the planting hole to create a basin that will catch water and direct it to where the new roots are. When you water, just fill up this basin and let the water naturally drain into the soil.

6. **Add a 2- to 4-inch-thick layer of bark mulch over the root zone.**

   The mulch helps preserve the soil moisture and keeps weeds from growing and competing with your tree. Keep the mulch a few inches away from the trunk of the tree or shrub. Mulch that sits right next to the trunk can cause disease problems, especially during wet weather.

Unless you live in a windy area or you plant a large tree, you probably don't need to stake your trees and shrubs. But if you want to add stakes, here's how:

1. **Place two stakes opposite each other and perpendicular to the prevailing winds.**

2. **Use commercial tree ties or soft cloth to wrap around the stakes and tree at a height just above a side branch or about halfway up the trunk.**

   Don't tie the tree tightly. You want to allow your tree to rock in the breeze; the natural movement of the trunk in the wind builds trunk and root strength.

3. **Remove the stakes after one year when your tree is well enough established to stand on its own.**

The miracle of mycorrhizae

Although you don't want to add fertilizers and other additives to your planting hole unless you have very poor soil, one beneficial additive is being more widely used. It contains *mycorrhizae,* naturally occurring beneficial fungi that are critical to tree and shrub health. These fungi colonize the roots of plants and extend into the soil so the plant can better absorb water and nutrients.

Adding mycorrhizae at planting time is especially beneficial to city trees and shrubs, helping them survive extremes in temperature, poor soil, soil compaction, neglect, and various other problems. You can purchase mycorrhizae powder to sprinkle in your planting hole to help establish these beneficial fungi on your newly planted trees and shrubs.

Getting your trees and shrubs off to a good start

How well your tree or shrub grows in the first year depends on a number of factors. Planting the right tree in the right location and selecting a variety that's adapted to your area are probably the two most important pieces to the puzzle (turn to Chapter 16 for details on choosing the right plants). But after your tree or shrub is safely in the ground, you can help keep it healthy by following these basic guidelines:

✔ **Keep watering.** Your young tree or shrub needs a constant supply of water throughout the growing season to keep growing well. If your native soil is mostly heavy clay and doesn't drain quickly, you need less water than if your soil is sandy and drains fast. Water once or twice a week if you don't get a soaking rainfall.

When you water, really soak the soil instead of just lightly sprinkling the ground. Frequent light watering encourages the roots to stay close to the soil surface to get the water, but you want them to grow deeper into the soil. After all, if they stay close to the soil surface, your tree or shrub will be more prone to drought stress when conditions are dry. You can always check the soil around your plant to see whether it's dry. Dig down about 6 inches into the soil. If it's dry at 6 inches, then water. Most trees and shrubs need 1 to 3 inches of water a week. To visualize how much water that is, consider this: Five gallons per square yard is about 1 inch of water.

Gotta love those gators. No, we're not talking about the Florida football team. *Treegators* are plastic bags that you fill with water and place around newly planted trees or shrubs (see Figure 6-3). They have small holes in the bottom and slowly drip water into the soil around the plant, keeping it moist. They're popular in public areas where tree crews don't have the time to water the trees regularly. When the bag is empty, simply fill it with water again for another dosing. Use Treegators only on new trees and shrubs because they drip water just around the planting hole and don't encourage older tree roots to venture into the native soil.

✔ **Hold off on fertilizing.** Although new trees and shrubs do need a fertile soil to get off to a good start, hold off on adding any fertilizers until the second year. Let the roots get established and the tree or shrub adjust to its new home before adding any more fertility to the soil.

✔ **Replenish the mulch.** In warm summer areas, the bark mulch or pine straw used around trees and shrubs may decompose by the end of summer. You can add more mulch in fall as long as you don't increase the mulch depth to more than 4 inches overall and you keep the mulch away from the tree trunk. In cold winter areas, the mulch helps insulate the roots, protecting the plant.

✔ **Add some protection, please.** If you plant an evergreen tree or shrub in fall in a cold area or if that evergreen is marginally hardy for your area (we explain what this means in Chapter 16), protect it by wrapping burlap around the plant in late fall. Pound four stakes around the plant and wrap the burlap to protect the bark and branches from the cold winter winds. Remove the burlap wrapping in spring.

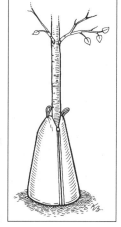

Figure 6-3:
Treegators
around a
tree.

Illustration by Kathryn Born.

Planting Perennial Flowers, Bulbs, and Roses

Perennial flowers are a treat to grow in the city. They come back each year, providing flowers at specific times, depending on the species, and they don't require as much soil preparation each spring. Plus, many perennial flowers *self-sow* (meaning they drop seeds that naturally grow into new plants) or grow large enough to be divided (meaning you can split apart your perennial plant to create new ones). It's like having free plants in your yard! To enjoy perennial flowers to the maximum, select a range of perennial flowers, bulbs, and roses that bloom in spring, summer, and fall. That way, you're guaranteed color throughout the growing season.

We explain everything you need to know about choosing the right perennial flowers for your urban garden in Chapter 15. Here, we concentrate on how to buy the perennials you want to grow and plant them to get them off to a great start.

Buying and planting perennial flowers

Assuming you know which perennial flowers you want to add to your garden, how do you purchase them? Although you can grow many perennials from seed, buying transplants is much easier, so that's what we focus on here.

Perennial flower transplants are sold the following two ways:

- ✔ **Mail-order perennials:** These perennials generally come as bare root or small container plants. They offer a broad selection of types and varieties that may be perfect for your conditions, and you can mix and match them to suit your tastes. The price is generally lower than plants sold at garden centers; however, the plants are small, young, and more likely to succumb to the weather than larger, more well-established plants. Plus, you have to wait for your plants to be shipped to you, which can be a problem if you miss a free window of time or ideal weather to plant.

- ✔ **Local garden center perennials:** These plants have been grown by professionals and tend to be larger, better-developed plants than their mail-order counterparts. Plus, they're more expensive, and the variety selection is often more limited. But you can purchase them when you want to plant them, you can see what you're buying, and they're more likely to survive, grow, and thrive the first year. They're also available at garden centers for longer periods in the summer and fall than mail-order plants.

When planting your newly purchased perennial flowers, use the same method we describe for planting annual flowers in the section "Planting annual flower and vegetable seedlings." Follow the instructions on the flower tags to make sure you give your flowers the proper sun and soil conditions and room to grow to their full size. Depending on when you purchase your perennials and how mature the plants are, they may not be flowering when you plant them, so you may have to go by the description of flower color on the tag or use your knowledge of the plant in a friend's garden as a guideline.

Flower color isn't a static thing. It changes depending on a number of factors. For instance, the color may be lighter if you grow the plant in direct sun and it likes part shade. Conversely, it may be darker if you grow it in part shade and it prefers full sun. To get a more accurate idea of what flower color a particular plant will have, find an example of that plant growing in your area under similar conditions to those in your yard. That way, you can avoid the dreaded "it's not quite the shade of blue I thought it would be" syndrome.

Buying and planting bulbs

If you want to grow spring and summer flowering bulbs, such as tulips, daffodils, lilies, and gladiolus, you can plant them in the fall (for spring-flowering bulbs) or the spring (for summer-flowering bulbs). Planting bulbs is especially fun in urban gardens because you always get a pleasant surprise in the spring when they start popping up around the garden. Plus, they flower and then die back, giving way to other later blooming flowers that will take their place. It's like having a succession of flowers in your small space.

Like perennial flowers, you can buy bulbs through the mail or at a local garden center. The advantages and disadvantages for each are the same. Generally, spring flowering bulbs are available for purchase in late summer and fall, while summer flowering bulbs are available mostly in spring. When shopping for bulbs, keep these tips in mind:

- **Pay attention to size.** The larger the flowering bulb, the more likely it is to produce not just one but multiple flowers. Bulbs are graded by size, and of course, the largest bulbs are the most expensive. So if you're planting a lot of bulbs, buying smaller bulbs is more cost effective. They'll still flower, but they'll need some extra nursing along, too. As long as they grow well, they'll eventually produce flowers like the larger bulbs. If you have a small space and want an immediate effect, go for the big ones.

- **Give them a squeeze.** When buying bulbs locally, give them a squeeze. Avoid any bulbs that are soft, mushy, or spotted with disease. The papery husk around the bulb is called the *tunic*. Don't worry if this is peeling off. It's just a covering, and your bulb will grow just as well without it.

- **Avoid bruised bulbs.** Stay away from bulbs with dents, bruises, and cuts. The bulb itself may be solid and firm, but the bruise could be an opportunity for rot organisms to start growing inside the bulb. Better to be safe than sorry.

- **Buy the right bulb for your yard.** Check the hardiness zone rating for your bulbs and select ones that are adapted to growing where you live (see Chapter 3). Also, consider bulbs with specific traits, such as fragrant bulbs, shade-loving bulbs, and vole- and mice-resistant bulbs.

After you buy your bulbs, the steps for planting them are very straightforward:

1. **Prepare the soil.**

   Bulbs grow best in well-drained, loose, fertile soil. Prepare your garden before you plant your bulbs, amending the soil with compost, especially if you have heavy clay soil.

2. **Decide where to plant your bulbs.**

   Plant your bulbs in groups for the biggest visual effect. Bulbs look best when you plant them in odd-numbered groups, such as 3, 5, 7, or 9 bulbs per group. This type of grouping looks more stunning than growing them individually like little soldiers in a row.

   You can plant bulbs closely together, but don't let them touch. Leave space between them so the bulbs aren't so overcrowded that they have to compete for nutrients. Most packages have proper bulb planting instructions.

3. **Dig a hole.**

   Planting depth is important here. You want to plant each bulb so the top tip of the bulb ends up being about twice as deep as the bulb is tall. For example, if your daffodil measures 2 inches from tip to base, dig the hole 6 inches deep so you end up with 4 inches of soil on top of the tip of the bulb.

   The ideal planting depth can vary, depending on where you live and the type of soil you have. Gardeners in warm climates may plant a little deeper than gardeners in cold climates. Gardeners with sandy soil plant 1 to 2 inches deeper, and gardeners with clay soil plant 1 to 2 inches more shallowly. Check your local Master Gardener or Extension Service office for information for your region.

4. **Plant the bulb with the flat end down and replace the soil on top of it.**

   On most bulbs, the flat end is the end with the roots, so naturally, you want the roots to go toward the deeper soil, not the surface. However, bulbs are smart, so no matter how you plant them, their shoots will find their way skyward and the roots will grow down into the soil.

5. **Add fertilizer.**

   Although compost is a good general soil additive, bulbs like phosphorous, so we recommend adding a small handful of a granular fertilizer rich in this nutrient, such as bulb booster, mixing it into the hole before you plant. Be careful using bone meal because animals may think a dead animal is buried where your bulbs are and dig up the ground after you plant them.

If mice, voles, chipmunks, and other creatures treat your bulbs as a free meal, artery out the following tips to keep them away:

- **Plant your bulbs in a wire mesh cage so animals can't dig down to them.** Just make sure the top of the cage has wire mesh wide enough for the bulb shoots to poke through.

- **Plant types of bulbs that these underground critters detest, such as daffodils and fritillaria.** Ringing susceptible bulbs with these less palatable ones may be enough to keep critters away.

Buying and planting roses

Roses are really just specialized shrubs, so planting them is similar to planting other trees and shrubs, except for a few additional considerations you need to remember. Check out Chapter 15 for details on the many types of roses you can choose from. Here, we focus on the buying and planting parts of urban rose gardening.

Roses are best purchased as bare root or container plants at the local garden center. When purchasing bare root roses, follow these tips:

- ✔ Check that the roots are moist.
- ✔ Select plants with the largest canes (at least ½ inch in diameter).
- ✔ Select plants that aren't leafing out yet.

When purchasing container roses, look for plants with all of the following:

- ✔ Dark green leaves
- ✔ No pests or diseases
- ✔ Unbruised stems
- ✔ Flower buds that are starting to swell

To get an accurate idea of the flower color, you can look at plants with a few open flowers as well.

After you bring your new rose home, you want to plant it in a convenient location as soon as possible. If you can't plant until a few days later, store your bare root rose in a cool, dark location, or place your container rose in a partly shaded location and keep it well watered until planting time. The following steps explain how to put your rose in the ground in just the right place:

1. **Choose a site in full sun (at least six hours a day) on well-drained soil with a near-neutral pH (6.5 is ideal).**

2. **If you're planting a bare root rose, unwrap the rose and soak the roots in warm water for one to two hours before planting.**

3. **Dig a hole at least twice the diameter of your container rose or the spread of your bare root rose.**

   Loosen the soil along the wall of the hole to encourage the rose roots to grow into the native soil. In cold winter areas (hardiness zones 3 through 5; see Chapter 3), dig the hole deep enough to bury the *graft union* (the bulge in the rose stem located just above the roots; see Figure 6-4) 3 to 5 inches into the soil. In warmer areas, dig the hole deep enough so the graft union is at or above the soil line. In heavy clay soils, consider mounding up the soil to plant the rose a little higher.

   The graft union is where the rose variety with the desired flower habit is grafted onto a rootstock with the desired hardiness, disease resistance, and vigor. It's important that this union not fail, or only the rootstock variety will grow, meaning a different colored flower or no flowers for your rose.

4. **Amend the soil with compost.**

   Create a volcano-like cone from the soil and compost for bare root roses; you need to drape the roots over the cone when planting.

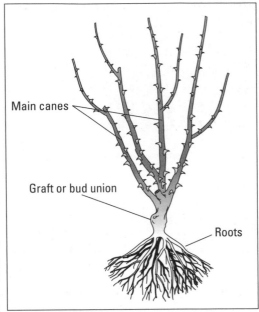

Illustration by Ron Hildebrand.

Figure 6-4:
A rose graft
union.

5. **Position the rose in the hole and backfill the hole with the native soil you dug out of the soil.**

   Drape the roots of your bare root rose over the soil cone you made in Step 4. If you're planting a container rose, just place it in the hole. Again, if you have poor native soil, amend it with topsoil and compost.

   Add water as you backfill the hole to remove any air pockets. Reposition the rose if it has sunk during the backfilling process.

6. **As with trees and shrubs, create a basin around the planting hole to fill with water.**

7. **Add bark mulch around the rose, keeping it away from the rose canes so they don't rot.**

   If cold weather threatens in spring, cover the graft union with bark mulch to protect it. After the weather is consistently warm, remove this extra mulch.

To make growing roses a little easier, particularly in the city, try growing *non-grafted* or *own-root roses*. These roses have been bred to the desired characteristics on their own rootstocks. The main advantage of planting these roses is that if the rose top dies back for any reason, the shoots that re-grow from the roots will be the same variety as the original top. You don't have to worry about graft unions. Many newer landscape roses are grown on their own roots and are good choices for city dwellers.

Part III
Places and Ways to Garden

The 5th Wave   By Rich Tennant

"I was thinking of adding wind chimes, but that seemed redundant."

In this part. . .

So where can you garden in the city? Part III provides many answers to this question, starting from the ground up — from changing a parking space into a mini-garden to making an elevated rooftop garden with a view. We've also covered everything in-between; including container gardening, apartment gardens, and urban community gardening. We discuss some of the detailed ways you can grow vertically, and the technical differences between *green roofs* versus *roof gardens,* and you'll' find a step-by-step approach to building a rooftop garden. We also including some cost-effective strategies to green city buildings or transform vacant lots into unique urban green spaces.

Chapter 7

Creating an Outdoor Room

. . . .

In This Chapter

▶ Extending your interior use of space into an outdoor room

▶ Accenting your garden with special gateways

▶ Selecting a focal element for your outdoor room

▶ Using recycled materials and junk as accent pieces in your outdoor space

▶ Creating an experiential space with interactive and engaging garden features

. . . .

A well-designed urban garden can provide a useful and aesthetically pleasing extension of your indoor living spaces. Think of it as knocking down a wall and expanding your kitchen, dining room, living room, or even bedroom outdoors. Where and how you place furniture, paving, lighting, plantings, art, and focal accents are all part of the design process for your outdoor room. Placing outdoor elements appropriately within your urban garden helps define, stylize, and create an enjoyable and functional exterior living space for you, your family, and your friends to enjoy.

Many urban gardeners use plants to help define their outdoor rooms and exterior spaces. Even though the outdoor landscape presents itself much differently than an indoor room, people nevertheless have a tendency to follow the edges of exterior surroundings with their eyes. In an urban setting, the eye is often drawn outward to neighboring buildings, walls, fences, and, of course, the city skyline.

Unfortunately, many homes built today pay little attention to the design and use of the exterior space surrounding the residence. Side yards are typically too small, while front and rear yards are undeveloped or simply landscaped with foundation shrubs, missing opportunities for the thoughtful use of space. But you don't have to settle for such a lackluster space!

In this chapter, we show you how to create an outdoor room that's a functional and aesthetically pleasing extension of your home. We show you how to analyze your existing conditions, decide what you want to get out of your exterior space, and plan functional aspects by creating unique entryways, focal elements, and artistic garden accents. Throughout this book we describe many different ways to develop an urban garden; one approach is developing an outdoor room.

Analyzing Your Outdoor Space

Just as the design of an interior space is defined by walls, floors, and furnishings, an outdoor room is architecturally defined with plants, paving, structures, and seating. But keep in mind that the design of your outdoor room is dynamic. Plants grow and mature, so you need to plan your garden appropriately to accommodate a continuously changing landscape.

Before you begin to define your outdoor room, develop your urban garden, or even add a work of exterior art, you must understand your existing site conditions. Be sure to take some time to completely analyze your existing space, making notes in this process. Here are some things to consider:

✔ **Take an inventory.** Analyze sun exposure, shade, soil conditions, existing plantings, direction of winds, slope/topography, temperatures, views you want to enhance or hide, and surrounding landscape features.

✔ **Think about the qualities of the existing space.** What's good, what's bad, and what's ugly?

✔ **Make a note of what activities the existing space is used for.** This way you can determine what you want to save, what needs to go, and what areas need to change.

A helpful tool to use when analyzing your outdoor space is a digital camera. Take a series of photographs of your existing space. When you download the images to your computer, adjust your printer to print out the photos on a lighter setting. Later, after printing large images of your existing space, use a marker to draw in some of your ideas on top of the printed photos when planning ideas for your outdoor room.

As you're analyzing your existing urban space, remember that views from the house to the garden are much more important than views from the street to your home. So focus less on how your garden is viewed by passersby and more on your own garden needs.

Fencing In Your Space

Most urban gardens are defined by walls or fencing along the property line or perimeter of your garden. The challenge for many urban landscapers is discovering how to provide privacy while maintaining enough space for an enjoyable and usable urban garden area. According to some folks, good fences make good neighbors. A little bit of screening can provide some privacy or perhaps hide an unsightly view.

When carefully selected and placed, plants can provide a living fence to screen neighbors, muffle noise, and create interest as a backdrop to your urban garden. Evergreen plants provide year-round screening and are usually the best choice for a living fence.

Wood fencing can also be used to create a barrier between you and your neighbors or help define a distinct area of your garden. This fencing is commonly 6 feet high, and the styles vary widely from traditional scalloped and rustic styles to a variety of "board" styles that look more like solid walls.

Before constructing your fence, be sure to check your local municipality for any local limitations on height, front yard setbacks, or any other restrictions.

Planning Your Outdoor Room

After you've taken a thorough inventory of your existing conditions, you're ready to begin planning how to develop your outdoor room into a useful extension of your home.

When planning the development of an outdoor room, consider current uses and activities as well as those you'd like to have. For example, where do you currently entertain and prepare food? Where do the children play? Do you have pets? Do you want to use the space for outdoor dining? Or do you want to create an outdoor living space with comfortable and restful seating? How do you want to develop the space aesthetically, and what is your budget?

The planning and design process helps you develop and enhance your existing garden space by adding garden entries and arbors, outdoor furniture, paving, patios, decks, water features, unique plantings, and garden art. The next sections of this chapter expand on some of these garden features and amenities to complement your outdoor room.

Creating Your Garden Entrance

Your garden entry is one of the most important aesthetic features, so it shouldn't be overlooked. The entry provides a sense of arrival to your garden, and it sets the mood for the garden within. We aren't garden therapists (yes, they do exist!), but we do believe that a garden gateway feature can really provide an uplifting and positive experience for garden visitors. Adding an architectural entry feature, whether with plantings, a trellis structure, or a moon gate, also helps define the entrance of your outdoor room. We explain the most common garden entry options in the following sections.

Just as a frame encloses a picture, your garden entrance highlights what lies beyond the entry. Whether it's a distant view to the natural landscape or a channeled view toward a unique garden feature, capturing the visual aesthetics beyond the entrance helps lure people into your outdoor room.

Installing moon gates for a Zen-like feel

In China, moon gates (see Figure 7-1) have long been used as a traditional entry feature to gardens. The purpose of these beautifully designed gateways is to invite passage into the garden area. These circular architectural features provide a well-defined sense of entry, and the circular form delightfully draws your eye away from the edges and into the garden space beyond. Although moon gates originated in China, they're now used as a garden entry feature in many countries throughout the world.

Figure 7-1:
A moon
gate.

Illustration by Kathryn Born.

Before installing a moon gate, make note of the directions from which people will be coming toward your garden entry. Are they approaching your garden from a nearby walk or directly from the driveway? Also, consider the developed garden space beyond the gate and how this space is viewed from outside the gate. Be sure to design your outdoor room with these view corridors in mind. As previously noted, the views through a gateway invite/lure passage to your garden.

We've never seen ready-made moon gates offered for sale at big-box home stores, so you have to custom-build this unique structure onsite. If you aren't confident in your construction skills, you can hire a contractor or landscaper to build one for you. Either way, it's truly worth the time, money, and effort to enhance your garden with this wonderful accent feature. Moon gates can be constructed with a number of different materials, including stone, wood, concrete, steel, or even climbing plant materials.

Showing off your space with garden arbors

A garden arbor, shown in Figure 7-2, is a good (and more affordable) alternative to the moon gate feature in the preceding section. You can usually find pre-made wooden arbors at your local garden center or home store. They're typically at least 3 or 4 feet wide by 2 feet deep, and tall enough for you to walk beneath. You can purchase an arbor that's unfinished, pre-stained, or painted (usually white). However, if you're interested in constructing your own, you can create whatever specifications you need for a custom design. You can even add a gate to your arbor to help enclose an area and help keep pets contained (if needed).

Figure 7-2:
A cottage garden arbor.

Illustration by Kathryn Born.

Opting for other types of entry features

You don't have to purchase or build a physical entry garden feature. You can opt to use larger plants, boulders, or other landscape materials (or combinations of these) to accent your garden entryway.

Some ideas for entry features include a strikingly colorful assortment of flowering shrubs, perhaps a garden bench surrounded by groundcover plantings, large rocks or stones turned upright alongside a path, or a walkway passing through a massing of ornamental grass plantings.

Defining the Uses for Your Outdoor Room

Earlier in the chapter, we discuss taking an inventory of your existing conditions and how to plan for the development of your outdoor room, including listing current and proposed uses.

Of course your analysis also identifies other important features such as the size of your garden area, solar orientation, existing utilities, site features, and topographical conditions, to name a few. The subsequent planning phase helped diagnose your desired uses, such as whether the outdoor space is used for pets, children's activities, outdoor dining, or leisurely seating.

After you know what type of space you have and what you plan to do, how can you define these uses for the outdoor room? Draw up specific details on a plan and coordinate them to meet your budget requirements. The following list provides a few defined uses you may wish to consider for your outdoor room:

✔ **An Outdoor dining area.** One of the most popular urban outdoor uses is dining. Much different than dining inside the home, an outdoor dining space provides a relaxing and enjoyable place for meals and is great for entertaining! A landscape of surrounding edible plants can complement this defined use. (For more on edible plants, see Chapter 13.)

✔ **The backyard kitchen.** With everything including the kitchen sink! An outdoor kitchen can be a delightful addition to your urban garden, with gas grills, wood-burning stoves, countertops, and any gourmet kitchen accoutrements. Vertical gardens, trellis structures, and arbors can also complement the outdoor kitchen plan. (For more on vertical gardens, see Chapter 10.)

✔ **A rooftop retreat.** Creating an outdoor lounge on a rooftop is quite like extending your living room outside, where you can enjoy the urban atmosphere and the sunset, and surround your seating areas with rooftop container gardens and plantings. (To find out how to build a rooftop garden, see Chapter 9.)

✔ **The sunny place.** The outdoor room may provide you an opportunity to channel the sun's rays for your plantings and you, too! Perhaps with a beachy theme, design your space with full-sun plantings including rosa rugosa and ornamental grasses. Oh, and don't forget the sand!

✔ **The hangout.** Designed with the teenager in mind, this space is defined with tables, moving chairs, and space to play board games or for reading activities. A variety of different yet complementary furnishings with a cool yet cozy approach to layout may be the way to go. For the surrounding landscape, think about using some cool-looking plants too, like 'Harry Lauder's Walking Stick' to compliment this approach.

✔ **The fireplace gathering spot.** Some urban dwellings, apartments, and condominiums do not have (or aren't capable of adding) an interior fireplace. However an outdoor room may allow this opportunity. A beautiful stone fireplace or even a small fire pit can become the focal point to any outdoor room.

✔ **The grill room.** The grill room garden has a sports bar approach with an efficient design. Of course the grill itself is likely the focal element to this garden, but also be sure to include a weatherproof big screen television, seating for you and several guests, and an outdoor refrigerator. How about some edible plantings surrounding the grill room such as peppers, salad greens, and climbing beans?

Don't limit yourself. Depending on the size of your outdoor room, you may wish to combine some of the ideas discussed above, such as the backyard kitchen and the outdoor dining area. Also, even in small spaces, mixing edibles and ornamentals allows for all sorts of interesting landscape design possibilities. It all depends on how much space you have and what your interests are.

Creating a Focal Element

Much like adding a painting on a wall or a centerpiece on the dining room table, creating a strong focal element in your outdoor room helps provide an interesting feature to draw your eye in the garden. You can create a focal element successfully with these techniques:

✔ **Contrast:** *Contrast* refers to differences in texture, shape, and color. Combining different forms together in the garden, such as multiple textures, shapes, and colors, increases contrast. The focal element is featured because of its difference from the other contrasting variations.

✔ **Placement:** Of course, placing an object, such as a unique plant or garden ornament, at the center of your outdoor room makes that object a focal element. However, keep in mind that most artists prefer to place focal points off-center.

- ✔ **Isolation:** Whenever you separate one feature distinctively from everything else, you create a focal element through *isolation*. An example would be planting a single yellow flowering annual among a sea of dark green groundcover plantings.

- ✔ **Convergence:** The eye is drawn to landscape edges and tends to follow neighboring buildings, walls, fences, other urban structures, and, of course, the city skyline. Drawing your eye toward an object or focal element is called *convergence*. A water garden feature located at the end of a planting bed or the edge of a patio is an example of this technique.

- ✔ **Surprise:** A fun way to create a focal element in your outdoor room (or other urban garden setting) is to place an unusual element within the scene. A gazing globe within a bed of hostas is an example. The object stands out and demands attention as a focal element in the garden.

Keep these elements in mind as you plan, design, and develop your urban garden space. It's also important to note that you can have more than one focal element in your garden; however, "less is more" because with one, you will have more attention given to that focal element when there are no other competing garden features. Plants, water features, and manmade structures are some of the most common focal elements. We delve into these in the following sections.

Using a unique plant

The placement of unique accent plantings to complement your exterior landscape is an important and critical step in the development of your outdoor room. The analysis of your views and sightlines is important when deciding where to locate these accent plantings within the landscape. This is where your previous efforts of recording your existing conditions and then planning your garden are important.

Here are some examples of ways to use unique plants:

- ✔ Place a small accent shrub or tree at the end of a terminating view where the walkway bends left or right.

- ✔ Add some colorful potted annual plantings in one corner of your patio.

- ✔ Plant a climbing flowering vine all along an entire wall of your garden.

- ✔ Grow a mass of low groundcover plants in the distance along the edge of a wooded landscape.

Here's a quick list of some interesting accent plant varieties that are suitable in most planting zones:

Plant Name	*Unique Characteristic*
Trees:	
Weeping Cherry	Cascading flowering branch structure
Laceleaf Japanese Maple	Brilliant lace-like leaves
Shrubs:	
Harry Lauder's Walking Stick	Unique contortion and branching
Red Twig Dogwood	Brilliant red branches
Winterberry Holly	Bright red berries in late fall and winter
Golden Euonymus	Yellow leaf color through all seasons
Witch Hazel	Striking yellow blooms
Rose of Sharon	Flowers in late summer through fall
Ornamental grasses:	
Zebra Grass	Pale yellow stripes on leaf blades
Purple Fountain Grass	Feathery blooms and majestic purple color
Groundcovers:	
Creeping Phlox	Low growing with abundant colorful blooms
Big Blue Liriope	Jumbo spikes of purple-blue flowers

Creating serenity with a water feature

Water features create inviting areas in landscapes. They offer a spot to stop and gaze at ripples moving across the water's surface or at a fish gliding gracefully beneath. Water draws people in and brings a sense of calm. A water feature can be big or small and simple or elaborate, but it always adds an enchanting focal element to an outdoor room.

You can bring water into a landscape in many ways, from small to complex:

- ✔ **Small:** A half-barrel water garden containing just a few small fish and a water plant can provide a low-maintenance water feature to your outdoor room. Small, prefabricated water features typically include a recirculation system. Creative gardeners can even devise their own versions with sealed pots or old galvanized buckets and tubs.

- ✔ **Large:** The next step up is a larger in-ground pond made of precast material. These water features are suited to holding a few larger fish and perhaps a plant or two. Many come with recirculation pumps and are simple enough to install yourself.

- ✔ **Complex:** When you're officially hooked on water features, you'll find that the sky is the limit on building a water garden in your outdoor room. Larger ponds and elaborate rock waterfalls really turn a plain landscape area into an elegant one. Custom forms and shapes for larger water gardens allow you to thoughtfully integrate your water garden plan into your garden space.

Water plants you can use in your water features include submerged plants, such as water lilies, and marginal or bog plants, such as papyrus, iris, and cannas that grow near the edge of the pond. Check local garden centers for recommended plants for your zone, and see Chapter 3 for guidance on determining your hardiness zone.

See whether you have a water gardening club or society in your city or town. You can draw guidance from its members. They can offer wisdom and advice, and some may even open their gardens to visitors to share ideas and inspiration.

Going with a man-made feature

Adding man-made ornamental art to the garden is one of the fastest growing trends today. Artful garden accessories are now sold everywhere, from grocery stores and big box chains to booths at the local farmers markets. We describe some of your ornament options and how to determine which ones to use in the following sections.

Exploring your garden ornament options

Ornaments in the garden are an extension of your personality, so why not make a statement? Whether whimsical or classical, a well-placed garden ornament tells visitors something about your personality and your outdoor room. They also provide a unique focal element.

Ornaments are limited only by your imagination. They can be functional if used to support or contain plants, can be used to hide an unsightly corner, or can set apart your outdoor room (or indicate divisions between other areas of your garden). Whatever their purpose, ornaments can make a statement.

Some common examples of ornaments include statues and sculptures (both serious and playful), wind chimes, plant stakes, water features, birdhouses, rocks, furniture, decorative vertical features, a sundial, gazing globes, pergolas, or an outdoor thermometer.

Of course there are uncommon examples too that can be added to an outdoor room like an outdoor television, a picture frame of weatherproof art, even an outdoor-ready wall clock or a recycled item you found at a yard sale.

Choosing the right look

You don't have to follow any hard-and-fast rules when selecting and placing ornaments in your garden, but we offer a few suggestions here:

✔ **Make sure the size of the art matches the scale of the garden.** You don't want the piece to be cramped in too small a space or lost in one too large.

✔ **Keep the style of your outdoor room in mind.** Certain ornaments lend themselves to particular styles. For instance, a white marble classical statue looks at home in a garden of neatly clipped boxwood and symmetrically arranged stone urns but would look out of place in a desert garden filled with terra cotta, graceful grasses, and spiny cacti, *unless* the element of surprise is the effect you want to create.

✔ **Find a good home for your ornament.** The most popular spot to place an ornament is at the end of a vista, like at the end of a walkway, or as a focal element beyond a moon gate. A fountain or statue can also serve as a pivot point between two spaces in the garden. You may also find just the right sculpture, rock, or gazing ball to place in an unexpected spot, just for fun.

Don't overdo it with ornaments and clutter up your outdoor room. Again, a "less is more" approach provides more attention to a single focal element in the space.

Turning Recycled Materials into Chic and Useful Garden Art

One man's trash is another man's treasure! You can recycle many materials as garden features in your outdoor room or urban garden, from old skis and bicycles to antique furniture and bed frames. We're sure you can find at least a few old items around your home or at yard sales that you can repurpose into a garden art feature.

Repurposed garden art is great because it can illustrate your personal interests (such as skiing) and provide great conversational elements when entertaining guests. Studies even show that art can help redirect feelings and improve one's mood. Of course, gardening is an experiential process that helps improve mood as well.

We hope the ideas in the following sections help you begin to think about what you can do in your own outdoor room to create a unique and signature garden art feature and great conversation piece for entertaining.

Using yard sale items

Yard sales often offer inexpensive finds that you just can't pass up, such as old records, classic books, and perhaps bicycles or other outdoor equipment. Occasionally you can even find some wonderful yard sale items that can be reused for the outdoor room or garden area. You never know what you'll find, but if you think creatively about repurposing materials for the garden, a trip to a local yard sale can be adventurous and purposeful. Here's a list of some yard sale items you may seek out as accents for your urban garden:

- **Antique bed frames:** Use as a stand-alone vertical accent feature or use it to help climbing vines, bean plantings, or climbing accent plants like roses, clematis, or ivy.

- **Bicycle frames:** Use for climbing vines or bean plantings by digging out a small trench in the garden and burying a portion of the frame to secure it in place vertically. Also think about securing the bike frame upside down as another option.

- **Chairs:** Antique chairs make wonderful garden accents. Think about securing a few older wooden chairs together to develop a distinctive sculptural piece. You can also use chairs as planters. See the nearby sidebar "Adventure gardening" for details.

- **Small dressers:** An old dresser can make a great planter. Pull out and secure each drawer to different lengths, with the top drawer opened slightly and the bottom drawer opened as much as possible to create a terraced planter. Cut a rectangular opening out of the cabinet top so you can plant in the top drawer area. Fill each drawer with soil mix, and then plant an assortment of your favorite plants to accent your new garden art feature.

- **Tools:** Old tools make wonderful and useful decorative garden features. If you have an old shovel, rake, hoe, or pitchfork, don't throw it away. Recycle and repurpose it as a showcase item for your garden instead. For example, a few old rakes can be secured together as a climbing structure for pole beans. Old wheelbarrows can stand as garden centerpieces and planters. And old watering cans make unique containers when filled with soil and cascading plants.

Adventure gardening

Plan one weekend this summer for a yard sale hop in search of creative garden containers. Traveling from one sale to another in search of unique containers to use in the garden can be exciting. Whether it's an old birdcage, a recipe box, a large cookie jar, or a toy wagon, repurposing items as garden containers can be a fun way to add accents your urban garden. We like to refer to this type of gardening as *adventure gardening.*

Make adventure gardening a game with your family. Challenge everyone to see who can find the most creative container at a yard sale. Part of the game rules can be that any real planters, such as clay pots, flower boxes, and garden planters, are off-limits.

After you're done collecting a few unusual containers, determine what you want to purchase from your local garden center to get them ready for the garden, such as colorful annuals, climbing vines, garden soil, coconut fiber liners, soil polymers, and fertilizer.

Repurposing materials (Reusing junk)

Many everyday household materials that eventually become junk can be recycled for use in your outdoor room. Following are some common examples:

- **Sign holders:** Metal frames that held campaign or business signs work well as repurposed supports for shorter vegetable plantings.

- **Cans:** Cover coffee cans with wallpaper samples or contact paper to create lovely vases. Fill them with flower cuttings and offer to friends, or use them as a centerpiece for your outdoor room. Cans also make handy and durable seed scoops for wild birdseed and for scooping soil into pots when starting seeds.

- **Cardboard boxes:** Lay large pieces of cardboard in garden paths and cover with straw or mulch. The cardboard provides a durable barrier layer to prevent weed growth.

- **Coffee filters (used):** Reuse your used coffee filters for collecting and drying seeds. You can also place them in the bottom of pots to keep the soil from running out the drainage hole and to prevent slugs from crawling in.

- **Paper:** Newspaper and all uncoated junk mail can be composted. Worms love it! Place the paper in the garden, cover it with grass clippings, and the worms will find it and break it down. You can also start a worm-composting project with a small trash can or bin. Shred the newspaper; moisten it; add a bit of soil, mulch, or fallen leaves; and then add some composting worms. The castings left by the worms make rich fertilizer for your garden plants!

- **Plastic milk jugs:** Help eliminate watering waste with these common jugs. Simply cut off the bottom inch or so of your used half-gallon plastic jugs, and bury the necks in soil next to plants that require a lot of water (pumpkin and tomato plants, for example). Then you can fill the upended jugs with water daily to provide targeted watering to your garden plantings.

- **String:** Hang pieces of old string or twine around the yard on trees or shrubs for birds to use as nesting material.

- **Toilet paper tubes:** These tubes are great for seed starting! Cut four 1-inch-long slits in one end and fold the tabs inward to create a pot with a bottom. Fill will soil and sow seeds. Plant the entire tube outside, and no fear, the tube does break down on its own so you don't have to worry about removing it. Give the plants plenty of light and air circulation to prevent mold growth.

- **Pallet gardening:** Pallets are being reused extensively in the garden today (see Figure 7-3). One idea is to reconstruct pallets into vertical garden features (which are great for small or tight spaces). You can remove and relocate some of the planks to form a series of tiered horizontal planter boxes along your pallet garden. (See Chapter 10 for more on vertical garden ideas.)

Avoid chemically treated pallets. Chemicals from the treated wood may slowly leach into the soil over time. We recommend using pallet gardens only for your flowering annuals and climbing vines, but don't use them for vegetable gardens because the pallet wood may have been chemically treated even if it might not look like it.

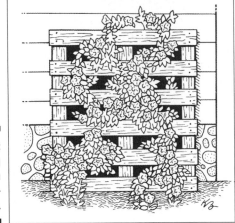

Figure 7-3:
Reusing pallets for a vertical garden feature.

Illustration by Kathryn Born.

Considering Interactive Garden Art

Interactive art helps define an outdoor room and also engages your senses as you experience your urban garden. You can engage your senses in many ways, including adding a simple sundial, hanging some wind chimes, or developing a water garden with trickling noises and calming features. We discuss sundials and audible art in the following sections, but don't forget to use your creativity to come up with your own ideas.

A garden sundial

For centuries people have calculated time based on the simple progression of the sun in the sky. Sundials, which were created to track this progression, can be an interesting addition of garden art for your outdoor room (see Figure 7-4). Sundials come in many different styles and may be made from wood, brass, bronze, stone, or cast iron.

Before purchasing a sundial, consider what you'll use as the base material or foundation for your sundial. You may consider placing the sundial on a level portion of a large boulder or purchasing a stone pedestal to mount it on.

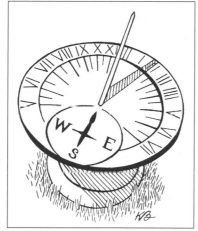

Figure 7-4:
A garden
sundial.

Illustration by Kathryn Born.

A sundial requires full sunlight throughout the day, so be sure not to place it in an area that's shaded by your home or trees. A southern exposure usually receives the most sunlight all day long.

Music in the garden

The trickling sound of a nearby stream, the rustling of leaves, the sounds of birds, and the whistling of passing breezes are nature's music in the garden. You can add to her symphony by including audible components to your urban garden. From simple wind chimes to outdoor instruments and weatherproof speakers, you can enhance your outdoor room and its entertaining capabilities by adding the element of music to your garden space. Here are some ideas:

✔ **Wind chimes:** Wind chimes can add a variety of harmonious and soothing tones to your garden. Similar to a visual garden entry, the gentle sound of music in your urban garden can provide a soothing relief when arriving home from a busy work day. Wind chimes can help signal this sense of arrival through their distinctive and soothing tones. Chimes can be made from a variety of materials including aluminum, wood, stainless steel, copper, or glass.

✔ **Talk tubes:** Remember the old tin can and string phones? Well, you actually build a real talk tube system in the garden as a fun and interactive feature. Talk tubes consist of a pair of funnel or horn-shaped end pieces with a connecting hose buried underground connecting one end to the other. These may be difficult to find locally; however, you may be able to find and purchase these online, especially since most playground manufacturers produce talk tubes.

✔ **Musical instruments outdoors:** You can now find a variety of instruments designed and tested for permanent outdoor use from many different manufacturers, from vertical chimes and outdoor xylophones to outdoor drum sets, to name a few. Companies like Nature Explore (`www.arborday.org/explore`) make professional hand-crafted instruments, including the marimba, akambira, and amadinda. Constructed of dense, high-quality ipé wood, with stainless steel hardware and aluminum resonators, these instruments are built to withstand extreme weather conditions.

✔ **Outdoor rock speakers:** Outdoor speakers designed to look like rocks are popular items that blend seamlessly in the garden. These weather-proof speakers are great for entertaining, and they can be left exposed to the elements in any climate.

✔ **Water features:** Water features bring the soothing sounds of a gurgling and splashing waterfall or fountain to the garden. Water can draw us in and make us calm. A trickling water garden adds both movement and relaxing sounds to the landscape. (See "Creating serenity with a water feature" for more on creating water features.)

Chapter 8

Containing Your Gardening

Container gardening is key to successfully gardening in the city. No matter how busy you are or how limited your yard, a beautiful container situated near the front door or back patio will help highlight, accent, and jazz-up your urban garden with color and pizzazz! A drab-looking porch, patio, balcony, or driveway can be transformed with the addition of flowering container gardens!

As an urban gardener, you may think that tight and small spaces limit your ability to garden, but don't worry! Containers to the rescue! Colorful, flower-filled containers can spruce up any space, no matter how small. Many varieties of ornamental annuals are suitable for container growing, and with the availability of more dwarf vegetable, fruit, and herb varieties, growing food in containers in the city is easier than ever.

Even for gardeners with plenty of space, containers provide a versatile way to accent an urban landscape. They can be moved around easily to create just the right effect. When a plant starts to decline, simply move the container out of view and replace it with another, or start over and replace your original planting with a new assortment of colorful flowers and foliage.

Surveying Container Options

This section walks you through some container choices you may want to consider in your urban garden. As you can see in Figure 8-1, you should have no trouble finding or creating the perfect containers for your space.

Figure 8-1:
A variety of
container
types.

As you consider which containers you may want to use, keep the following points in mind:

- ✔ **While almost anything can be used as a container, it's important that containers have an appropriate width-to-height ratio.** Tall containers tend to dry out quickly at the top, but stay soggy at the bottom. Shallow containers may not support deep enough root development and can result in drought-prone plants that lack good root anchorage.

- ✔ **Make sure that all containers either have drainage holes or are made of material that water can drain through freely so that excess water doesn't stand in the bottom of the pot.** If a container doesn't come with drainage holes, it is often possible to drill some in the bottom to make it suitable for growing plants.

- ✔ **Consider how a container's shape and style influence its "look."** A tall, narrow container provides a contemporary feel and allows the sharply toothed edges of an aloe to drape naturally out of the way. A low, round container enhances the circular symmetry of many succulents, such as hens and chicks or rosette-shaped agaves.

Be on the lookout for containers that will enhance plant features. Stockpile a few in your potting area so that you will be ready next time you bring home a plant purchased on impulse! Rather than having an interesting selection get lost among other plants in your garden, you can set it in its own pot and create an artistic focal point.

Cool commercial containers

In the old days you were pretty much limited to plastic or terra cotta contain-ers. Now, there are many materials used to make interesting and functional pots. Here are some commercial pot options you'll readily find in garden cen-ters and home stores:

- **Ceramic:** Ceramic containers are clay pots with a glaze. There are many beautiful glazed terra cotta containers on the market, and they are as much a decorative piece of art as a place to grow plants. Ceramic pots are delicate, so be careful where you place them. Since they have a glaze on them, they tend to dry out more slowly than unglazed terra cotta pots.

  You'll need to protect ceramic pots in cold winter areas by removing plants and soil and storing them in a dry location. If you leave these pots outdoors in winter with soil in them, they stand a good chance of crack-ing from the freezing and thawing.

- **Fiberglass:** Fiberglass containers are popular and have the advantage of being lightweight and long lasting. Some planters resemble terra cotta or wood, or even bronze or copper with a metallic patina, so the aged look is built in. Fiberglass is durable and will last for years; however, it can also be expensive and difficult to find.

- **Metal:** For a chic look, try metal containers. Like ceramic pots, many of these containers are pieces of art and add a contemporary look to your garden. Containers made from scrap metal or galvanized buckets add a decorative quality to any garden.

  Obviously metal doesn't breathe like terra cotta, so be sure to have adequate drainage holes in the bottom. It can also heat up excessively in the hot sun. Metal containers are tough and long lasting and don't have to be protected in cold areas in winter.

- **Plastic:** This is the type of container most gardeners are familiar with. Many plastic containers are now made to look exactly like terra cotta clay containers. Of course they are lighter in weight and usually less expensive, but have the disadvantage of never attaining the "aged" look a clay container can provide. However, plastic is easy to clean and long lasting. Since it isn't porous, it holds moisture, which can be a good or bad thing, depending on the type of plants you plan to grow.

- **Polypropylene:** The newest type of containers are made from a tough, flexible, woven polypropylene material. The advantage of this material is that it breathes like terra cotta, yet still holds moisture well. It doesn't heat up like a plastic or metal pot, so the roots grow better, especially in hot climates. They're great for the urban garden because when you're finished with them at the end of the season, simply empty out the plants and soil, then fold them into a stack and store them in a closet. They come in cool vibrant colors such as red, blue, and orange.

110 Part III: Places and Ways to Garden

Self-watering containers

The latest craze in containers is self-watering containers. Keeping the soil in your pots consistently moist is one of the toughest maintenance tasks of container growing. Self-watering containers make that task a lot easier. Self-watering containers have a false bottom with a water reservoir under the soil. The reservoir is shaped so the water and soil have contact.

Through osmosis, the water is wicked up into the soil to keep the growing medium moist. Depending on what you're growing, how large the plants are, and the weather, you may be able to walk away from your containers in midsummer for up to five days without having to worry about watering. Let's go to the beach!

✔ **Terra cotta clay:** Clay terra cotta containers, such as the common reddish-orange, unglazed flowerpots, come in variety of shapes and sizes. One advantage of this material is that, over time, it acquires a beautiful patina. Also, salts and minerals are absorbed into the clay and drawn away from the roots of the plants. The disadvantages of clay are that it is breaks or cracks fairly easily and it is porous, so plants grown in clay pots dry out quickly and need frequent watering. Use terra cotta pots when growing plants that like a dry soil such as herbs, geraniums, portulaca, and lantana.

✔ **Wood:** Wood is another excellent choice and comes in a variety of styles, from traditional redwood barrels to square, upright boxes with feet. Since many wood containers are quite large, they can be heavy to move when filled with moist soil. Like unglazed terra cotta, wood is porous, so plants dry out more quickly than in plastic pots. Wood containers don't last as long as plastic or fiberglass ones, but plants commonly grow very well in wood containers.

When selecting a container for your yard, think of the plants you might grow in it, its durability, especially if it stays outdoors year-round, and whether you'll be moving it often. Large pots are great for big plants and give you lots of options for plant combinations, but they can be heavy to move.

Hanging, balancing, and other interesting containers

While a pot on the ground is the most traditional container type, there are many other ways of using containers in your urban yard. Since urban yards are often cramped for space, it's important to maximize every nook and cranny. Here are some container choices that allow you to grow lots of flowers and edibles:

✔ **Window box:** A standard fixture on many traditional homes, the window box has the advantage of turning unused space outside your window into a garden. Since window boxes don't have a lot of soil mass, look for self-watering window boxes to reduce the amount of time you'll have to spend watering.

✔ **Hanging basket:** Hanging baskets are great ways to use space under a balcony, fire escape, or outdoor roof. Most hanging baskets are 12 to 16 inch in diameter. You can grow shade-loving annuals, herbs, and even strawberries in a hanging basket. Plastic hanging baskets are most common, but you can also find wire baskets lined with sphagnum peat moss with a more rustic look.

Lowering and raising your hanging basket for watering once it's in full growth can be tedious and difficult. To make this task easier, consider using a simple pulley system to move the basket up and down or a long-handled watering wand so you don't have to reach up so high.

✔ **Railing planter:** Think of a railing planter as a window box on a deck railing. They are about the same size, made from plastic, and are molded to fit securely on the top of a two-by-four or two-by-six wooden railing without the need for braces or brackets to keep them in place. Like window boxes, they don't hold a large soil mass area, so you'll need to be diligent about watering them.

✔ **Strawberry pot:** This cylindrical terra cotta or plastic container gets its name from the many holes spaced around its circumference where you can plant these fruits. However, don't limit yourself to strawberries. We've often seen lobelia, alyssum, thyme, and other small cascading plants trailing from the planting holes.

Bathtubs, birdcages, bicycles, and more

All the containers we mention so far are commercially available, but don't forget to be creative when selecting or even making containers for your urban garden. An old boot, a rusted-out galvanized bucket, a chicken feeder, an old wheelbarrow, or even a bathroom fixture can be turned into a planter by an imaginative gardener.

Anything can be a container for plants as long as it has three qualities:

✔ Enough strength to hold soil

✔ Ample room for root growth

✔ Adequate drainage

If it suits your style, give it a try!

Water drainage is often the most important issue for a homemade container. Those attractive ceramic pots or other unconventional containers, like an old boot, can be drilled to allow water and air to flow.

How many holes should you drill in the bottom of your self-made container? The more, the better. If it's made of a sturdy material such as metal, make the bottom look like Swiss cheese. Use a hammer and large nail or a drill bit to create the holes. As a guide, a 14-inch container should have about six to eight ½-inch-diameter holes. When drilling holes isn't practical, use the attractive container as an outer sleeve with a little smaller pot that has drainage holes slipped inside it. Support the inner pot on a block of wood or a few inches of gravel so that its bottom doesn't stand in any water that drains through.

There are lots of containers to choose from. Look for bargains on used containers at garage sales and secondhand shops.

For more information on creative containers that can also function as outdoor art, see Chapter 7.

Selecting Soil for Your Container

The type of growing medium you put into your container can make the difference between gorgeous flowers and vegetables and a stunted, yellowing, sad-looking container garden. The soil mix needs to have enough bulk to anchor plant roots, good drainage so water moves freely through the mix, and the ability to hold nutrients. Potting soils will not have enough nutrients in and of themselves to support plant growth all summer long.

We talk more about fertilizing your containers later in this chapter, but first, we need to talk soil — or, more accurately, growing medium (since some may not contain any actual soil).

Container "soil" is a mix of ingredients such as compost, peat, sand, vermiculite, and perlite. It's used in containers because regular topsoil or garden soil would compact, leaving little air and water spaces for healthy roots, and may harbor insects and diseases that can attack your plants. If you're growing plants in containers, use a container soil mix, often called potting soil. The materials it's composed of give it the aeration, drainage, and water- and nutrient-holding capacity needed for proper growth.

That being said, not all container soils are equal. Some plants, such as African violets, like a heavier and more moisture-retentive soil mix. Other plants, such as cacti, need a soil mix that is very well drained. Some plants don't even need a soil mix at all. Orchids grow best in a medium dominated with bark chips. So know your plants' requirements before you select a soil mix.

Lightening up your pots

Soil mixes can be heavy, especially if you're filling large containers. To reduce the weight and save money on potting mix, fill the bottom of a large container with a light-weight material that will take up space but not add lots of weight. The old recommendation is to use packing peanuts. However, if you've ever worked with these before, you know they fly all over the place, get staticy and stick everywhere you don't want them to. Plus, when they're wet, they can turn into mush. A better solution is to use empty plastic soda or water bottles. Place a layer in the bottom of the container filling it about one-third deep. Cover the bottles with a layer of landscape fabric or plastic window screen so that the soil won't wash through. Then, fill the container with fresh potting mixture, set in the plants, and water. There should be plenty of soil mix to support plant growth and, if and when you move the container, it will be easier on your back.

For most garden flower, vegetable, fruit, and herb plants, a commercial soil mix is the easiest way to go. Experiment with different brands to see which one performs best in your containers. If you're growing large plants in large containers, consider using a soil mix that contains compost. Compost will not only help feed the plants over time (see Chapter 4 for more on the benefits of compost) but will add bulk for the roots to hold on to.

Excellent drainage is the most important attribute of a good soil mix. Purchase a good-quality potting mix that contains perlite, pumice, and/or vermiculite. These materials help provide air spaces between the soil particles to promote good drainage for your containers.

To make your own lightweight mix, use one-third each of good-quality potting mix, shredded peat moss, and pumice (or perlite). *Pumice* is a volcanic material that absorbs water and releases it slowly, helping to maintain a more consistent moisture level in the container. It's preferable to *perlite* (a form of volcanic rock) because perlite is extremely lightweight, doesn't absorb water, and tends to wash away with repeated watering.

Planting a Container

Once you have the container and the proper soil mix, it's time to plant. We cover the basics of planting everything from a petunia to a poplar in Chapter 6, but container planting requires some special considerations. This section shows you how to prepare and fill your pots and properly plant in containers.

Prepping your pots

Getting your pots ready for planting requires a few easy steps:

1. **Make sure your pots are clean.**

2. **Check your pots to ensure they have adequate drainage holes in the bottom.**

   If a pot doesn't come with enough holes, use a hammer and nail or drill to create more.

3. **Cover the drainage hold with window screening (see Figure 8-2), cheesecloth, or landscape fabric.**

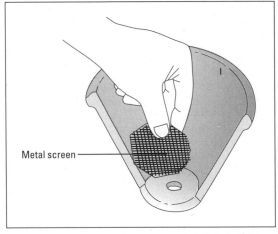

Figure 8-2: Window screening allows water to pass through while keeping the soil in the pot.

Metal screen

Illustration by Ron Hildebrand.

4. **Fill the container about two-thirds full with your selected container soil.**

Planting your containers properly

Here are the basics for planting annual or perennial flowers, veggies, and herbs:

1. **Take the seedling plant you grew or purchased from a garden center and pop it out of its plastic pot.**

   If it's in a biodegradeable peat or cow pot, simply break apart the bottom of the pot with your hands, then plant it, pot and all. Keep the root ball intact.

2. **Select a Container at least 2 inches deeper and 2 inches wider than the original pot so the plant will have enough room to grow (see Figure 8-3).**

It's important to select the right-sized container for the plants you wish to grow. Smaller-growing annual flowers, such as alyssum, narrow-leaf zinnia, pansy, dwarf marigold, and viola, will grow fine in a 2-gallon containers. However flowers that reach a height of 2 to 3 feet need at least a 3- to 5-gallon container. Groupings of multiple plants may require something even larger. Be sure to read the labels when selecting the right-sized plants for your containers.

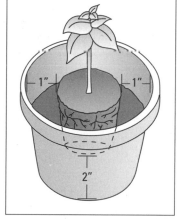

Figure 8-3:
Cross
section of
a container
planting.

Illustration by Ron Hildebrand.

3. **Plant your seedling at the same depth it was growing in the original pot.**

The exception is tall, leggy tomatoes that can be planted deeper because they form new roots along their stems.

4. **Fill the container with soil to within a few inches of the top.**

5. **Water well.**

If it's a small pot, consider placing it in a tub or basin filled a few inches deep with water. Let the pot sit in the water until it has slowly soaked up enough through its drainage holes to make the surface of the soil moist.

When planting berry bushes, trees, and shrubs in containers, water from the top slowly so the water has a chance to permeate the soil medium. Water once, let it sit for 10 minutes, then water again. When the water comes out of the drainage holes on the bottom of the pot and the medium is moist when you poke your finger into it, it's all set.

Bottom watering is best used for plants that don't like to get their leaves wet, such as African violets. Water on the leaves can cause staining and rot.

6. Set the plant in its desired location.

Elevate your containers. No matter how many holes you place in the bottom of your container, if there isn't a space between the bottom of the container and your deck or patio, the water won't drain away properly. It's best to elevate your containers a few inches off the ground with pieces of brick, wood, stone, or purchased "pot feet."

Jazzing Up Your Containers

How you arrange plants within the container is an important design factor. Use different leaf and flower colors and textures to make a bold or subdued statement. They also can play off the color and texture of the container.

But keep the arrangement of the containers themselves in mind as well. Cluster containers in compatible groupings or use a striking individual pot as a focal point in your deck or patio garden. Ahh, so many considerations.

The most important thing is to have fun with your containers and come up with designs that appeal to your personal tastes. After all you're the one who will see them every day!

Placing containers for visual interest

Use your creativity and mix container shapes and sizes for the most attractive arrangements. The beauty of containers is that you can move them around until you find the most appealing and complementary arrangement.

You may even wish to apply the rule of three to your container placement. Try one tall, one small, and one in-between. Sometimes it takes a mixture of container forms and an arrangement of plants to create the look you're after!

For vertical garden placement, consider using some half-round containers attached to a wall or fence to bring a cascade of color to an otherwise flat surface. Or set a large container near a trellis or porch pillar and plant a vine to grow vertically! (For more on vertical gardening, head to Chapter 10. For more discussion on containers that work well along walls and balcony railings, head to Chapter 11.)

Coordinating colors

Color coordinating both plants and containers can add to the visual qualities and distinctiveness of your urban garden. A container may be a similar color to the plants it holds, which harmoniously enhances the intensity and volume of the plant's character. Or perhaps instead you would like to showcase the distinctiveness of a plant by selecting a container color with a high contrast.

Thinking about which color scheme to pursue for your container can help you make good decisions when showcasing your plants and enhancing their features. This will certainly help jazz up your garden! (For more on color harmonies and textures see Chapter 14.)

Analogous color schemes

Selecting similar color schemes is generally a good approach. Using similar colors creates "analogous" schemes with colors that are next to each other on the color wheel. These colors match well and create a serene and comfortable design. Analogous color schemes are harmonious and pleasing to the eye.

If you decide to go with an analogous color scheme, make sure you have some contrast. Choose one color to dominate, one to support, and a third to accent, along with black, gray, or white.

Complementary color schemes

Contrasting plant and container colors add energy to the overall effect and can be used to brighten up an area. High-contrast colors are colors that are opposite each other on the color wheel (like green and red or orange and blue). These are known as "complementary" color schemes. The high contrast of complementary colors creates a vibrant look but can be tricky to use in large doses. Complementary schemes do make your plants stand out and get noticed!

Try using two of the primary colors (red, yellow, or blue) or two colors that are opposite each other on the color wheel (red/green, orange/blue, or yellow/purple). For example, a golden barrel cactus in a midnight blue saucer bowl can add some striking color to an otherwise dull corner of a patio.

Cool container combos

General design recommendations are a great way to get an overall view of possible great container combinations, but examples always help us when we're designing containers. The following sections offer some tips on designing with various plants in the container garden.

Annual flowers

It's easy to get overwhelmed at a garden center with all the annual flower choices (or tender perennials grown as annuals) available. Many garden centers make it easier by grouping plants by color. That way you can mix and match colors as we discuss in "Coordinating Colors."

But don't stop with flower colors. Consider leaf colors and textures, too. Dusty miller, coleus, and ivy are just some of the plants with interesting foliage that can add a great contrast to your container.

Or consider planting one large, stunning plant such as pineapple sage, a dwarf sunflower, or a geranium in a container. Then you can group containers that work well together.

Of course, if you're really stuck, there's the thrillers, fillers, and spillers design concept we highlight in Chapter 14. That's always a winner.

Perennial flowers

Perennial flowers work well in containers, especially in warm climates. In colder areas you'll have to protect them in winter or treat them as annuals.

Many low-growing perennials, such as coral bells, dead nettle (lamium), coreopsis, and gaillardia, are perfect container plants. They either stay small in stature or have a cascading habit, fitting nicely in a small space. There are also many dwarf varieties of classic perennial flowers; for example, the dwarf purple coneflower variety 'Kim's Knee High' gets only 15 to 24 inches tall and works well in containers.

Of course, perennials usually only flower for a limited time period, so the best way to use them in containers is to combine perennials with different flowering times such as forget-me-nots, salvia, and sedum, to get color all season. There's also no rule against mixing and matching annual and perennial flowers in the same pot. In this way you'll have the constant color you want, plus get to use some cool perennial varieties in your planting.

Edibles

We talk a lot about growing edibles in urban landscapes, and we highlighted many dwarf varieties in Chapter 13. The container is an excellent place to augment any edible garden. Pots of lettuce, beans, cucumbers, summer squash, peppers, and dwarf tomatoes fit beautifully in the landscape. They look beautiful and provide food for you and your family.

Eggplant is one of the most ornamental vegetables. Varieties with striped fruit, such as 'Rosa Bianca', make a stunning statement in a container. Hot peppers varieties, such as 'Pretty in Purple' and 'Sangria', create a rainbow of colorful fruits that contrast with dark purple stems and leaves.

Even dwarf fruit trees, such as columnar apple and dwarf peaches, can be grown in containers with care. Exotics, such as fig, citrus, and pomegranate, can make excellent container plants, especially in warm climates; in colder climates they will need to be given winter protection or brought inside for the winter.

Trees and shrubs

Growing shrubs and dwarf trees is definitely possible in containers, but you'll need a large container and a good watering system in place. Because of their size, trees and shrubs often become the focal point of a container planting. They are often grown alone in containers because of the impact they make and their size would overrun other plants. Choose the best variety for your climate and space. It's not unthinkable to have dwarf boxwoods or dwarf conifers in a pot. There are some nice dwarf varieties of flowering shrubs that work in containers, including potentilla, fothergilla, daphne, spirea, and weigela. Scout around garden centers for dwarf versions of blue spruce, Alberta spruce, and pines to try, too.

Just keep in mind that woody plants will be more susceptible to injury from winter cold when grown in containers than when grown in the ground. A good rule of thumb is to choose plants with a hardiness zone rating two zones lower than yours for container planting. For example, if you are in hardiness zone 6, choose plants rated to hardiness zone 4 for use in containers.

Taking Care of Your Container Plants

No matter what plants you grow in your container, keeping them healthy is of the utmost importance. Watering, fertilizing, and controlling pests are some of the key maintenance activities for a healthy container garden.

Watering

Containers need frequent watering. How often to water depends on the types of plants and the weather conditions. Vegetable and flower containers in full sun generally need watering two to four times per week in spring, increasing to daily watering during the summer.

Container soils can dry out quickly and restrict the plant's root growth. You'll need to water your container plants more frequently than plants grown directly in the garden. This may be as often as once or twice a day during especially hot weather. Add enough water so that the entire root zone gets moistened and some water drains out the bottom of the container, but make sure that the soil isn't soggy. Maintaining consistent soil moisture will help keep flowers blooming and veggies producing without skipping a beat. (We talk more about watering and water conservation in Chapter 19, so head there if you want some more ideas for how to water plants with as little waste as possible.)

When watering a container that has really dried out, don't just pour on the water. When a container plant's soil mix dries out, it often shrinks away from the sides of the container. Then when you water, the moisture just runs down the sides and out of the container without actually wetting the soil mix. You see the water on the ground and think you've watered enough, but the soil is really still dry.

If a container plant gets very dry, it's best to soak the container in a pail of water, letting it soak up the moisture through the drainage holes. Check the soil mix and remove the container when the soil surface is moist, indicating that the water has permeated all the soil in the container.

Another way to reduce the need for frequent watering is to double pot your plants. Place the planted container inside a larger pot. Fill the space in between with crumpled newspaper to act as a layer of insulation. A majority of the direct sunlight will be absorbed by the insulation layer between the two pots. This helps keep the soil cool and moist for longer periods when in direct sunlight.

Ice is nice. A fun and efficient way to slowly water a container is to drop some ice cubes onto the soil. They'll slowly melt, watering the plant in the process. It's a fun way to let your kids help out in the container garden world.

Maintaining your containers

Certainly, growing the right plant in your container and keeping it well watered helps it to thrive, but your plants also need fertilizer, pruning, and an eye kept toward pest control.

Containers in the city can heat up fast and furious in full sun. Even plants that are labeled as heat-loving can overheat on a hot summer day. Watering regularly helps keep them cool, but you also should consider the plant placement. Even a plant that needs full sun may benefit from some shade during the hottest part of the day. If you're planting container vegetables and annual flowers, situate them where they'll get morning sun but have some protection from intense afternoon sun or set them in the filtered light of a high tree canopy. For more on sunlight and the urban microclimate, see Chapter 3.

Fertilizing

Most potting soils don't contain enough nutrients to keep your plants growing to perfection all summer long. However, some potting soils have time-release fertilizers added to them that slowly release their nutrients in response to watering. These are probably the easiest potting soils for the urban gardener to use, as long as you're okay with using the chemical fertilizer product included in the soil. These slow-release granules last at least three months, with some hanging on up to nine months. Their effectiveness may be reduced by frequent watering in summer, so monitor your plants for signs of nutrient deficiency, such as yellowing leaves and stunted growth. You can also buy these slow release fertilizers and add them to potting soil yourself at planting time. Apply them again later in the season, according to the instructions.

You can also use organic fertilizer products such as compost, fish emulsion, and cottonseed meal in your containers. We cover these and other fertilizers in Chapter 5. The key to adding these fertilizers is to stick with it. Since the nutrients are lost through leaching due to frequent watering, and there's a limited amount of soil mass to hold nutrients, you'll need to apply these fertilizers as often as every few weeks to keep your plants growing strong.

Pruning

The beauty of most annual flowers is that they never stop flowering. However, if individual plants in a container become tired-looking, cut them back. They'll regrow and begin flowering again. If the plants are beyond rejuvenation, spruce up the planters with replacement annuals, choosing similar plants and colors to complement the remaining flowers. Or remove the whole planting and start over with a different theme. For an immediate full effect in your container, place plants close together.

Another way to keep annual flowers blooming is to deadhead the flowers after they finish blooming. Simply pinch off the dead flower. It not only cleans up the plant, it encourages it to form more flowers.

Some newer varieties of annual flowers are *self-cleaning*. This means they drop their dead flowers to the ground when blooming is done. See more on these types of flowers in Chapter 14.

Pest inspection

Since your pots are elevated and in the city, you'd think you wouldn't have to contend with pests. Amazingly enough, pests will find your plants, even in urban areas. Certainly, problems with deer or woodchucks may be minimal, but squirrels, raccoons, and mice all may find your plants. Insect pests with winged adult stages such as cabbageworms, Japanese beetles, and whiteflies all can find your plants. Diseases such as powdery mildew and black spot are ubiquitous in the environment and likely to occur when the weather conditions are right.

Here are some tips to keep the pests away (for more details on specific pests, go to Chapter 20):

✔ **Keep your plants healthy.** This almost goes without saying, but a healthy plant is less likely to suffer from insect and disease attacks than a stressed one. Keep your plants well watered and fertilized all summer long.

✔ **Keep watch.** Check leaves, stems, and flowers regularly. You'll be admiring your beautiful plantings daily anyway, so just take an extra minute to look under the leaves and peer closely at the stems. Often you'll see the first signs of damage or young insects lurking there. Simply squish them to prevent any problems from taking hold.

✔ **Cover them up.** Create barriers to keep squirrels away or use floating row covers to prevent insects from laying eggs on your prized plants. If you can prevent problems from occurring, rather than trying to cure them once they happen, you'll get the best from your container gardens.

✔ **Be realistic.** If your plants have been attacked and aren't recovering or have disease or insect infestations that are spreading to other plants, be realistic. Consider ripping out those damaged plants. The beauty of containers is you can easily start over and over again. Why live through a rotten summer of ugly plants when it's simpler to just start over?

Moving containers

Small containers are easy to move to a new location or to follow the sun during the course of the growing season. But larger containers can be a real challenge to move. If you're growing trees, shrubs, or flower plantings in large containers, the combined weight of the soil, water, and plants may make it too heavy to budge. Here are some tips if you have to move a big pot:

✔ **Casters.** Purchase a container or a dolly with casters on it. These wheels help you roll heavy containers around with less effort. Of course, they work best on level, smooth surfaces. Trying to push a heavy pot uphill on bumpy ground is a drag.

✔ **Straps and a friend.** There are products on the market that use straps and handles to allow you and a friend to easily lift a heavy pot. Just remember to bend those knees.

✔ **Leave it until fall.** If you have a heavy container filled with vegetables or flowers, consider just leaving it in one place until fall. Once the plants die back, remove them, let the soil dry out, and then the pot will be easier to move.

Chapter 9

A Garden with a View: The Rooftop Garden

- -

In This Chapter

▶ Reviewing some important rooftop gardening basics

▶ Creating a sound design for your rooftop garden or green roof

▶ Going the less expensive route with rooftop container gardening

- -

*F*or many people, the urban environment lacks the space needed to garden. Buildings dominate the typical urban city block, and parking, sidewalks, and pavement take up whatever space is left. With so little green space available (especially on the ground level) to homeowners, builders, and community planners, the practice of building green roofs and rooftop gardens is an increasingly important option.

In the 1970s, green roof experts in Germany and Switzerland began to identify and label the various types of roof gardening systems. Since then, gardening experts around the world have done more and more research on these systems, focusing on waterproofing, drainage, lightweight growing media, and plant suitability.

In this chapter, we cover the basics of rooftop gardening from the initial planning and assessment of your roof conditions to understanding the difference between green roofs and roof gardens. We also show you what you can plant on a roof and how deep to plant it. Finally, we share some cost-effective roof gardening strategies, such as rooftop containers, so you can build your very own urban rooftop garden oasis.

Finding Out the Rooftop Gardening Basics

Green roofs are like green machines providing a natural approach to capture and manage storm water, as well as reduce the urban Heat Island Effect. A roof garden can also help reduce air pollution and provide an aesthetically useable green space in an urban environment. While a deep and heavy roof garden that can support trees, shrubs and people may be costly, in this chapter, we cover other affordable light weight green roof solutions you can pursue.

A mere 4-to-6-inch-thick bed of growing medium may just do the trick and provide you with a beautiful green roof of plantings without adding heavy loads to your roof.

You can find numerous strategies to develop your roof into a green garden. Some of the limitations are based on your budget, while others depend on an analysis of your structural rooftop conditions and local zoning regulations. This section covers the types of roof gardening you can pursue.

Why grow up? Reviewing reasons for planting on the roof

What are some of the reasons to garden on the rooftop and why is gardening up on the roof becoming increasingly popular in our urban environments? Here are some reasons why we believe this trend seems to be (ahem) *growing*:

- **Aesthetics:** Much like adding an "outdoor room," a developed roof garden provides a valuable and attractive green space in the urban setting. Roof gardens are great for entertaining, rooftop vegetable gardens, raised beds, pergolas, grilling and dining, and spaces with relaxed outdoor seating. Whichever approach you pursue, a rooftop garden can provide both beauty and useable space.

- **Better growing conditions:** Although rooftop conditions may include increased wind and temperature extremes, you may find that a rooftop garden in the city has better growing conditions, better soils, and better exposure to the sun and rain as compared to a street-level city garden. A roof garden is also less likely to suffer problems from compacted soil and the damaging effects of road salting in the winter season.

- **Roof protection:** If built properly, a rooftop garden or green roof can help protect the constructive qualities of a roof. The added layer can help extend the life and usefulness of the roof and in some cases, extend warranty periods as well.

✔ **Insulation:** Long before air-conditioning systems were invented, people constructed roof gardens to insulate their homes against extreme temperatures. In cold climates, this extra layer of plantings and soil helped retain heat, while in warmer climates, it helped keep buildings cooler.

✔ **Water and air quality:** Rooftop plantings are one way to help reduce water runoff, decrease higher temperatures caused by the Heat Island Effect, improve air quality, and reduce pollution — something many municipalities are now recognizing (thankfully).

✔ **Wildlife:** A rooftop garden provides a habitat for butterflies, other insects, and songbirds. Even small rooftop gardens can support a variety of wildlife. The deeper the growing medium, the greater the diversity of critters your rooftop garden can support.

What's your type? Choosing a green roof or roof garden

Green roofs and roof gardens commonly come in two types: *extensive* systems and *intensive* systems. Deciding on which system to use is best determined after a structural analysis of your existing roof conditions and allowable loading capacities. *Extensive systems,* or *green roofs,* are less expensive and are best for people who want to put a few inches of lightweight soil and some low-growing plantings or grasses on their roof. *Intensive systems,* or *roof gardens,* are for people whose roof can structurally support a deeper rooftop garden, one where you can hang out on the roof and entertain guests. These gardens include larger plantings, trees, shrubs, and even outdoor furniture and garden structures.

Of course, many roof gardens can also be constructed somewhere between the two as *simple intensive* or *hybrid systems.* Here's how the systems compare (see Figure 9-1):

✔ **Green roof/extensive system (shallow):** An extensive garden has a shallow depth of a lightweight growing medium (approximately 2 to 6 inches deep) and hardy, thinly rooted plants that require very little maintenance. The garden itself weighs much less than an intensive rooftop garden and is much cheaper to install and maintain. In the United States, these shallow systems are described as *green roofs*, and they're becoming more popular in cities across the country and being used on both level and sloped roofing surfaces.

✔ **Hybrid model/simple intensive system (moderate depth):** The simple intensive system has a growing medium that's approximately 6 to 10 inches deep. Also called the *hybrid model,* this moderate-weight system incorporates aspects of both extensive and intensive systems. It requires periodic maintenance, can be accessible, and has a medium cost compared to extensive and intensive systems.

✔ **Rooftop garden/intensive system (deep):** The intensive rooftop system has a growing medium that's more than 10 inches deep. Intensive rooftop gardens are the most like gardens on the ground, with deeper growing media, a variety of plantings, and higher maintenance needs (such as irrigation and pruning). They're also heavier and more costly to install than extensive systems.

Container gardening on the roof is a low-cost alternative to a green roof or rooftop garden. For details, see the section "Staying In Bounds with a Container Rooftop Garden" later in this chapter.

Terminology is important when you're submitting plans to obtain approvals from your local city planning and zoning offices. For instance, a *rooftop garden* may be presumed to be accessible and, therefore, require appropriate perimeter railings, heightened exhaust stacks, minimum walkway widths, and appropriate pedestrian exits. Make sure you're using the correct terms if you're applying for permits.

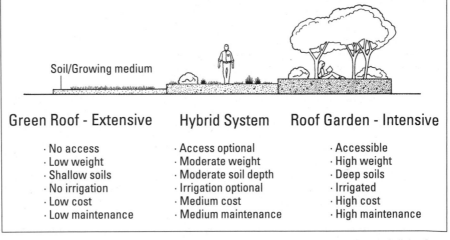

Figure 9-1: Cross-section of a green roof and hybrid and rooftop gardens.

Soil/Growing medium

Green Roof - Extensive
· No access
· Low weight
· Shallow soils
· No irrigation
· Low cost
· Low maintenance

Hybrid System
· Access optional
· Moderate weight
· Moderate soil depth
· Irrigation optional
· Medium cost
· Medium maintenance

Roof Garden - Intensive
· Accessible
· High weight
· Deep soils
· Irrigated
· High cost
· High maintenance

Illustration by Kathryn Born.

How much is enough? Looking at your limits

Before you start building a rooftop garden, you need to do some planning to assess your options. Here are some of the factors that limit what you can do on your roof:

✔ **Budget:** While the structural review will dictate the type of garden you can build, another large consideration is your pocketbook. Of course costs will vary greatly between a green roof, a hybrid, and a roof garden, but here are some general cost comparisons.

Modular systems: Installing a pre-grown green roof

If you're into simplicity, you may want to consider installing a modular system rather than starting a green roof from scratch. Complete modular green roof systems are ready-to-go, with fully grown plants inside the container. The installers simply set the containers in place for an instant green roof.

The *LiveRoof* system is one of our favorites (see the accompanying figure). The design includes an elevated soil system and moisture portals that seamlessly unite one panel to another. This physical unity allows for the natural sharing of water, nutrients, and beneficial organisms across the entire rooftop strata. Because the product is naturally interconnected with an elevated soil system, hot, wet, and dry zones are minimal. In addition, this design avoids compartmentalizing the growing medium into unnatural "grids," as is the case with other modular systems. LiveRoof systems range in a variety of planting depths from 2½ inches thick with shallow rooted plantings to heavier 8-inch-thick systems that are able to support vegetable and perennial plantings.

For more on *LiveRoof* Modular systems, visit www.liveroof.com.

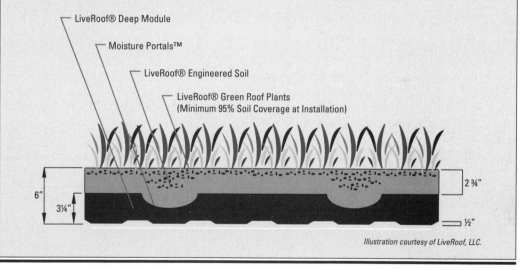

LiveRoof® Deep Module

Moisture Portals™

LiveRoof® Engineered Soil

LiveRoof® Green Roof Plants
(Minimum 95% Soil Coverage at Installation)

6"

3¼"

2¾"

½"

Illustration courtesy of LiveRoof, LLC.

The approximate cost for a modular green roof system ranges from $15 to $35 per square foot (PSF) to build. A hybrid system will likely be between $25 to $45 PSF, and a roof garden may cost anywhere from about $35 PSF to $100 per square foot *and more,* depending on how deep and intensively it is constructed.

Again, keep in mind that costs will vary widely depending not only on which of the three types of systems you select but also on project size, building height, whether paving is used, the types of planters, whether the roof garden is accessible, and the overall design complexity.

✔ **Amount of weight your roof can hold:** The structural load capacity of your roof largely dictates the type of rooftop garden you can create.

For example, a typical 4-inch-deep roof garden weighs 20 to 25 pounds per square foot. Intensive rooftop garden systems can easily reach 80 pounds PSF or more when accommodating trees and shrubs. An engineer's structural analysis determines whether your rooftop can support a garden and how thick the soil layer or growing medium can be. See the later section "Structural considerations: Making sure your roof won't cave in!" for details.

✔ **Roof access and pitch:** If the pitch of your roof is rather steep or your rooftop is inaccessible, you may want to develop a shallow green roof with hardy, low-maintenance plantings rather than a deeper intensive rooftop garden.

✔ **Local zoning regulations:** Check your local regulations for specific requirements that may relate to the development of your rooftop garden. These local requirements likely regulate proposed structures, allowable building heights, fire rating requirements, access, and roof exiting requirements. After you've developed a plan, you need to submit your drawings to your municipality for their review and obtain the proper permits before construction begins.

Table 9-1 provides info on garden uses and features as well as recommends sizes based on cost and coverage requirements. For instance, larger areas are better suited for extensive green roof systems with self-sustaining plant communities as opposed to large, costly intensive roof gardens. This table may be a useful tool for you when deciding your initial approach to develop your roof garden space appropriately.

Table 9-1   Rooftop Garden Uses, Features, and Water Needs

	Green Roof/ Extensive System	*Green Roof/Hybrid/ Semi-Intensive System*	*Roof Garden/ Intensive System*
Depth	Approx. 2–6 inches	Approx. 6–10 inches	Approx. >10 inches
Area	Most suitable for large expansive roof areas, can also be used for sloped roof sur-faces	Most suitable for average-sized roof areas where access is optional, but larger than a patio garden space	Most suitable for smaller roof areas, with room for larger plants like an outdoor room or patio garden space
Design complexity	Simple	Simple or complex	Complex

	Green Roof/ Extensive System	Green Roof/Hybrid/ Semi-Intensive System	Roof Garden/ Intensive System
Plant types	Self-sustaining plant community; limited range of plant varieties	Varied selection of plants available including vegetable plants	Wide range of available plantings, including native varieties
Food growth	Limited food growth	Good for growing food	Great for growing food
Insulation properties	Good	Better	Great
Watering	No irrigation necessary	Irrigation optional, depending on plant varieties selected	Regular irrigation recommended
Weight requirements	Low weight	Medium weight	High weight
Access	Inaccessible	Accessible (option)	Accessible
Cost	Low cost	Moderate cost	High cost
Maintenance	Low	Medium	High

What's next? Getting started and developing a plan

Developing a roof garden can get complicated, so where do you begin when it comes to planning a roof garden without being overwhelmed? The following steps are a brief step-by-step guide to develop a rooftop garden plan:

1. **Think about what you envision your rooftop garden to be.**

   Review your goals, intended use, aesthetics, timing, and budget considerations.

2. **Research local regulations.**

   Review any local codes and zoning regulations with your local planning and zoning officials. Be sure to also review any neighborhood association rules or covenants.

3. **Hire a structural engineer.**

   A structural engineer will review the existing conditions and assess the roof properly for your rooftop garden considerations and limitations. This assessment helps you clearly select the type of system your roof is capable of supporting.

4. Hire a landscape architect.

Once you know applicable zoning regulations and structural considerations, consider hiring a designer to appropriately develop your vision.

5. Have a peer review of the plans.

Once the plans are complete it is best to have the structural engineer come back in to assess the proposed design plans, review the weight-bearing conditions of the proposal, and provide further recommendations or an approval for the proposed design.

6. Submit your drawings to the city for approval.

Once completed, you want to submit your plans to all appropriate city agencies for your local municipal approvals. Also provide a record copy to your homeowners association. Do not begin construction until all necessary approvals have been obtained.

7. Install your garden or hire contractors to do the work.

Follow the plans and install your garden. While you may find that modular green roof systems may be easy enough to install on your own, we urge you to hire a contractor to install the larger and more complex systems.

8. Maintain the gardens as needed.

Both green roofs and roof gardens require periodic maintenance. While green roof and modular systems require less maintenance, deeper roof gardens require more periodic maintenance, especially frequent watering or irrigation. Ask your landscape architect to provide a maintenance plan so you will have a good understanding of how to take care of the garden.

You may be surprised to discover that your initial vision to develop the garden ends up very different once you understand various limitations and structural considerations. For any rooftop garden, we highly recommend you to hire the right professionals who can help guide you through this process appropriately. The following list of resources may benefit your management of this process:

- For a professional landscape architect start by visiting the American Society of Landscape Architects at www.asla.org. Click on the Chapters tab to find an interactive map where you can select your state and region to find a professional landscape architect near you.

- For a structural engineer, we've found the easy way is to Google "structural engineer" and include your state as well. From there you should be able to find a list of engineers in your area. You can also ask your designer for a recommendation or use the (old-fashioned) phone book method to find a local engineer.

- As for contractors, it may be best to also obtain a recommendation from your designer, however if you're looking on your own, be sure that your contractor is experienced in rooftop construction and will obtain all appropriate permits and approvals to complete all the work.

Many *green building technologies,* like green roofs, have positive impacts on communities and the environment, including reduction of storm water runoff, improved air and water quality, mitigation of the urban Heat Island Effect, and energy savings. The American Society of Landscape Architects supports efforts to encourage the use of these technologies and other design techniques to create sustainable communities. For more visit: www.asla.org/sustainabledesign.aspx.

Designing a Rooftop Garden or Green Roof

A green roof or roof garden has many different layers, and often such gardens are unique and custom designed. But generally, here are several different layers for a rooftop system from top to bottom:

- **Layer 1:** Plantings
- **Layer 2:** Growing medium
- **Layer 3:** Filter fabric separator
- **Layer 4:** A drainage layer
- **Layer 5:** Insulation barrier
- **Layer 6:** A waterproof membrane
- **Layer 7:** The structural roof deck surface

Although a rooftop garden design can incorporate your personal garden interests, aesthetics, maintenance, and environmental goals, the initial planning requires a technical assessment by a structural engineer, who will verify whether your roof can support the weight of a garden. Your design also needs to consider watering, drainage, growing medium, plant choices, and other rooftop garden features. In this section, we cover some special considerations when designing gardens on the rooftop.

If you need help designing a good rooftop garden plan, a landscape architect can guide you in the process of developing a suitable garden that will meet the loading capacity requirements, local regulations, and your design aesthetics. Visit www.asla.org to find a professional near you.

Constructing a roof garden during a new build or when the roof needs repair work allows for the greatest design options and is the most cost-effective approach. Specifically, this approach helps you budget-in and allow for the construction of a waterproofing membrane and root-resistant barrier as part of a new project.

Structural considerations: Making sure your roof won't cave in

If your proposed roof garden will be placed on your existing roof, you need to start your design plan by calculating how much weight the garden will add and whether your existing roof is structurally capable of handling this load.

For this assessment, call in a structural engineer to do a thorough review of your record plans and construction drawings and to conduct a site inspection to determine whether your roof is capable of supporting a rooftop garden. The record drawings and site analysis help the engineer determine the *total load capacity* (the total weight your roof can hold) for your rooftop.

You can have your rooftop designer recommend an engineer or you can search the Yellow Pages for a structural engineer near you. Generally, a structural engineer is required by local authorities when you're adding 17 pounds per square foot or more to a rooftop. A flat roof with a minimum pitch will be the easiest to install and the least complicated. Steeper, sloped roofs may require additional cross-battens to support both soil and drainage layers for your garden.

Understanding live and dead loads

Your roof's total load capacity must be greater than the sum of both the dead and live loads:

✔ *Dead loads* are permanently affixed materials such as the roof itself and other securely attached structures including both green roof and rooftop garden systems. Dead loads are physical and can easily be measured and calculated into the structural engineering analysis.

✔ *Live loads* are moveable and temporary materials, such as people, snow, and other objects, that contribute to periodic weighted loads on a temporary basis. Live loads are harder to measure since they are infrequent and vary greatly. Estimates for live loads are usually given in a range because of this.

For a roof garden, additional dead loads typically include a growing medium, filter fabric, an insulation layer, waterproofing, fixed vertical planters, and plantings. Keep in mind the depth of the growing medium.

The engineer first determines the existing roof loading capacity in allowable pounds per square foot (PSF) and then subtracts potential live loads, such as snow and people. You can use the resulting number — the PSF balance — to choose your roof garden materials, depth of the growing medium, decking, and other rooftop features.

Being sure of typical load requirements

The PSF requirements for rooftop garden systems vary depending on what you use to build your garden. The following general load estimates help you understand the weight and capacity limitations for some common dead and live loads associated with rooftop garden planning:

Dead Load Approximations

Green roof (extensive system)	20–35 PSF
Green roof hybrid (simple intensive system)	35–80 PSF
Roof garden (intensive system)	80–150 PSF

Live Load Approximations (check local municipal requirements)

Snow	25–35 PSF (check state and local building code requirements)
Water	About 8 PSF (stored in rain barrels, tanks, or other rooftop containers)
People	About 15–20 PSF per person

Your engineer must add all existing dead loads and potential live loads to his structural calculations to determine your roof's *total load capacity*. Keep in mind that the total load capacity may vary for different areas of your roof, depending on existing structural conditions and building additions, and all live loads shall be determined in accordance with a method approved by your local municipality.

Depending on how tight your allowable PSF numbers are, consider restricting or eliminating rooftop access to small gatherings of people during periods when other loads (such as snow) are present.

Managing rainwater

Roofs can collect a surprising amount of rain during a storm. Instead of letting all that water flow off the roofs, run off, and go down the driveway or road, you can collect it to water your plants and gardens. In this section, we show you the basics of storm water runoff and some water conservation strategies and techniques you can use to conserve, retain, and recycle rainwater from the rooftop.

Storm water management

One of the keys to developing a successful rooftop garden is creating a balanced storm water management system that efficiently captures, stores, uses, and drains rainwater. You don't want to just collect the water as fast as you can and drain it away, because if you do, you lose out on a great resource. On the other hand, you don't want to collect every drop of rainwater and just let it sit because pooling or standing water and oversaturated soil conditions can cause root suffocation, decay, and rot, not to mention severe damage to your rooftop surfacing and waterproofing layers.

Surface storm water can be directed to planted areas where it can be absorbed and used. Do this by designing your rooftop garden to pitch rain water toward your planted areas. Any excess water beyond what is needed for rooftop plantings then drains through the growing medium and is captured, stored, and reused as needed. For details on harvesting rainwater, see Chapter 19.

Rooftop erosion

Sloped planting beds and even level rooftop garden beds can be subject to erosion caused by heavy rainstorms. These downpours can wash away soil, and if they're severe enough, they can interfere with root systems, keeping plants from becoming established. In addition, many rooftop gardens are less protected than their ground-level counterparts from direct sun and high winds.

If erosion is a severe problem on your roof, you need to take a twofold approach to fixing it:

✔ Control and direct surface runoff appropriately.

✔ Stabilize the surface with proper techniques and plantings.

In some cases, you can control and stabilize by planting a mixture of plants in your rooftop garden. Doing so provides various plant root types and depths that are better at holding the soil in place. In other cases, a mass planting of just one kind of plant may be enough to stabilize the soil from erosion.

Other than choosing what to plant, you can pick from many different techniques that are specifically designed to help control runoff and stabilize the garden's surface. Some solutions include biodegradable stabilization products, while others are more permanent. Either way, you should place your soil stabilization products before doing any planting on a sloped green roof.

Until your roof garden plantings establish their root systems and fill up the growing surfaces, the risk for erosion is greater. Here are two stabilization products that can help control erosion:

✔ **Erosion blankets:** Also called *erosion matting,* these blankets are typically made of natural fiber or straw, and they lay over the surface of the growing medium. Erosion blankets are lightweight and easy to install. They eventually biodegrade as your plantings establish their root systems.

✔ **Stabilization netting:** For more steeply sloped rooftops, you may need to use a more permanent approach like stabilization netting. Stabilization nets are typically made of polyethylene and come in various thicknesses, depending on the depth of your growing medium. You place stabilization nets and anchor them by using horizontal steel cables before filling in with soil or other growing medium. The netting is perforated to allow the flow of air and water to reach the root systems.

Whether you're planning to develop a green roof or a rooftop garden, we strongly suggest consulting a landscape architect or other professional with formal training in grading and drainage to help you determine the best way to handle water runoff from heavy rains and reduce the risk of erosion before planting. If you're dealing with severe erosion issues after planting, don't try to address them without first talking to an expert trained in controlling runoff.

Water service and irrigation

By design, a green roof typically includes hardy, low-maintenance plantings with no irrigation requirements. Rooftop gardens, on the other hand, have varying irrigation needs, depending on the depth of the planting beds. But no matter what type of rooftop garden you have, the best way to fulfill your irrigation needs is to harvest rainwater and direct it toward the planted areas, where it can infiltrate and be reused.

Hybrid rooftop gardens with 6- to 10-inch-deep planting beds may require an irrigation system, depending on the types of plantings and their water needs. To reduce the need for supplemental irrigation, design your hybrid rooftop garden by using low-maintenance and native varieties that are more likely to thrive on their own.

An intensive rooftop garden with planting beds deeper than 10 inches usually requires periodic monitoring and watering of plants, especially if it includes trees and shrubs. See Figure 9-2 for an example of a deep *rooftop garden,* including a detailed installation drawing for tree planting. (***Note:*** Figure 9-2 is for preliminary design only, not for construction. Check all federal, state, and local code requirements and coordinate with a structure engineer if you wish to proceed with an deep rooftop garden.)

You can water your garden by hand or install an irrigation system to provide for your plants' water needs. Be sure to monitor your garden regularly, especially during periods when rainwater is insufficient. If you want to go the manual watering route, install a hose-bib system on your roof. If you want to use an irrigation system, you can install moisture sensors to help regulate your watering use. A landscape architect can help you design an appropriate irrigation system capable of meeting the needs of your rooftop garden.

Deciding what to grow

A rooftop garden has its own microclimate with different conditions than the nearby ground-level landscape environment (see Chapter 3 for details on microclimates). For example, many rooftop gardens are subject to higher winds, more direct sunlight, and lower winter soil temperatures. With these conditions in mind, you need to select plantings that can survive and establish well in such extremes. Low-growing plants with shallow root systems capable of tolerating a shallow growing medium are likely to be the best candidates for your roof garden.

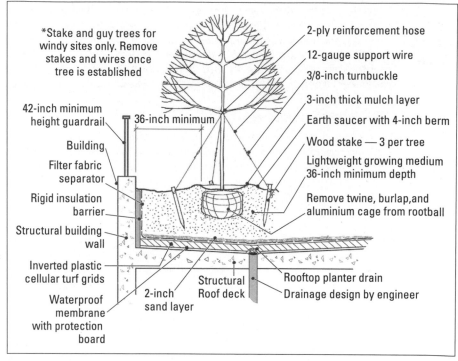

*Stake and guy trees for windy sites only. Remove stakes and wires once tree is established

2-ply reinforcement hose

12-gauge support wire

3/8-inch turnbuckle

3-inch thick mulch layer

Earth saucer with 4-inch berm

Wood stake — 3 per tree

Lightweight growing medium 36-inch minimum depth

Remove twine, burlap, and aluminium cage from rootball

42-inch minimum height guardrail

36-inch minimum

Building

Filter fabric separator

Rigid insulation barrier

Structural building wall

Inverted plastic cellular turf grids

Waterproof membrane with protection board

2-inch sand layer

Structural Roof deck

Rooftop planter drain

Drainage design by engineer

Figure 9-2:
Cross-section of a rooftop tree planting.

Illustration courtesy of Paul Simon.

After you complete a structural analysis and know whether you want to construct a green roof or a roof garden (see the earlier section "Structural considerations: Making sure your roof won't cave in"), you can start planning your project appropriately. The following chart can guide you in selecting suitable plantings for either shallow- or deep-rooted systems.

Green Roof (Extensive System): 2–6 Inches Deep	*Green Roof Hybrid (Simple Intensive System): 6–10 Inches Deep*	*Roof Garden (Intensive System): > 10 Inches Deep*
Sedum	Ornamental grasses	Lawns
Moss	Various herbs	Grasses
Herbs	Small shrubs	Shrubs
Grasses	Some edible plants	Edible plants
Or combine plantings:	Some perennials	Perennials
Moss, sedum and herbs	Sedum	Small trees
Sedum, grass and herbs		
Grasses & herbs		

Whatever plants you decide to include in your garden, avoid using regular garden soil, which is heavier and denser and may contain undesirable insects, weeds, and pathogens. Instead, purchase a lightweight growing medium designed specifically for roof gardens. A quality, engineered growing medium weighs less, reduces the possibility of weeds and insects, and is engineered for both green roofs and rooftop gardens. Visit www.rooflitesoil.com and www.myplantconnection.com to find out how to buy extensive, semi-intensive, or intensive growing mixtures.

Planning electrical service and lighting

If you plan to build an accessible roof garden, a lighting plan can add interest and help highlight garden plantings, trees, shrubs, garden paths, walkways, perimeter railings, and perhaps a special garden feature or sculpture. Fortunately, you can plan the wiring and conduit necessary for your lighting system right along with the design of your irrigation system.

Make sure your contractor installs all the utilities below your growing medium to keep the conduit shielded from direct sun exposure so that it doesn't decay over time. Specialized installation of rooftop utilities is also necessary to avoid puncturing the waterproofing membrane. If you plan to install larger vertical lighting features such as post lighting or bollards, you'll likely need to puncture the waterproofing membrane. In that case, just be sure to carefully seal these fixtures appropriately to the roof for water tightness.

Transporting materials

Before you jump past the planning stage to the construction stage, you have to assess how you intend to access your rooftop garden. Consider the size and weight of all your construction materials. For instance, you may need to assemble a large garden arbor on the roof instead of preassembling it at ground level and transporting it up if it can't fit through the doors and stairways to the roof itself. As you assess how you and your contractors (if you have them) will access the roof during construction and transport materials. Don't forget about how you'll access your garden for continued maintenance throughout the growing season.

Ease of transport

Transporting materials up to a roof can be quite challenging and time consuming. If you're installing your own garden, gather a group of your friends together to help you haul all your materials to the roof, including building materials, containers, soil, fertilizer, and other equipment necessary to build your roof garden. Try not to take on all the work yourself as the transport itself can be a back-breaking endeavor.

After everything is on the roof, have your team assemble and fill the containers so you're ready to go. Just be ready to order in lots of pizza when the work is done!

To transport your roof garden materials more easily, consider hiring a crane and lift bucket on an hourly basis. Doing so will likely add a considerable cost, but it can save you an enormous amount of time, considering how tall your building is and how long it would take to manually transport your materials. Check local codes and obtain permits and an approval from the building owner before you begin.

Staying In Bounds with a Rooftop Container Garden

Budget is usually one of the biggest issues many people face when working to develop their rooftops into gardens. One popular low-cost alternatives to rooftop gardens and green roofs are containers and potted plantings. Containers and potted plantings provide many of the same benefits and most importantly keep your cost under control. One of the big differences however is that a green roof or roof garden will have greater insulating properties and is able to help capture and reduce storm water runoff.

A simple low-budget rooftop garden can be created with potted plants and containers. This kind of garden is the one most commonly constructed by homeowners because it's relatively low in cost and easy to maintain.

Container gardens can also provide many of the same benefits as more elaborate roof gardens, including shade and increased reflectivity and evapotranspiration. But compared to an extensive or intensive green roof system, they are not as effective at providing insulation or reducing storm water runoff.

Constructing an elaborate rooftop garden can be quite an expensive endeavor, from the initial engineering analysis to the customized rooftop construction needed to support a roof garden. Lucky for those of you on a tight budget who still want to give rooftop gardening a try, many rooftop gardens involve basic raised beds or rooftop containers (see Figure 9-3), both of which usually cost less and allow for some separation between the raised beds or containers and the roof's surface. As a result, you can save money, and the roof and its waterproofing layer are easily accessible for inspection, maintenance, and repair.

Rooftop containers and raised beds also allow for more design flexibility because you can change your layout from year to year simply by rearranging the individual containers.

Don't forget to account for your roof's total load capacity even if you go with the raised bed or container route! An analysis of the existing roof condition is still important no matter what option you decide to pursue. When planning your rooftop containers, select lightweight products that fall below the roof's load capacity.

If you're looking for a way to garden on the roof that's even cheaper than a raised bed, consider converting small containers that you already have or that you can purchase cheaply into rooftop planters. For instance, you can use a 4-to 6-foot-wide child's plastic wading pool (noninflatable, please!). These 12-to 15-inch-deep pools are readily available, cost efficient, and provide a decently sized growing area for a small garden.

Figure 9-3:
A rooftop container garden.

Illustration by Kathryn Born.

To provide drainage, drill a series of 3⁄4-inch holes about 1 foot apart around the bottom perimeter crease of the wading pool. The holes allow excess water to drain onto the roof's surface.

Then fill the container with a lightweight growing medium to a depth less than the allowable total load capacity determined in your initial structural analysis (see the earlier section "Structural considerations: Making sure your roof won't cave in" for details). Place your pool planters on a level surface with enough room between them for easy access.

Chapter 10

Going Vertical in Your Garden

A lack of space is no reason to give up gardening. Think of a sprawling melon plant or cucumber vine. Now picture it growing up a trellis. Same vine, foliage, and fruit but with a fraction of the gardening footprint! Vertical gardening has numerous benefits, but for urban gardeners, the most important one is growing more in a smaller area.

You can go vertical in a variety of ways — with a vine on a trellis, a green wall, or simply a row of shrubs to define the edges of your urban garden. This chapter helps you think in 3D and understand the benefits of vertical gardening. We also cover techniques and some products that can help you build a vertical garden.

Discovering the Benefits of Growing Vertical

Here are some of the many benefits to growing a vertical urban garden:

✔ **Space saving:** You can grow more plants in a smaller area because you can train your plantings to grow vertically instead of competing with one another for space horizontally.

✔ **Simplified efforts:** It is easier to harvest from a trellis than to stoop and harvest from the ground. It is also easier to get around the garden when there aren't vines sprawling around to step over.

✔ **Less chance for plant disease:** Growing plants vertically may also help reduce disease problems like powdery mildew by improving air circulation through the foliage. In addition, keeping your plants away from direct contact with the soil helps reduce the risk of soil-borne fruit rot diseases.

✔ **Easier to weed:** Every square foot of garden you have is a square foot of soil that may require weeding. The vertical garden encompasses less space and thus less area to keep weed free!

✔ **Easier to fertilize:** Vertical garden beds are more accessible and easier to fertilize when needed.

✔ **Water conserving:** Vertical gardens help you save water. They take up less planter space, reducing water needs.

✔ **Shade providing:** Vertical gardens can provide shade, reduce temperatures, and create a cooler, more comfortable microclimate.

✔ **Greater sun exposure:** Vertical plantings have less competition with one another for sunlight exposure, which is also why this gardening technique can provide you greater shading capabilities.

✔ **Wind shielding:** Vertical plantings and structures can help protect against harsh winter winds while also working to channel summer breezes into your urban garden area. For more on wind direction and seasonal climate conditions see Chapter 3.

✔ **Visually pleasing "Wow Factor":** Whether as a backdrop to your outdoor room or as a special focal element and garden feature, vertical gardens provide a visually stimulating accent to your outdoor space and a great conversation piece for entertaining guests.

Facing the Challenges of Growing Vertical

Here are some of the challenges to growing vertically:

✔ **Room to grow:** Placing a trellis up against a wall may hinder plant growth since room is needed on both sides of a trellis system. When fixing a trellis to a wall, add 2"-by-2" wood lath strips along the façade first and then fix your trellis to these. This will help keep the trellis system far enough away from the wall, allowing ample room for plants to climb and grow well.

✔ **Building regulations and municipal review:** For larger vertical construction, one of your challenges may be obtaining approvals from your condo association and local municipality. Be sure to call or visit your local city planning and zoning and fire prevention departments to find out what requirements you may need to follow.

✔ **Protection from winter frost:** Vertical plantings are more susceptible to low temperatures and freezing soil conditions in the winter when compared to planting at ground level. For small container plantings, consider moving planters indoors during the winter months if possible. The south and west sides of your home provide greater sun exposure to keep plantings warmer in the winter.

✔ **Finding the right plants:** Selecting suitable hardy plantings for your vertical garden is key to having a beautiful and successful garden. When purchasing plants, be sure to ask questions.

✔ **Watering:** Hosing down the plants horizontally will only moisten surface growth because the majority of the water splashes back onto the ground. Be sure to develop your vertical garden with watering in mind. In addition to drainage holes, provide adequate room for irrigation or watering efforts that can penetrate through the soil or growing medium appropriately.

✔ **Drainage space:** Make sure that your vertical containers allow ample room and drainage so water doesn't get trapped inside your planters and cause root decay. Containers like terra-cotta clay pots provide excellent drainage capabilities, making over-watering less likely. For more on container gardening see Chapter 8.

Rethinking Your Space: Up, Down, and All Around

You should have adequate access in your vertical garden for periodic maintenance, good drainage, decent irrigation and watering capabilities, and a good support structure for your plantings. There are several vertical gardening techniques you can build in tight urban spaces from climbing vines on simple trellis systems to raised containers. For inspiration, here are some ways to rethink your spaces:

✔ **Growing up.** Vining vegetables, including cucumbers, melons, squash, indeterminate tomato varieties, and vining beans can be trained up a trellis, where they take up very little horizontal garden space. This allows you to increase the amount of plantings in your garden bed as you take advantage of vertical space.

✔ **Growing down.** Vertical doesn't just mean growing up. You can also *grow down.* A second story porch or balcony can be a great place to set a large container of vining plants that will cascade downward. An apartment dweller can grow a crop of sweet potatoes in a large balcony container, allowing the vines to hang down over the ledge in a curtain of attractive foliage. Make sure the pot is attached to a railing or post and secured against strong winds.

✔ **Growing all around.** Think of an urban garden space as an outdoor room that functions as an extension of the home. Of course, when planting, many people think of only the ground floor of the landscape. Vertical planting structures can help define the walls and ceiling space of your outdoor room. Consider enclosing an area of your outdoor space by gardening vertically on at least three sides to create a special, enclosed gathering area.

Getting Plants to Grow Up

So where do you begin when it comes to vertical gardening? How do we get our plants growing up — on trellises, fencing, tepees, arches, and arbors? And how does it look? There are a number of reasons, both aesthetic and practical, for growing plants on vertical structures. To help, the next two sections provide some very detailed information on many different types of vertical structures and some tips on growing fruits and vegetables vertically.

Vertical structures: Providing a place to climb

Vertical structures come in many different sizes, shapes, and forms, and like a picture frame, they provide a structural canvas to place your colorful garden materials. Imagine a pergola covered with colorful morning glories or a rose-covered arbor with a comfortable bench that will welcome visitors to your garden. Perhaps your urban garden could use a trellis panel system to screen you from a busy road and provide a bit of privacy? Or maybe you would like to create a fun-tunnel of your own with a two-sided teepee trellis system you're able to walk under. Whatever you're looking for, adding a vertical structure to an urban garden is a space saver and can provide a three-dimensional element of colorful and creative context to your urban garden.

A trellis garden

Growing on a trellis is an efficient and cost-effective way to develop your vertical garden. Even a 12-inch-wide planter can accommodate a wood trellis. Today you can find a variety of trellises at local garden centers. Better yet, you can construct a custom trellis to fit your space perfectly! Trellises now come in a variety of styles, including the standard fan, woven patterns, vertical woven accent styles, slender pole-trellis styles, and various rectangular or square grid-style panel shaped arrangements. See Figure 10-1 for an example of a vertical trellis panel.

Figure 10-1:
A vertical panel garden trellis.

Illustration by Kathryn Born.

Besides acting as a plant support, a series of trellis panels can work well as a privacy screen between you and your neighbor or provide a vine-laden fence to block an unattractive view.

Some common plants to grow on trellises include climbing roses, clematis, morning glory, bougainvillea, various ivy plants, and grape vines, to name just a few. You can also grow cucumbers, peas, and summer squash. However, one of our favorite plants for a garden trellis is the pole bean. Pole beans are easy to grow, require little maintenance, and grow fast enough for you and your children to notice a daily difference. Eventually your bean plant will easily yield lots of long, tasty bean pods for you and your family to harvest and enjoy!

If the trellis is going to be placed adjacent to a wall, it needs to be attached with supports. You can support the trellis with small, wooden blocks between the trellis and the wall. Securely mount your blocks to the wall and the trellis to the blocks. Be sure the blocks hold the trellis a minimum of 4 inches away from the wall to provide plenty of room for plants to climb through and create a cooling shadow on the wall.

Modular trellis panels

Today there are numerous three-dimensional, welded wire vertical trellising systems available. Trellis panels can transform a blank concrete or masonry wall into soft-textured, vine laden, and flower-covered surfaces. The elements are simple and the possibilities are endless. You can mount these modular shaped panels near entries and around windows, to support a living plant matrix that can cover all or part of a building façade. One of our favorites is the Greenscreen modular system because of the many different assembled possibilities, from modular trellis panels to planters and custom construction. This is a great product to meet the needs of your urban garden space. For more on this product visit: www.greenscreen.com.

Illustration by Kathryn Born.

Garden arbors and pergolas

Woody vines planted and trained to climb an arbor or pergola create a beautiful and definitive urban garden space. Once the plantings are established, they provide a break from direct summer sun and also help screen unsightly views. Consider adding an arbor or pergola to your urban landscape and turn a hot outdoor area into a cool urban retreat!

What is the difference between an arbor and a pergola? Not much. Arbors are just smaller, simpler structures than pergolas. A garden arbor (see Figure 10-2) is typically used as an entry feature and is at least 3 or 4 feet wide and is often arched above. A pergola (see Figure 10-3) is a much larger structure and usually given much more architectural treatment than an arbor. Both structures are extensively used to support vining plants and other vertical plantings.

Both arbors and pergolas form a ceiling that not only blocks out the sun, but also creates a cool, shady spot in which to sit. These structures can support a variety of flowering or fruiting plants, including grapes, vining vegetables, climbing roses, or clematis vines to name a few.

Figure 10-2:
A garden
arbor.

Illustration by Kathryn Born.

Figure 10-3:
A garden
pergola.

Illustration by Kathryn Born.

Annual and perennial vines are wonderful but they do take some time during the growing season to get big enough to provide needed shade. Woody vines can cover an arbor or pergola structure in a few seasons, providing years of beauty and the bonus of summer shade. Here are a few different recommended varieties of woody vines; however, check your hardiness zones to ensure these plants are appropriate for your region.

- **Trumpet Honeysuckle** (*Lonicera sempervirens*) — This climbing vine is noted for its colorful, trumpet-shaped flowers, sweet scent, and attractiveness to butterflies and hummingbirds and can grow 10–20 feet. Select a site with full sun to shade and moist, well-drained soil. The plants will flower more profusely in full sun. Zones 4–10a.

- **Crossvine** (*Bignonia capreolata*) — The native vine sports rusty brown-red to yellow blooms. The dazzling variety 'Tangerine Beauty' is a show-stopper with its tangerine-to-coral blooms. It blooms profusely in spring and more sparsely later in the season, and also attracts hummingbirds. Plant in full sun to part shade. Zones 5–9.

- **Trumpet creeper** (*Campsis radicans*) — The "wild" version is often cursed as a rampant weedy vine. Newer cultivars like 'Madame Galen' and 'Georgia' offer larger blooms and have a place as a strong vine for a large arbor or to cover the expanse of a western wall. Full sun to part shade. Zones 4b–10a.

- **Wisteria** (*Wisteria* spp.) — Several species and varieties are available. Long cascades of blue-to-purple flowers in spring. Looks great trained along the top of a fence and cut back heavily each winter. Also outstanding for the side walls and ceiling of a large, sturdy pergola. Full sun to part shade. Be careful not to plant wisteria vine too close to foundation walls as the root system is very vigorous! Zones 5–9.

- **Carolina jessamine** (*Gelsemium sempervirens*) — This evergreen vine puts on a spring show of trumpet-shaped yellow blooms. Great for a post or vertical lattice-type outdoor wall. All parts of the plant are poisonous. Full sun to part shade. Zones 5b–9b.

- **Lady Banks rose** (*Rosa banksiae*) — Long, arching, thornless canes bear yellow blooms in spring. Needs lots of room and a sturdy trellis support to do its thing. A lightly fragrant, white blooming form is also available. Full sun. Evergreen in zones 9–11 and deciduous in zones 6–8.

Again, be sure to check the availability of plants and whether any of the above are suitable for your hardiness zone before purchasing.

Teepees

Of course many city residents, condominium owners, apartment dwellers, and urban residents have limited space to develop a complete vegetable garden each season. Vertical garden teepees can create the additional space needed to help urban gardeners grow a larger and more abundant vegetable garden. See Figure 10-4 for an example of a garden teepee.

Illustration by Kathryn Born.

Teepee garden structures can be built in many different, creative ways. They add visual interest and a fun aspect to your garden since you can build the teepee high enough to allow you to walk beneath your plants. These structures are also an engaging and fun way to teach your children to garden.

Repurposed materials

Of course there are many ways to grow vertically beyond using a premade structure. Here are a few more creative solutions specific for vertical gardens:

- ✔ **Porch and balcony posts.** Turn a porch or balcony post into a column of cukes or cherry tomatoes. Just set a large planting container at the base and tie the vines to the post as they grow. Plant another container with sweet potatoes and allow the trailing vines to dangle over a balcony.

- ✔ **PVC pipe framing.** Build your own vertical garden frame, using PVC supports and piping. Add strings or simple lattice netting to help train your climbing plants. The benefit of a customized frame is that you can build it to fit a specific size wall of your outdoor room. Or have some fun with the framing and build a unique and strangely shaped PVC feature as a vertical focal element.

- ✔ **Livestock panels.** Livestock panels make great trellises for vining plants. Bend a full-sized panel (about 16 feet long) into an arch and secure it with a couple of T-posts to make a cool structure you can walk beneath. Several in a row make a fun tunnel!

Growing vertical veggies and fruits

Here are some of our favorite vegetable varieties that will grow well or can easily be trained vertically:

- ✔ **Pole (climbing) beans** — Excellent climbers and many varieties.
- ✔ **Cucumbers** — Although not real climbers, cucumbers can easily be trained by weaving it along your trellis as it continues to grow.
- ✔ **Grapes** — Excellent climbing perennial vining varieties.
- ✔ **Melons and pumpkins** — Provide additional support to fruit.
- ✔ **Peas** — For large harvests, plant tall growing varieties.
- ✔ **Squash** — Be sure to select vining varieties.
- ✔ **Tomatoes** — Select indeterminate varieties to train up a trellis or use tomato cages.

Keep the size of your vertical support system in mind with the size of your garden planting. A simple square-foot vertical grid system made of garden twine may support your climbing beans, even the cucumbers too, but you'll likely need a stronger and more rigid system to support heavier squash, melon, and pumpkin plantings.

Yes, even heavy muskmelons and watermelons can be grown vertically. Simply support the fruit with a "sling" made from pantyhose, a piece of T-shirt fabric, or a mesh bag that produce comes in.

When you garden vertically, you can tighten up the spacing of your plants. It is usually the horizontal competing growth that restricts the spacing of your plantings. With vertical growing plants, there is much less horizontal competition between each plant, thus allowing you to grow more. For example, one cucumber plant can take up 15 square feet or more when left sprawling on the ground. Grow your cukes on a trellis, and you can have four plants in that same amount of space.

You can turn a sunny balcony or patio into a productive vertical garden by growing vining veggies on a lattice panel. Securely attach a lattice panel to a fence or wall and cover it with cucumber vines to provide protective shade from the hot afternoon sun.

Keep in mind that sun exposure is important for good vegetable production. Locate your trellises, teepees, or other vertical structure where the foliage will receive good sunlight without shading other areas of the garden.

Giving Containers a Lift

Containers are another good solution to help you develop a vertical garden. Urban would-be gardeners with limited space can now make room and develop their small outdoor spaces for a productive vertical gardening use. This section covers some container gardening tips, including general planting information and helpful vertical planting products available.

Understanding the special considerations for vertical container gardening

Garden soil is generally not the best choice for container growing. Instead a soilless growing mix composed of ingredients such as compost, peat, sand, vermiculite, and perlite is usually used for best results. A mix provides good aeration and drainage, as well as water- and nutrient-holding capacity. A soilless growing medium is much lighter than soil and is preferred when gardening on rooftops, balconies, and other areas where weight and loading capacities (as discussed in Chapter 9) need to be considered.

Choosing vertical containers

In this section, we introduce some do-it-yourself containers for vertical gardening as well as some ready-made products you can buy.

Making your own containers

Almost any plant will grow in a suitably sized container, so be creative and have fun! Making your own vertical containers is creative, unique, and can also demonstrate your special style in your garden area. Don't forget watering and maintenance considerations when reusing and building your own vertical container systems. Keep in mind that you are not limited to things intended for plants; virtually any receptacle that can hold artificial soil mix and adequately drain excess moisture will work. Here are a few unique vertical container gardening ideas to help get you started:

- **Wall hanging pots.** Try hanging small terra-cotta clay pots, old coffee cans, or other containers to your wall using large pipe clamps or other creative techniques. Assemble dozens of small pots on a wall in a zigzag design or in a more structured approach, like columns. Again, be sure to drill holes in the bottoms of containers for adequate drainage.

- **Pallet gardening.** Pallets can also be used to grow vertically. You can take portions of the pallets apart, build some shelving, and customize your pallet container to accommodate your plantings. For more on using pallets as a vertical garden feature see Chapter 7.

✔ **Rotating bicycle rim(s).** If you really want to win the grand prize as the eccentric urban gardener, why not construct a series of unique planters using several aluminum bicycle rims? In place of a bicycle tube along the perimeter, wrap the surrounding rim structure with filter fabric and your growing medium. Secure the perimeter soil mixture and fabric with garden twine. While planting, lay the rim flat, and puncture holes around the perimeter of the wheel for seed starting. Keep the rim in a horizontal position until your plantings have sprouted and established a root network. Once your small greens have grown enough, you're ready to hang up your rim vertically. Be sure to spin slowly while watering!

Finding vertical gardening products

Many wonderful gardening products are designed to help you grow vertically. Here is a list of some of our favorite vertical gardening products:

✔ **Vertical containers.** Many interesting containers that are made for hanging on a fence, wall, or post are on the market now. Imagine a wall filled with flowering containers of cascading plants, or a monoculture of salad greens!

✔ **Pot hangers for containers.** Instead of using pipe clamps, some garden centers now sell attractive pot hangers from which a terra-cotta pot can be hung on a post, wall, or fence. These hangers can be used to create a multitiered garden of radishes, chard, kohlrabi, lettuce, or other small greens. Other "half-round" containers are made for attaching to a wall or fence and make great use of limited space in city gardens.

✔ **Planter walls.** Manufacturers now include options for planting vertically along both freestanding and retaining walls. Another option to consider when building high retaining walls is to divide the wall height and include a terraced area for planting between the walls (see Figure 10-5). For instance, instead of building an 8-foot-high wall, build two 4-foot-high walls with a 2-foot-wide planter between the two wall structures.

✔ **Straddling containers.** Numerous products are available that (like a saddle) can straddle both sides of your balcony railing, even along the top of a fence. The Steckling plants container designed by German designer Michael Hilgers is one example of a modern design that has a look of a simple circular planter (see Figure 10-6a), whereas more traditional balcony containers are more boxy like window planters (see Figure 10-6b).

✔ **Wall hanging pocket gardens.** Wall hanging pocket gardens (see Figure 10-7) are simple pocket planters which can easily hang and affix to walls, rails, and fences and can be used indoors or outside. They all come with simple fasteners and anchors that work on masonry, drywall, sheetrock, wood, and metal walls.

Figure 10-5:
Example of
a modular
planter wall.

Illustration by Kathryn Born.

Figure 10-6:
Different
types of
straddling
containers.

a.

b.

Illustration by Kathryn Born.

Figure 10-7:
A wall hang-
ing pocket
garden.

Illustration by Kathryn Born.

The WoollyPocket garden is a great example and includes a "smart watering" system and reservoir, allowing water to slowly wick as needed to the plants root systems. WoollyPockets were developed to conserve water and promote plant health. In addition, the breathable felt liner allows excess moisture to evaporate. The pockets are made in the United States, using recycled plastic bottles. For more on WoollyPockets visit www.woollypocket.com.

✔ **Stacking planters.** Imagine picking the fruit from a stand of strawberries 3 feet high! Stacking planters are specifically designed so that when you stack them, they create a column of multiple and interconnected growing facets that may be suspended or just left freestanding. Nancy Jane's Stacking Planters are one product specifically designed so that when you stack them, they create a column of multiple and interconnected growing facets that may be suspended or just left freestanding. Grow a collection of your favorite herbs and enjoy them year-round or display a collection of your favorite cacti like you've never seen! Available in multiple colors, these products are designed to produce cascades of flowers or greenery on all sides and have been designed specifically with vertical gardening in mind. Check them out at www.gardensupplyinc.com.

✔ **Vertical aeroponic garden systems.** Numerous new aeroponic garden systems are available to help you grow vertically. A tower garden planting system is one example of a state-of-the-art vertical aeroponic growing system. It's perfect for rooftops, patios, balconies, terraces — just about any relatively sunny place outside. Because of its unique technology and vertical design, the Tower Garden uses less than 10 percent of the water and land required by traditional, soil-based agriculture. The Tower is easy to assemble and maintain, and it can be placed in any relatively sunny place outside. There's no soil, no weeds, and no ground pests to worry about with these systems. For more on this product, visit www.towergarden.com.

✔ **Vertical Garden Solutions.** If you're looking for an assortment of different vertical gardening products, www.verticalgardensolutions.com offers many different vertical gardening systems. You can create a vertical green wall by using felt pouches, modular trays, or planting tubes. They have products available for small spaces, too, including self-watering vertical living walls made from modular tray systems.

Chapter 11

Apartment Gardens

*Y*our apartment garden may be small in size, but it can be big in impact and personal expression. A small apartment garden can offer a great place to show off favorite plants and garden accessories that reflect your personal style.

Perhaps best of all, a small space garden can be intimate, encourage conversation, and offer quiet, contemplative moods. Put a chair in a corner, or a bench if you want company. Arrange an assortment of pot shapes, plant an assortment of colors and lines that lead your eye in to the scene. Imagine yourself there, enjoying the comfort of a small space apartment garden.

This chapter provides you with a variety of ideas to develop an apartment garden space, with tips for urban patios, balconies, deck areas and indoor growing. In addition, we offer tips on flowerbox gardens, windowsill herb gardening, even how to build your own vertical picture frame garden!

Balcony Gardens

An apartment balcony or patio, however small, can provide an opportunity for you to develop a garden with perimeter potted plantings, hanging baskets, and planters affixed to railings. To save on usable space, you can also incorporate vertical garden structures (see Chapter 10 for more on vertical gardening). Apartment balconies and patios can become a small but effective garden space.

Using containers on your balcony

Potted plants have a lot to offer for the urban gardener. Their obvious advantages include control over water and soil mixes and the ability to garden in otherwise impossible locations. Beyond that, the design possibilities are endless. Containers are a great way to bring instant color to the landscape, and the plantings can be changed out as the colors fade from season to season. Container plantings offer versatility and add a unique look for otherwise boring city porches, balconies, and patio areas.

Larger balconies and deck areas allow for a nice mix of container styles, shapes, and sizes of pots and plant material, while small spaces look better filled with different-sized containers made from the same materials. And don't discount the value of adding hanging plants or wall-mounted planter boxes to your container garden. You can add some height and visual interest by including a trellis or by training vining plants up and over the rail of your deck or balcony.

Following are some points to keep in mind when creating your balcony container garden:

- ✓ **Discovering design options.** For a striking and classic look, line your balcony with a row of pots that match to unify the setting. Decide whether to pick a monoculture of plants for a complementary look, or pick a diversity of plantings for a variety of color and textures. For more contrast, select some to trail, some to grow upright, others for flowers, and still others for colorful leaves.

- ✓ **Minding the rule of three.** Remember the *rule of three* when selecting plants for containers. Put together a tall, spiky plant, one that flowers, and another that sprawls or crawls. Or use matching pots filled with different flowering plants to add color spots wherever you want them. Containers are all about the gardener's choices; you're not limited to tillable soil or the one sunny spot in the yard.

- ✓ **Knowing that weight matters.** In choosing pots and mixing soils, go light to save your back, especially when carrying and transporting soils to your balcony. Remember clay and other pottery materials are heavier than plastic and resin containers. Use mixes called "soilless" for even lighter loads.

- ✓ **Choosing container size.** Choose large containers if possible. There are many charming tiny container designs out there, but they are a problem when hot weather arrives. Remember the more soil volume, the less often you have to water and the more resilient the plants can be. Rolling casters are a nice way to keep these large, heavy containers mobile.

- ✓ **Finding sun or shade.** Be sure to place your container plantings in their preferred sun exposure. It takes lots of light to get most plants to bloom. However the more shade you can provide, the less stress your plants will suffer and the less often you will have to water them. As always, read your plant labels since some plantings prefer full sun exposure, while others prefer shade.

✔ **Using drought-tolerant options.** Various succulents and dwarf agaves work well as heat and drought-tolerant options for your container gardens. There are also many ornamental grasses, such as dwarf fountain grass and Mexican feather grass, that work great in a large container. In a part-shade spot, try pentas, begonias, and coleus. For a densely shady area, try Mexican petunias, impatiens, and caladiums.

✔ **Growing veggies in containers.** Flowers are great, but for the urban gardener looking to grow some edibles, don't be afraid to add some vegetables and specimen plants to the mix. Lettuce plantings, cherry tomatoes, carrots, beets, and herbs all do well in container gardens.

✔ **Knowing your climate.** Remember that the container gardens on your balcony and deck are subjected to temperature extremes the rest of your garden may not experience. This is especially true for our urban environments as we learned in Chapter 3 on microclimates. Since roots are above ground level, they can suffer heat stress. In hot spots, use lighter-colored containers to lessen heat absorption.

✔ **Trading out plants.** Remember, gardening is always a process, and be ready to trade things out when needed. The nice thing about containers is that they are mobile. When one plant starts looking ragged, simply replace it with another one. Flowers have their peak seasons so you may want to plan on changing some of the plantings in spring, summer, and fall seasons.

✔ **Moving your containers.** One of the great things about growing plants in pots is that containers can be moved with very little effort. Depending on your mood, you can reposition containers into dozens of different combinations.

✔ **Hanging off the balcony.** If you have limited space on your balcony and square footage is valuable, you can save space by securing containers along the perimeter to the outside railing (see Figure 11-1).

✔ **Using your imagination.** From traditional terra-cotta to the many creative containers covered in Chapter 8, let your imagination be your guide in choosing just the right container for the look you want to create. Don't be afraid to try a planter box, watering can, a coffee can, or toy wagon to display your treasured plants on your balcony. Just remember to poke holes in the bottom for drainage.

Most importantly, have fun! Experiment with containers. Fill them with your favorite annuals or combinations you've never tried before. If it doesn't work out, you can dump it out and try something new. (For more on container gardening see Chapter 8.)

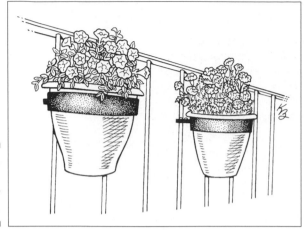

Illustration by Kathryn Born.

Creating a picture frame garden

One idea to save space on your balcony or condo or apartment patio is to place your garden along the walls surrounding your space. Much like hanging a beautiful painting indoors, a picture frame garden can help define and complement your outdoor room, patio, or balcony and add some beautiful color, texture, and a focal point to your exterior living area, not to mention it will be a great conversation item for your guests!

A picture frame garden (see Figure 11-2) is an assortment of plantings that are planted within a growing medium behind woven wire mesh. Many different succulent varieties and sedums are good recommendations for a picture frame garden. Sempervivum (hens and chicks) are cold-hardy, drought-tolerant plants and have many different colors, textures, and forms. Some are large, some are small, and all have baby chicks which can later be transplanted. Be sure to select varieties that stay small.

Assembling your garden

Building a picture frame garden is easy too! Just follow these steps:

1. **Find an old picture frame or buy one at a yard sale.**

2. **Deepen the frame by constructing a shadow box of 1" × 3" material the same size of the frame to contain your growing medium.**

3. **Set your woven wire mesh (½" hardware cloth is recommended) inside the frame.**

4. **Back the frame by using ¼" plywood sheeting.**

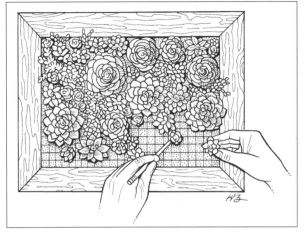

Figure 11-2:
A picture
frame
garden.

Illustration by Kathryn Born.

Growing your plants and hanging your frame

Once assembled, add your growing medium through the screen, and you are
then ready to begin planting small succulents along the wire mesh surface.
Plant closely and keep your picture frame garden flat. Leave your frame
in a cool space away from direct sunlight. Succulents do not need excessive watering, so lightly water about once a week. Your succulent plantings
should be securely rooted in place in about six to eight weeks' time.

In time, your plantings will establish in your picture frame garden. Then you
will certainly be eager to raise your picture frame vertically and secure it to
an exterior wall.

Before raising your frame, drill small holes along the top of the shadow box
(behind the frame) for continued watering care.

Using flowerbox planters

Many apartments and urban residents who are lacking front yards can decorate their facades, entrances, and windows with flowerbox planters like the
one shown in Figure 11-3.

These small garden touches can add the accenting colors and texture needed
to highlight and distinguish your apartment, townhome, or urban dwelling
and can be changed yearly with annual plantings.

Foliage color, texture, and shape are some of the elements to consider when
creating plant combinations. Gather ideas for planting from garden catalogs,
public gardens, your local retail nurseries, garden centers, or other gardeners.

Figure 11-3:
A flowerbox
garden.

Illustration by Kathryn Born.

Of course, annuals are a natural in flowerbox gardens. With care, they can provide long-term color. It's common to combine tall, bushy plants with those that trail over the sides of your flowerbox container. For example, surround lacy-leaved dusty miller plants with sherbet-colored portulaca flowers. But you also can't go wrong with a flowerbox planter full of petunias for sun, or impatiens for shade. Here are some creative and colorful flowerbox gardening arrangements to help get you started:

- Try a great cascading display of Wave petunias with salvia and purple verbena included for additional purple color highlights.

- Simply display multiple shades of pink petunias in sunny areas, or a variety of different pink impatiens for shady areas.

- Try using all trailing plants for a unique look, or if your flowerbox planters are placed very high, trailing plants will draw some attention. Include petunias for color along with green leaf sweet potato vine and vinca vine.

- Red and white petunia plants can be highlighted well in a flowerbox with dracena spikes for added height and texture. Include vinca vine as a trailing plant.

- Plant coleus, salvia, and periwinkle for a variety of color along with ferns and trailing vinca vine plantings.

- Try mixing a variety of colorful annuals in your flowerbox such as geraniums, purple salvia, with nasturtium or verbena and trailing vinca vine.

- Plant dracena spikes for height and texture along with red geraniums, periwinkle, and dusty miller for a variety of color. Add vinca vine for a trailing look as well.

- Try planting light pink shades of petunias with surrounding and trailing dark leaf sweet potato vine.

✔ Great for celebrating the Fourth of July, plant petunias, using equal amounts of red, white, and the bluest one you can find, along with cascading vinca vine.

Keep in mind, annuals grown in a flowerbox container will need more water than ones grown in the ground or in a pot on the ground. Rainfall is seldom adequate to keep pots moist, so you need to be ready to supplement. Air circulating around all sides of the box may cause the soil to dry out quickly.

To keep annuals blooming all summer, water them well if rains aren't coming consistently, fertilize every few weeks with a diluted solution of a liquid fertilizer (or use time-release pellets such as Osmocote), and pinch them back if they get rangy. Pinching back annuals in mid-summer may sacrifice some flowers, but in a few weeks the plants will put on new growth and continue to flower the rest of summer.

Indoor Gardening

We discuss numerous strategies to develop an outdoor urban garden throughout this book, including many different creative techniques and solutions you can pursue. However, for those of us lacking the room outside, you can grow plants indoors with the help of an indoor lighting system. Here, we discuss a few urban gardening strategies for indoor growing, from planting along windowsills to artificial lighting strategies, plus some watering tips so you can create a thriving indoor garden in the city.

Creating an indoor herb garden

Have you ever wanted a fresh sprig of rosemary to garnish a roasting chicken? Maybe some fresh mint leaves to top off your tea or garnish a dessert? Wouldn't it be nice to go to the kitchen window and harvest your own plants instead of going to the market? Apartment gardeners can't go wrong with a windowsill herb garden like the one shown in Figure 11-4.

Good herb choices include basil, cilantro, dill, oregano, rosemary, sage, and thyme. You can start herbs from seed or purchase small plants. Annual herbs are especially easy to start from seed; most perennial herbs take longer to germinate and grow, so it's easier to start with plants.

Figure 11-4:
A window-
sill herb
garden.

Illustration by Kathryn Born.

The trick to growing herbs inside is providing the right amount of light, water, fertilizer, and humidity needed by the different herbs. Here are some tips to help you enjoy caring for a small windowsill herb garden in your apartment:

✔ **Use individual pots for each plant so you can give each herb the specific care it needs.** Be sure containers have drainage holes and water-proof saucers.

✔ **If you're starting seeds, use a seed-starting mix or potting soil, or a 50:50 combination of the two.** Avoid using garden soil, which tends to be heavy, doesn't drain well, and may contain disease organisms. Don't skimp on the potting soil or use the least expensive brand. Herbs do best in moist, yet well-drained, soil mixes. If the soil is too dry when removed from the package, lightly moisten it before planting your herbs. Sow seeds, checking the seed packet to determine planting depth.

✔ **A sunny, south-facing window is adequate for most herbs, although supplemental fluorescent lights help in winter.** Most herbs need at least five to six hours of direct sunlight daily. The amount of sunlight or supplemental light your plants receive dictates what kinds of herbs you can grow. In a sunny, south- or southwest-facing windowsill, try growing sage, rosemary, thyme, and even spicy-tasting nasturtiums. The east- or west-facing windows will do nicely for aromatic mints, chives, parsley, and old-fashioned scented geraniums. If you don't have enough natural sunlight, don't worry. Herbs can be grown under grow lights.

✔ **Don't allow foliage to touch cold windows.** Herbs prefer relatively cool temperatures at night. The daytime regimen can be around 65 to 70 degrees F, while the night can drop to around 55 to 60 degrees F. Also be sure that the plants are spaced adequately for good air circulation and to offset any problems with leaf diseases.

✔ **Water to keep soil moist but not soggy, and drain saucers after watering.** Most herbs are sensitive to overwatering or soggy soils. Check the moisture by pressing your finger into the top inch of potting mix. If you can detect moisture, don't water. When the soil is dry to the touch, water until the excess drains from the bottom of the pot.

✔ **Fertilize every two weeks with a half-strength solution of an all-purpose fertilizer.** To grow herbs with more intense flavor, be stingy with the fertilizer. Only fertilize when the potting mixture is damp, never dry.

✔ **One of the most important elements to growing herbs is ample humidity, perhaps even more so at this time of year since our forced-air heating systems rob the air of needed humidity.** Dry air not only dries out our skin; it can cause houseplants to develop brown or dry tips.

Growing under lights indoors

Short of a greenhouse or very bright sunroom, growing plants under lights is another great option for the urban gardener. Flowering plants, such as orchids, African violets, citrus, and other tropicals, as well as annuals, can be kept flowering under lights. It's even possible to grow tomatoes, herbs, and lettuce with lights as well.

Urban gardeners lacking the room for outdoor gardens can certainly grow indoors with the help of an indoor lighting system. Today there are multiple types of lighting and multitiered systems available for your choosing.

Garden catalogs, hardware stores, and garden centers offer a variety of light fixtures to choose from. Fluorescent light bulbs are the most common, while high-intensity discharge (HID) bulbs are used by avid gardeners and commercial growers.

A good choice for growing indoors is a full-spectrum fluorescent bulb. Full-spectrum fluorescent bulbs actually duplicate the solar spectrum of light, providing a balance of cool and warm light output to your indoor plantings. The full-spectrum bulbs also use less energy and last longer than standard fluorescent bulb fixtures.

Tiered multilevel indoor lighting units can also save space and help you efficiently garden indoors. Although somewhat expensive, the multiple-level units provide a lot of growing space and lighting for small areas and may be worth it for an urban gardener who lacks the room for outdoor growing and perhaps is looking to save valuable square-foot area.

When selecting your grow light options and equipment, look for convenience. For example, how easy is it to raise and lower each light fixture? Is there a separate on/off switch for each fixture? How big are the plant trays? Is the unit on casters for easy moving if needed? Will the unit fit your apartment, condo, or urban dwelling space efficiently?

Another factor is how many bulbs each fixture holds. A light fixture that holds four fluorescent bulbs provides the most light. If the fixture only holds two bulbs, consider if the reflector is specially designed to distribute light effectively to your plantings.

 Unlike the sun that provides multiple directions of light throughout the day, your indoor lighting typically doesn't move, so rotating your plants (at least weekly) is recommended for best growth. Be sure to clean and replace bulbs as needed to maintain quality lighting for your indoor garden.

Practicing indoor plant care and watering

Keeping plants happy and healthy can be a challenge in an apartment garden, particularly if you have to contend with varying light and dry air conditions. However, the most likely killer of houseplants is soggy soil conditions caused by overwatering indoor plants. Many of us actually kill a plant with kindness. We want to nurture our plants so we give them too much water and stunt their growth. Plants with soggy soil conditions for long periods will end up with root rot and may die.

 To avoid overwatering your houseplants, periodically check your container soil conditions. If your soil is damp one inch below the surface, continue to hold off on watering and be sure to check back in a couple days.

Then there is the other extreme, where we are too busy and may forget to water. That can be just as damaging as overwatering unless you select plants that can take the indoor drought conditions such as cacti or the snake plant.

Good drainage is important for your houseplants. Check the drainage hole for your indoor plant containers to make sure it hasn't clogged up with root growth. You can check by pushing a pen up through the hole to make sure the container is able to keep water flowing and draining properly. Deep planters or pots wrapped-up with foil will create stagnated soil conditions with little or no available oxygen. This could lead to disease and root rot.

Chapter 12

Community Gardening and Urban Farming

*I*f you're one of the many urban dwellers who get excited about gardening as spring approaches, but you don't have the space to garden, have no fear. You are an excellent candidate to join in a group community garden project.

Urban community gardens are becoming more and more popular, as our cities increase in population and the demand for locally grown food increases. Community gardens and small urban farms are popping up everywhere, from empty lots in the inner cities to designated sites and programs within city and county parks. Many municipalities are also recognizing the demand for local gardening and making changes, if needed, to allow for urban gardening.

This chapter provides you with a variety of ideas on making inner-city community gardening and urban farming a reality, but perhaps the most important point is recognizing that collaboration with your community and municipality is the real key to success.

Community Gardening 101

Community gardening is truly about growing — growing vegetables and fruits, growing flowers, and, most important, growing a community of people who can share their love of gardening while taking good care of the earth.

Community gardens provide a place to meet new friends and share gardening experiences. In fact, many community gardens offer workshops to help gardeners learn about seeds, crop rotation, companion planting, and organic pest control solutions to help keep the soil and their plants healthy.

Sometimes gardeners have their own designated plot, and sometimes the work and the harvest are shared by all the gardeners in one large community garden. Some community gardens encourage their volunteers to grow a row for local food banks, kitchens, or shelters. Figure 12-1 shows one possible setup for an urban community garden, but each community garden has its own personality, its own flavor, and its own pace. They are sites where families can produce their own food, help one another by sharing their experiences and enthusiasm for gardening, and beautify their neighborhoods in the process.

Figure 12-1:
An urban community garden.

Illustration by Kathryn Born.

A brief history of community gardening

Community gardens have been a part of American culture for many decades. The U.S. government encouraged people to grow their own food in "liberty gardens" during World War I because it was one way that every American could contribute to the war effort. During the Great Depression in the 1930s, "relief gardens" were promoted to improve people's spirits and enable them to produce their own fresh food. During the Second World War, growing food in a "victory garden" was again considered a contribution to the war effort.

In the 1960s and 1970s, community gardens regained popularity, both as a way to get back in touch with nature and to address the growing concerns about the amount of pesticides used in the production of fruits and vegetables.

The 2007 through 2012 global financial crisis is considered by many economists as the worst financial crisis since the Great Depression. No doubt many families have struggled during this period and have learned to be very resourceful during this time. Some have learned to save money by growing their own food. We believe there has been a very strong resurgence of community gardening throughout the world since the financial crises began in 2007. The good news is that we have learned during this time to be very resourceful, live more sustainably, and connect with and help one another through the practice of community gardening.

How community gardening works

Community gardens can fill a variety of needs and are accessible to everyone. A community garden can function in so many ways, whether it's as a beautiful display garden or a garden of flowers, vegetables, and fruits or a combination of all three.

Anyone can rent a plot or volunteer as part of a larger community garden project and be surrounded with the camaraderie and knowledge of plant lovers. Volunteers at some community gardens grow produce to supply food banks. Urban community gardens often rise up from abandoned lots as a means to revitalize a neighborhood and remove eyesores.

All community garden programs depend strongly on volunteer support. Volunteers provide the majority of the labor for day-to-day operations, as well as the leadership required to keep any educational workshops and the programs current and interesting for their community. There is value in all of the different ways of staying in touch with the earth, both for the individual and the community.

Starting a Community Gardening Program

To start a community garden program, begin by assessing the level of interest in your community. The first step is to find like-minded folks to help you organize the project. Ideally, you'd like to recruit at least five to ten families interested in helping. Survey neighbors to see who would like to participate and hold planning meetings at least monthly to get the ball rolling.

Consider getting a partner or sponsor for the project, such as a local church, parks and recreation department, a nonprofit organization, or a local business. They may be able to provide land, supplies, organizational help, and money to get the garden up and running.

Once you've established that there is a strong community interest in beginning a community gardening program, and you've checked to see if there isn't already an established community garden nearby, you're ready to organize and start one yourself! The following sections offer some guidance to help you get started.

Selecting a site

Look for an open piece of land that might serve the purpose, and contact the owner for permission to use it.

Make sure the site gets at least six hours of sun per day. And be sure to test the soil for nutrients and for contaminants such as lead and other heavy metals. The site will also need a water source, easy access, and, possibly, parking.

The best scenario is to find a landowner who is enthusiastic about the plan and is willing to provide a written, multiyear lease. You don't want to establish your garden just to have to move it in two years' time!

Developing your site

Once the site is secured, your group can start to plan its development! Involve as many stakeholders as is practical. The more people involved in the design and planning of the gardens, the more help you'll have in building and maintaining your community garden.

Schedule workdays and clean-up days. Measure the site, determine the size of individual plots, and mark them. Amend the soil as necessary with nutrients and compost to build up the health of the land. Water is crucial to a garden's success. If you're irrigating, plan and install an irrigation system before opening the garden to residents.

Consider including community areas where you can plant trees, shrubs, and flowers for general beautification. Some community gardens have special areas just for kids to garden. Create some shady areas where people can sit to rest, have a picnic, and gather and socialize.

Organizing the garden

Your garden group must be well organized if the community garden is to be successful. You'll need to determine how much to charge for plots and create a budget for spending the money. While most of the money will probably pay for tilling, soil amendments, and water bills, consider soliciting donations from individuals and local businesses for special additions such as a tool storage shed, a sign, and a bulletin board (a good way to notify gardeners of upcoming events and meetings).

Build a compost pile in one area of the garden where everyone can dump their dead plants, and add a trash barrel for dumping non-biodegradable materials, but only if you can arrange for it to be emptied on a regular basis.

Don't forget rules! Community gardens should have rules of conduct that all the plot holders read and agree to when they register. Rules can govern pesticide use, watering, planting deadlines, weeding requirements, and the clean-up schedule for garden plots at the end of the season.

Managing the garden

A group of dedicated, organized volunteers will help keep your urban garden growing well and diffuse misunderstandings before they become problems. That said, here are a couple of common issues that arise for community gardeners:

- ✔ Most private landowners will not sign a lease unless your group has liability insurance, so secure coverage before opening the gardens.

- ✔ Provide signage that clearly identifies the area as a community garden, and include names of sponsors and contact people. Let the neighbors know this is their garden, too — this will help thwart vandalism.

Celebrate and have fun. Be sure to hold social gatherings in the garden, especially in the summer and fall, to celebrate the garden and all its bounty. See "Hosting harvest festivals" for more on harvest festivals and community gatherings.

Urban Farming = Urban Renewal

The health of a neighborhood can be determined by looking at its open land. A vibrant community features parks, public gardens, and gathering places for the neighborhood. Unfortunately, a disconnected and disenfranchised community often has vacant lots that are used as trash dumps and breeding grounds for criminal activity such as drug dealing.

Farm to table

Farm to table refers to all the stages involved in producing food, everything from initial planting to harvesting, packaging, processing, storage, sales, and finally, consumption.

When you grow something yourself, you know exactly how it was grown and have total control over the "farm to table" process. You know what has or has not been sprayed on your food and what fertilizers were used or not used.

You can also choose exactly when to harvest from your garden. When your harvest arrives in your kitchen, it's probably about 1,000 miles fresher than much of what you purchase from the supermarket. And then there's that simple satisfaction of knowing that you — yourself — have grown your own food!

So how does a community make use of its vacant lots to better a neighborhood, making it a safe, bright, and healthy place to live? One way to transform abandoned urban areas into healthy, productive land is to build community gardens and small urban farms. Not only are these lands useful for growing healthful food and lovely flowers for residents, they can provide public gathering places for festivals, meetings, and classes.

Community gardens have the reputation of being a great first step in a renewal process, transforming rundown areas with little civic pride into thriving neighborhoods with increased property values and enthusiastic resident involvement. The same is true on a larger scale where large, vacant city land areas can become urban farms, where the practice of growing, cultivating, processing, and even distributing food is done on a local level. Sometimes small community gardening operations expand over the years, evolving into market gardens or urban farms.

Another variation of the community farm is the Community Supported Agricultural operation (CSA). A CSA allows people to buy "shares" in the farm in advance of the growing season. For each share, individuals receive a regular supply of fresh, seasonal produce throughout the growing season. CSAs started in Europe, and the first in the United States was launched in 1985. Today there are thousands of CSA farms across the United States and Canada.

Whether you decide to transform a vacant urban space into a community garden, develop a small urban farm, or become involved with a CSA program, you're helping better our neighborhoods and making safer, brighter, and healthier places of renewal in the city. In this section, we explore some ways to bring farming to the city.

Benefits of gardening together

Urban dwellers live in a busy world that seems to move faster and faster as time goes on. Many aspects of modern life combine to add complexity and confusion, not to mention stress. However, a community garden can change all of this! Gardens help make things quite simple. Although infinitely complex in its inner workings, a garden moves at a slow, peaceful pace. We are free to create or to just sit and watch. Whether you spend the day at your community garden or just a few minutes, you can look back and see instant results from your efforts and connect with your community.

The American Community Gardening Association lists numerous benefits on their website for the practice of community gardening. Some benefits include helping neighbors communicate, encouraging beautiful neighborhoods, providing nutritious food, and discouraging crime while at the same time adding green space to urban areas, as well as many others.

The American Community Gardening Association is a valuable resource for all community gardening organizations, whether you're in the beginning stages of starting up a community garden, or are part of an established garden looking to connect with other gardeners or advocacy campaigns. For more on the American Community Gardening Association, visit ACGA at: www.communitygarden.org.

During the period of the 2007 through 2012 global financial crisis, many municipalities, planning departments, and local governments saw an increase in urban farming, community gardening, and other urban agricultural practices. These efforts benefited local communities and helped transform some of our urban areas from blighted wastelands into thriving farms and gardens. From reusing vacant or abandoned properties to developing rooftop gardens, such efforts have encouraged urban renewal initiatives in many municipalities across the U.S. in recent years.

Avoiding down zoning

With increasing trends to grow locally, many municipalities are now redrafting zoning regulations to allow for uses such as community gardens and urban agriculture. City planning departments and zoning administrators should understand that many of these initiatives *do not* require rezoning measures that reduce values and allowable densities of urban properties.

Although down zoning can reduce the density of permitted construction in urban areas, there is no need to down zone in order to accommodate urban agriculture, urban gardens, or green spaces.

Boston is a great example of one of the many cities taking measures to redraft their regulations appropriately for urban agriculture. The city has established the Mayor's "Urban Agriculture Working Group" to explore and address ways in which the existing zoning code may be impeding all forms of urban farming. Activities and uses that are not mentioned in the current regulations are assumed to be forbidden. The working group is developing recommendations to update the code to allow a variety of urban agriculture activities such as greenhouses, rooftop gardens, aquaculture, hydroponics, urban composting, and animal and beekeeping. The new regulations will not down zone or reduce property values but instead provide the regulatory flexibility needed for urban agricultural initiatives in the city.

Marketing Locally

Selling locally grown food can benefit the local economy and connect you directly with the community. Whether you decide to participate in a neighborhood farmers market, a harvest festival, or sell your produce to nearby schools, groceries, or restaurants, there are a variety of ways you can market locally. Here are some additional suggestions to help you market your produce within your community.

Selling produce at farmers' markets

Farmers' markets have a rich history in the United States and are enjoying a strong revival. With the increases in small market gardens, farm operations, and specialty food producers, farmers' markets cut out the middleman, making the transaction more profitable for purveyors and more economical for consumers. By bringing farmers and consumers face to face, it also creates a stronger sense of community.

Today, farmers' markets continue to expand in cities across the country. As consumers search for quality and affordable produce, local growers have stepped up to fill the need. For most shoppers, the large variety of locally grown produce is the main draw. Communities are recognizing this appeal and harvesting from community gardens and local farms to sell locally and reap the rewards.

Participating in farm-to-school initiatives

The growing concern over diet-related children's health problems has encouraged many communities to introduce fresh local food to school cafeterias. Usually, concerned parents and teachers and local nonprofit organizations are the driving force behind farm-to-school partnerships. Such programs ensure farmers a steady market for their goods and supply kids with more nutritious lunches.

Selling to local restaurants

Encourage local restaurants to purchase and use locally grown food. You may already see the growing trend of neighborhood chefs focusing on using local, in-season foods on their menus. Selling to community restaurants helps local growers expand their marketing and in turn, it's also beneficial for the restaurants to advertise locally purchased foods. A win for farmers, chefs, and foodies!

Hosting harvest festivals

You can celebrate the bounty of food harvested from the garden in many different ways. Harvest festivals can include garden tours, cooking demonstrations, performances, agricultural exhibits, and more.

Here are some suggestions to help generate ideas for your very own community harvest festival:

- ✔ Create a *vegetable-of-the-week celebration*. This could include feature information on that week's edible, its nutrients, and the urban farmer or gardener who grew it, along with a take-home recipe!

- ✔ Hold a community *salad luncheon or dinner party,* asking everyone to harvest and create their own special salad for a group gathering.

- ✔ Set up a *collaborative cooking event* using homegrown produce and shared harvests from all community gardening participants.

- ✔ Host a *local foods dinner* and invite families and community members to attend. You can prepare menus or brochures that explain the origins of the foods and perhaps interest some neighbors in local gardening.

- ✔ Hold a festival that focuses on just *one crop* that's important to your local or state economy. You can share some of the history and importance of the particular crop as a presentation during the event.

- ✔ Feature garden foods and dishes associated with the *ethnic and cultural* groups represented in your local school and community organizations. Learn about related harvest stories or traditions and invite visitors to participate.

Creating community gatherings and celebrations

Harvest festivals are one of the many ways you can come together with your community and share in the bounty of your garden efforts. Of course there are numerous other ways you can gather and celebrate your community gardening efforts, from gardening meetings, educational sessions, and book discussions to youth programs and celebrations.

Celebrate National Garden Month with your community in April each year. Back in the mid-1980s, the National Garden Bureau began collaborating with 23 other horticultural organizations nationwide to create a week-long celebration of gardening. Their dreams were realized when in 1986, President Reagan signed a proclamation designating the second full week in April as National Garden Week. In 2002, the National Gardening Association expanded the week into a month-long celebration of one of America's favorite hobbies.

Every April communities, organizations, and individuals across the United States celebrate gardening during National Garden Month. Gardeners know, and research confirms, that nurturing plants is good for us: attitudes toward health and nutrition improve, kids perform better at school, and community spirit grows. Join the celebration within your community with your own urban beautification project and help to make America a greener, healthier, more livable place!

Consider expanding your celebration by joining neighbors in a city beautification project. This could be as simple as spending a Saturday morning "greening up" an abandoned park by picking up trash. Or you might build and plant a raised flowerbed in front of your local library, or adopt a portion of your town green, or even start a community garden. Ask your neighborhood school if they could use your extra seedlings and volunteers to help students plant them in the schoolyard.

For more on National Garden Month visit: www.garden.org.

Sharing a Garden

When you garden, you grow! We can all do our part as responsible stewards of the earth by sharing in the environmental, social, and economic responsibilities as an urban gardening community. Encourage family, friends, and neighbors — and especially children — to dig in and share this community effort, however large or small, and to garden themselves. Here are some ways for urban gardeners to share this endeavor with others.

Gardening with roommates

Sharing an urban community garden or urban farm can be similar to sharing an apartment with roommates. Instead of splitting the electric bills and deciding who does the dishes, a shared urban garden has its own set of divided tasks and responsibilities. You can decide to divide the tasks equally or not, but sharing a garden can provide the extra hands to help ensure the success of your garden. Garden sharing is also useful for periods when you may be out of town or on vacation and you would otherwise need to seek the help.

Volunteering for others

Many urban gardens begin with the efforts of volunteers. Reach out and offer your gardening skills and enthusiasm to a youth group, scout troop, after-school enrichment program, community center, nursing home, or other public facility. Spend just a few hours of your time teaching seed starting or helping set out transplants, and you could spark a life-long love of gardening for a youngster or perhaps renew a forgotten interest for an adult.

Hiring out as an urban farmer

In hard economic times everyone wants to cut costs. While growing your own food can save money and produce fresh, healthy vegetables in your own yard, it does take time and expertise. People in cities are particularly hard-pressed to grow their own food since few have the skills and land to start a large vegetable garden. Unfortunately, many who live in the city may not have the extra time needed to develop a garden. However, there is a new solution.

Across the country, experienced urban gardeners are offering services to assist others who want to establish a garden. For a fee, these urban agricultural entrepreneurs will come into your yard; assess the site for sun, soil, and space; and design, plant, and even maintain a vegetable garden for you. Even in densely settled urban areas, there's room to grow lots of produce.

In cities such as San Francisco, Portland, Seattle, and Charlotte, North Carolina, professional urban gardeners are offering this service and getting an overwhelming response. Of course, fees can range widely, from a few hundred dollars to thousands. But if you're willing to spend the money, these professionals can help from the initial installation of your garden to periodic weekly maintenance, including weeding, watering, and even harvesting the produce for you. All you have to do is eat it!

Planting a row for the hungry

Also consider sharing your harvest. Plant an additional row in your garden and donate the produce to a local food bank. People across the country have joined forces to end hunger in their communities. "Plant a Row for the Hungry" was launched in 1995 as a public service campaign of the Garden Writers Association (GWA).

Community food security

In this land of plenty, most of us rarely think about where our food comes from or wonder if we will always have enough. But the fragility of our food system was highlighted in New Orleans when Hurricane Katrina isolated thousands of residents from fresh food and water. The aftermath demonstrated that local agencies in the area were *better* able to help residents than large bureaucracies. Food and water donated from area food shelves, churches, and agencies were able to reach people long before donations from outside the region arrived.

Community food security is more than just having a grocery store in the neighborhood. It means that residents of a region feel they have adequate access to a safe, culturally acceptable, nutritionally adequate diet through a sustainable food system. Other social benefits of a secure local food system include better health, job creation, and community self-reliance and collaboration. To some, access to fresh, wholesome food at a reasonable price should be considered a basic human right.

There are many faces of food security. The most visible are community gardens, community farms, farmers' markets, and farm-to-school programs.

To participate in the "Plant a Row for the Hungry" national campaign, you report your donations to the GWA, and they keep track of the totals. Many millions of pounds have been donated so far! The concept is simple; the benefits are far-reaching.

Going from Pavement to Parks

As our urban centers continue to grow, and impervious surfaces (like asphalt, rooftops, and buildings) continue to expand, we realize the need to accommodate for green space, but unfortunately, it's after the fact. In some cases, we can reclaim a vacant lot, an abandoned building, or even an old vehicular overpass into a beneficial community green space for all of us to enjoy and make use of. In the following sections, we share some strategies you can use to creatively transform these urban hardscapes into useful community green spaces.

Reclaiming urban green space

For most apartment dwellers, finding a place to garden can be quite the challenge. But even without any actual ground to garden in, there are many possible garden spots, including rooftops, balconies, patios, along walls and stairways, even growing indoors on a windowsill or under lights.

If you're up for a challenge, you might even try to reclaim a portion of paved roadway in front of your apartment building. Of course this means obtaining approvals from your local planning and zoning office; however, many cities are now realizing that many urban streets are under-utilized, excessively wide, and highly overdesigned to accommodate vehicular uses. These paved unused areas may provide an opportunity to be reclaimed for public green uses. The ideas to reclaim paved surfaces are numerous, from cordoning off areas for container plantings to actually ripping up the pavement to build a vegetative space.

In Chapter 3, we talked about the urban Heat Island Effect that results in higher temperatures in our cities, compared to rural and suburban areas. These higher temperatures are a result of excessive amounts of impervious, heat-absorbing surfaces, mainly roadways and rooftops. For many cities the roadways alone take up as much as 25 percent of the city's land area, contributing to these increased temperatures. Reducing the amount of paved surfacing can help decrease the Heat Island Effect, especially when we find opportunities to reclaim these paved surfaces by putting in urban gardens and other vegetated green spaces.

While our main city corridors are heavily trafficked, side streets and collector roads are less likely to be congested. The residential corridors may be wider than necessary for the traffic they bear. Many cities across the country are now taking an inventory of these under-utilized paved spaces and taking appropriate steps to reclaim them for small parks and community gardens.

The San Francisco planning department has developed a Pavement to Parks program inspired by similar New York City projects. The program is "intended to be a public laboratory where the city can work with the community" testing the selected locations to potentially become permanent public open spaces. The Pavement to Parks program includes temporary and moveable materials such as seating, benches, planters, trees, shrubs and other landscape enhancements that can easily be placed for a trial run.

Of course the city has developed criteria when selecting locations for the Pavement to Parks program, which include the following:

- ✔ Sizeable area of under-utilized roadway
- ✔ Lack of public space in the surrounding neighborhood
- ✔ Preexisting community support for public space at the location
- ✔ Potential to improve pedestrian and bicyclist safety via redesign
- ✔ Surrounding uses that can attract people to the space
- ✔ Identified community or business steward

Making the change from pavement to parks requires collaboration between city administration and the community. The San Francisco planning department has done well to coordinate with their community and welcomes suggested locations that meet the criteria listed previously. This is a great example to consider when taking steps to reclaim wasted paved surfaces into a variety of public garden uses in urban areas.

Creating urban parklets

Parklets are a type of *pavement to park* project many cities are now developing where they repurpose approximately two to three parallel parking stalls as a new pedestrian space. *Parklets* are built as elevated platforms within former street-side parking spaces matching the grade of sidewalks to create a larger pedestrian useable space. Just like a larger park, these mini-sized parks allow people to sit, relax, and enjoy the city environment.

Parklets can be uniquely developed to include site furnishings, benches, tables, bicycle racks, specialty paving, public art, landscaping, and gardens. So if your urban apartment lacks a balcony or patio, and you can find two or three under-used street-side parking spaces available, you may wish to consider developing a *parklet* for you and your neighbors to enjoy.

Be sure to coordinate with your city planning department for guidance and an understanding of all permitting requirements involved to develop a *parklet*.

San Francisco is leading the way with this trend, but as *parklets* increase in popularity, we may see more cities adjusting their regulations to allow opportunities for many mini-parks like this in urban areas across the United States.

PARK(ing) Day is a one-day version of a parklet and has now become a fantastic "annual worldwide event where artists, designers and citizens transform metered parking spots into temporary public parks." For more on PARK(ing) Day or to participate in the annual one-day program, visit: www.parkingday.org.

Part IV
Growing Plants in the City

The 5th Wave   By Rich Tennant

"Judy grew all the vegetables right outside the window. You can almost taste the fire escape."

In this part. . .

Whether you're gardening in a container on an apartment balcony, in the ground in a community garden, or just in your own backyard, you'll need to know the basics of growing all your favorites plants. In this part, we give you the how-to information on growing edibles, flowers, trees, shrubs, and lawns. We get into the nitty-gritty of how to plant your own vegetable garden and annual and perennial flower gardens. We help you understand how to select and plant the right tree or shrub for your yard and how to keep your urban lawn and ground covers growing strong. There's a lot of *how-to* packed into this part of the book.

Chapter 13

City Setting, Country Food

A big interest in food production is developing in cities (see Chapter 2) — and for good reason. City residents often don't have access to fresh, homegrown vegetables, or the vegetables that are for sale in the grocery stores are expensive. The solution is to grow some of your own food. You might be thinking you don't have room for a farm, but the reality is you don't need one to produce an abundance of greens, fruits, and herbs in your yard. The keys to edible gardening in the city are finding the right location, choosing the right varieties, and using planting techniques like succession planting and season extending to grow crops late into the fall and early in spring. You'll be amazed at what you can produce.

Making a Veggie Garden Plan

If you have a small yard, deck, patio, or balcony or access to a community garden, you can grow some of your own vegetables and herbs. You may just have to get creative with where and how you do your vegetable gardening. Using raised beds, containers, and small, forgotten spaces, you can grow the right vegetable in the right locale. But before you go popping tomatoes in willy-nilly around the yard, come up with a plan. Analyze the limitations of your garden areas and match the right vegetable to that location.

Choosing a site for your vegetable garden

The ideal spot for a vegetable garden is close enough to the house that you'll pass by it daily. Out of sight, out of mind holds true with vegetable gardening too. Of course, if you have an older house with potential lead paint in the soil nearby, it would be best to use a raised bed or plant a little farther away.

Look for a location that's protected from animals, passersby, and vandals. Try to have a water faucet close by to avoid dragging hoses around the yard. But most important, check out the light conditions in the location.

The very first consideration when looking for the perfect spot for your vegetable garden or containers is sunlight. Most vegetables need at least 6 to 8 hours of direct sun a day to produce their best. This is often a problem in crowded cities with tall buildings and trees close by. Spend a little time watching the sun. Go out in the garden area at different times on a sunny day to see how often and for how long the sun is hitting your veggie patch. Add up the hours. Full sun may mean a few hours in the morning, and a few in the late afternoon. No matter; as long as the time adds up to 6 to 8 hours, you can grow any of the fruiting vegetables crops, such as tomatoes, peppers, beans, peas, squash, cucumbers, eggplant, corn, and broccoli.

Go out in the garden monthly from May until October to see how the shadows change. Later in the summer the sun is lower in the sky, so what was a full sun location in spring may be partly shaded in September. Learn more about sun in the city in Chapter 3.

But don't be discouraged if the only space you have gets less than 6 hours of sun a day. You can still grow some veggies. Root crops, such as carrots, beets, radishes, and potatoes, can grow in part-sun locations that receive only three to four hours of direct sun a day.

If your garden or container location only gets one to two hours of direct sun a day, try growing greens, such as lettuce, spinach, Swiss chard, kale, and parsley. Although the plants won't be as productive as when they're grown in a sunny spot, you'll still get something to eat.

Sizing up your garden: How big is big?

How big should your garden be? The answer depends on your space and what you grow. Amazingly, some urban gardeners grow enough food to feed their families not only in summer but almost year-round. You may not be interested in becoming a self-sufficient, urban homesteader, but know that using the right varieties and techniques allows you to grow more food than you thought possible in a small space.

Be reasonable about how much you can grow and care for. It's better to have a small and successful veggie garden than a large one that gets out of hand because you don't have time to care for it.

Gardeners.com has a terrific garden-planning tool that can help you decide how much to plant in each square foot of your garden. Check it out at www. gardeners.com/on/demandware.store/Sites-Gardeners-Site/ default/Page-KGPJS.

Laying it all out

Once you have found the right location(s) for your vegetable and herb gardens, follow the recommendations for building the soil fertility and making raised beds that we talked about in Chapter 4. Then, with a list of your favorite vegetables to grow, it's time to make a garden plan.

If you are growing all your vegetables in one garden area, there are some guidelines to follow to get the most production with least amount of care.

- **Place big boys in back.** Reduce the amount of shade in your garden by planting tall growing vegetables such as tomatoes, corn, peas, and pole beans on the north side of your garden and shorter growing vegetables such as lettuce, carrots, and herbs on the south side.

- **Use raised beds.** Raised beds not only make gardening easier, they are more productive. Build them no wider than 3 to 4 feet so you can easily reach into the center of the bed from any direction. Also, raised beds help you avoid contaminated soils as we mentioned in Chapter 4. The key is not compacting the soil by stepping on the bed. See Chapter 6 for more on building a raised bed.

- **Make wide paths.** Make your pathways wide enough to walk through and pull or push a cart or wheelbarrow. Two feet wide is a minimum. If you use a small garden cart, 4 feet wide may be necessary.

- **Plan for shade.** Make note what parts of your garden get shade in the late summer and plan for it. Consider growing fall crops of kale, radishes, and spinach in those areas.

- **Plant in succession.** Planning what vegetables will be in which beds in spring, summer, and fall is a good way to increase your yields from your garden. See "Succession planting: Lettuce forever!" for details.

- **Rotate your crops.** Save your garden plans each year so you can see what you planted and then rotate. It's good to not plant the same family of crops in the same location for three years. This helps avoid insects and diseases building up in the soil. We talk more about crop rotation in Chapter 20.

- **Don't forget the flowers.** Consider mixing in annual flowers such as marigolds, cosmos, zinnias, and nasturtiums around the garden. Not only will they attract beneficial insects to help with pest control, they are beautiful and some are edible, too.

Keeping Your Veggies Happy

Planting vegetable and herbs from seed or transplants is a snap, and we describe how to do that in Chapter 6. Once they are in the ground and growing, veggies need some attention to produce their best. If you spend extra time in spring and early summer caring for your crops, you can spend the rest of the summer lounging, harvesting, and eating. What could be better? Okay, you might plant some more and weed and water a little, but the point is, planning helps make the vegetable garden a more pleasant experience.

Feeding

Vegetables like a fertile soil, and adding compost each spring is a good way to get started. But they also like to be fed throughout the summer to keep production going. Plants that grow all summer, such as melons and tomatoes, and heavy feeders, such as corn, need side-dressing a few times in summer. Other vegetables, such as beans, radishes, and lettuce, need little or no side-dressing because they make their own fertilizer or they mature so quickly. Use either 1 to 2 tablespoons of an organic granular fertilizer per plant or spray leafy vegetables and herbs with fish emulsion to side-dress.

Table 13-1 offers details on which crops will need side-dressing and when. We talk more about side-dressing and compost in Chapter 5.

Table 13-1	When to Side-Dress Your Vegetables
Vegetable	**When to Side-Dress**
Beets	Two weeks after leaves appear
Broccoli and Brussels sprouts	Three weeks after transplanting
Cabbage	Four to six weeks after planting
Carrots	Three weeks after planting
Cucumbers	When they first start to vine and again when they start to flower
Eggplant	Three weeks after planting
Lettuce, spinach, Swiss chard, and kale	Three weeks after germination
Onions	Three weeks after planting, when tops are 8 inches tall and again when bulbs start to swell.
Peppers	Three weeks after planting and again when first fruits set
Potatoes	When plants bloom
Melons/summer squash/ zucchini	When plants are 6 inches tall and again when they start to flower
Tomatoes	Three weeks after transplanting, at first picking, and again two weeks later

Weeding, mulching, and watering

Even with a raised bed, you'll have to keep an eye out for weeds. Weed seeds blow around even an urban area and can get established in your garden. Depending on the compost or manure you're using, you may get weed seeds in this as well. The key to success is to cultivate and weed early and often. It's much easier to pull and remove young weeds than older ones. Simply cultivate the raised beds a few times a week after seeds germinate and transplants start growing, and you'll be able to keep weeds at bay. Even if the weeds are tiny and few, cultivate anyway. You'll probably eliminate ones that are just starting to germinate.

When weeding, use a cultivator or small hoe and cut the weeds right below the soil surface. If you dig deeply in the soil you'll be bringing up other weed seeds to germinate.

The other weeding solution is to use mulch. Mulching not only prevents weeds from growing, it conserves soil moisture and can add beneficial organic matter to the soil. In cool summer areas, use dark plastic mulches around warm-weather-loving veggies such as tomatoes, peppers, eggplant, cucumbers, melons, and summer squash. These veggies love the heat and do best with plastic mulch. For cool-weather-loving veggies such as lettuce, carrots, peas, broccoli, and spinach, apply a 2- to 3-inch-thick layer of an organic mulch such as hay, straw, or pine straw. This will keep the soil cool and moist. In hot summer areas, use this organic mulch on all vegetables since the soil is already well heated. We talk more about mulching, weeds, and weeding in Chapter 18.

The mulch will help keep the soil around your vegetables moist, but you'll need to add supplemental water, especially if Mother Nature doesn't help out. Water newly planted seed beds daily if it doesn't rain to keep the soil moist. Seeds need constant moisture to germinate properly. Water transplants every few days. Once established, water your gardens weekly or as needed. We talk more about watering in Chapter 19.

Raising the Top City Vegetables

With so many vegetables available, it's hard to know what to grow. The best way to get started is to grow what you like to eat. Try one or two varieties of each type of vegetable to see which grows and tastes best in your garden.

We've gathered the top city vegetables into similar groups to make it easier to know how to grow them. We've included information on planting, growing, and harvesting. For more details on pest problems, refer to Chapter 20. For more detailed information on growing vegetables check out *Vegetable Gardening For Dummies,* by yours truly, coauthor Charlie (Wiley).

Leafy greens

Probably the easiest urban garden vegetables to grow are leafy greens. They take little time to mature, withstand less than ideal sun conditions, and fit in the smallest of places.

Choosing your greens

Grow spinach varieties such as 'Tyee', kale such as 'Red Russian', Swiss chard such as 'Bright Lights', and, of course, lettuces. Colorful and unusual lettuce varieties to try include 'Oakleaf', 'Red Salad Bowl' and the heat tolerant 'Summertime'.

A fun way to grow greens is to sow a mix. Mesclun mix includes a blend of lettuces, spinach, and kale with other spicy greens such as mizuna, arugula, chicory, and mustard, depending on the blend. They are a great way to add zip to a spinach or lettuce salad.

Growing great greens

All greens like it cool and moist. Plant in spring before the last frost, then every few weeks in succession until early summer to get a continuous harvest of greens. Plant again in late summer or early fall for a late fall harvest. In warm climates you can have greens in winter by planting in the fall for a winter and early spring harvest.

Amend the soil with compost and plant in rows or broadcast the seeds (see Chapter 6) in raised beds. Greens like nitrogen fertilizer, so water the young plants with fish emulsion or worm poop tea to keep them growing strong. Watch out for slugs and snails, rabbits, and leaf miner insects. See Chapter 20 for more on these pests.

All these greens are ideal for containers and small spaces because you can harvest them when they're only 4 to 6 inches tall as baby greens for salads. Also, many are cut-and-come-again types, meaning you can snip them with a pair of scissors just above the ground and they'll regrow for another harvest. If the stems become tough or if the plant bolts (sends up a flower stalk), they're done producing.

The tomato family: Eggplants, peppers, and other relatives

There's a good reason tomatoes are the most popular vegetable grown in home gardens. Nothing beats a sun-warmed, vine-ripened fresh tomato oozing with sweetness and juice.

Peppers and eggplants are also in the tomato family and like similar warm growing conditions with fertile soil. Sweet and hot peppers and eggplants are smaller plants than tomatoes, so they fit well in the urban garden. They're also great container plants if you only have room for pots in your garden.

Potatoes are the odd cousins in the tomato family. Unlike the warm-weather-loving tomatoes, peppers, and eggplant, potatoes like it cool, so plant before your last frost date. They require room to grow, so potatoes may be a limited option if you only have a small space garden. However, growing potatoes in a barrel is a great urban option — we talk about that in Chapter 8 and Chapter 22. Some good potato varieties to try include 'Yukon Gold' and 'Red Pontiac'.

Choosing the right size plants

For a city garden, look for *dwarf* or *determinate* varieties such as 'Pixie II', 'Mountain Spring', and 'Celebrity'. These tomato varieties grow to a certain height and then stop, making them more manageable in the space-starved urban landscape. If you do have room for bigger plants look for *indeterminate* varieties such as 'Big Beef', 'Better Boy', 'Green Zebra', and 'Brandywine'. They produce more fruit, but take up more room. Mix in some cherry tomatoes for the kids (young and old) such as 'Sungold' and 'Sweet Million'. Try plum-shaped tomatoes for sauce such as 'San Marzano' and 'Viva Italia'.

A few pots of 'Cayenne' peppers will keep you in hot peppers all summer long. Some widely adapted varieties to try include 'Blushing Beauty' and 'Ace' sweet bell peppers, 'Gypsy' and 'Carmen' long, thin sweet peppers, and 'Jalapeno' and 'Super Cayenne III' hot peppers.

Growing the tomato family

Amend the planting area with a 1- to 2-inch thick layer of compost before planting. Wait until the soil warms to at least 60°F before planting your tomato, pepper, or eggplant transplants into the garden. All three grow best in cool areas if planted in a black or red plastic mulch laid over beds 2 weeks before planting to heat up the soil. Poke holes in the plastic mulch to plant a few feet apart. If you don't use plastic, mulch with hay or straw after planting to reduce weeding and watering.

Although peppers and eggplants are stout plants and don't need help standing upright, tomatoes (especially tall growing varieties) can use some support. Stake or cage your tomatoes after planting so you keep the fruit and branches off the ground and free of insects and disease (see Figure 13-1). For tomato varieties that produce large vines, such as 'Brandywine' choose the largest cages available or make your own from concrete reinforcing wire.

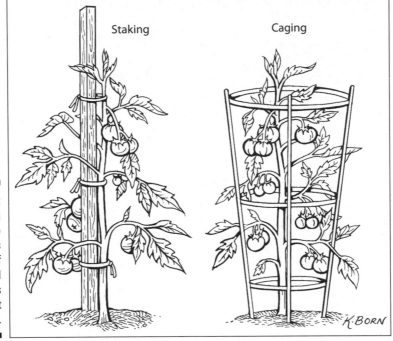

Figure 13-1:
Supporting
tomato
plants keeps
the fruits off
the ground
and less
likely to get
damaged.

Illustration by Kathryn Born.

Side-dress your plants monthly with a complete organic fertilizer (see Chapter 5 for more on side-dressing) and keep plants evenly watered. See Chapter 19 for more on proper watering techniques. Look out for tomato hornworms, leaf blights, and blossom end rot on your plants. Harvest when the tomatoes turn the mature color of the variety you are growing, peppers have reached their full size, and eggplants at any size as long as the skin is still shiny. When the skin color dulls, the fruit is over-mature and mushy.

Melons, squash, and other vining vegetables

Vining vegetables, such as cucumbers, pumpkins, squash, and melons, love to run and take up space. This may be a problem in an urban garden with limited space. But plant breeders have come to the rescue with bush varieties of many of these popular vining plants. These can fit in a smaller garden, even a container.

Trellising these veggies up is a way to plant more crops per square foot of garden space. They grow best on an angled trellis that allows better support for the fruits. Check out Chapter 10 for tips on vertical gardening.

Choosing varieties of vining vegetables

Here are some good varieties for an urban gardener. 'Salad Bush' is a good slicing (long and thin) cucumber, while 'Bush Pickle' is a good small-space pickling (short and prickly) cucumber. Most summer squash varieties stay in a bush form, such as 'Black' zucchini, 'Sunburst' patty pan, and 'Yellow Crookneck' summer squash.

Pumpkins, winter squash, and melons all tend to take up room and need large spaces to grow their best. Some bush varieties are available, though, that make growing these space hogs possible in a small garden. Try 'Cornell Bush' delicata squash, 'Butterbush' butternut squash, 'Honeybun' cantaloupe and 'Sugar Baby' watermelon.

Most vining vegetables have separate male and female blossoms and need bees to pollinate the flowers in order to get fruits. Although bees can fly for miles to find your vegetable garden, pollination may be an issue in some urban areas with few native or honey bees around. To ensure success, look for self-fertilizing varieties such as 'Diva' cucumber and 'Parthenon' zucchini, that don't require cross pollination. Also, plant bee-attracting flowers such as alyssum, marigolds, and cosmos in the garden to lure these winged friends in.

Growing the vining crops

Vining crops like heat, water, and fertile soil. Amend the soil before planting with compost. In cool areas lay black plastic mulch on the beds or planting area to heat the soil. Plant after danger of frost has passed in your area, following the spacing guidelines on the seed packet.

Keep the soil consistently moist and side-dress with an organic fertilizer as recommended earlier in this chapter. Watch out for squash vine borers, cucumber beetles, and powdery mildew disease on your plants. See Chapter 20 for more on these bad guys.

Harvest cukes and squash when the fruits are small. They'll have fewer seeds, and harvesting young stimulates the plants to produce more fruits. Harvest cucumbers when they are 4 to 6 inches long, summer squash and zucchini when the flowers are still attached to the fruit, and winter squash once the true color forms and the skin is tough and thick. Harvest cantaloupes when they naturally slip off the vine when you lift them up.

Root vegetables

Root crops such as carrots, beets, and radishes grow well in small space gardens because they hardly take up any room.

Choosing varieties of root vegetables

Some good carrot varieties to try include 'Scarlet Nantes', Danvers Half-Long', 'Cosmic Purple', and 'Atomic Red'. Try 'Red Ace', 'Golden', and 'Chioggia' beets. For radishes, look for 'Cherry Belle' or ' French Breakfast'.

All three root crops mentioned grow well in small spaces, but if growing in a small container or on heavy clay soils look for dwarf varieties such as Thumbelina carrot, Little Fingers carrot, and Baby Ball beet.

Growing the root

Root crops need well-drained, deep, fertile soil to grow their best. Raised beds are a great place to grow root crops because the soil stays loose, making it perfect for root crops to fill out. Root crops like cool weather conditions. Sow seeds in spring a week or so before your last frost date. For quick maturing roots, such as radishes, sow every few weeks until early summer to get a constant supply of these tasty roots. Sow radishes, carrots, and beet seeds again in late summer for a fall crop. Carrots and beets can grow through the winter in milder climates, providing sweet roots during dark days.

The key to a healthy root crop is thinning. Since the seeds are small, it's easy to overplant. Thinning is removing crowded seedlings so the remaining ones can grow to full size. If you don't thin early and often, you won't get many radishes, carrots, or beets forming. Thin roots to 2 to 4 inches apart one month after planting. Thin so plants are closer together for radishes and farther apart for beets. Use the beet, carrot, and radish thinnings in salads. The greens are tasty.

Watch out for rabbits munching on your carrots, leaf miners tunneling into your beet greens, and flea beetles on your radishes. See Chapter 20 for controls of these pesky critters.

Harvest radishes within one month of sowing seeds when the root ball has formed. Keep harvesting or the roots will split and get large and pithy. Harvest beets and carrots once they develop their true colors. Carrots and beets have a sweeter flavor when exposed to cold temperatures, so consider leaving some in the garden in fall for a winter harvest before the ground freezes.

Peas and beans

Peas and beans are legumes that are able to create their own nitrogen fertilizer. That makes growing these vegetables a snap. But they are different crops. Peas like cool weather to grow and mature, while beans like it hot. Both are well suited to the urban garden. Grow tall varieties of peas or pole beans on a fence or trellis to save space. Grow bush peas or beans in rows in the garden or tucked into containers.

Peas fall into three different groups: English (eat only the peas), snap (eat the pod and all), or snow (flat and eat pods and all). Beans are eaten fresh as snap beans or allowed to mature as dried beans.

Choosing pea and bean varieties

Some good climbing pea varieties include 'Alderman' (English), 'Sugar Snap' (edible pods), and 'Golden Sweet' (flat, yellow pods). Some good pole bean varieties to grow include 'Romano', 'Kentucky Wonder', and 'Blue Lake'. In fact, these same varieties of pole beans are available as bush bean versions too. Plus, you can grow yellow bush beans such as 'Concador' and purple-colored bush beans such as 'Royalty Purple'. For dried beans, try 'Pinto' and Red Kidney'.

For pea varieties that stay in a bush form, try 'Sugar Ann' (edible pod), 'Dwarf Gray Sugar' (flat pod), and 'Little Marvel' (English).

Growing legumes

Peas and beans are some of the simplest veggies to grow. The seeds are large, they're easy to space properly, and they germinate quickly under the right conditions. Peas like it cool, so as soon as the soil dries out in spring, plant your peas in double rows spaced a foot apart in raised beds. If you're growing tall varieties, place a fence in between the rows for them to climb on or plant next to an existing fence. You can also grow peas as a fall crop sown in late summer.

Beans like it hot, so wait until after your last frost to sow bean seeds. Plant them around tall poles for pole bean varieties or in rows for bush varieties. If you keep the plants weeded and watered, there's not much more you'll have to do to get a crop

 Pole beans love to twirl, so grow them up an 8-foot tall pole or fence. Consider making a pole bean teepee to support them (see Chapter 10 for details). Tall varieties of peas cling, so grow these up a fence. Peas are a great way to decorate an ugly chain link fence in a city. Some gardeners like to make pea trellis out of tall twigs and build a rustic fence.

Watch out for Mexican bean beetles and white mold fungus on your bean plants. Peas are relatively pest free except for aphids and the occasional rabbit. Go to Chapter 20 for controls of these pests.

Harvest your snap and English peas when the pods swell, and while the peas are still sweet tasting. Eating a few in the garden is the best way to tell if they are ripe. If you wait too long to harvest, the peas turns chewy and bitter. Snow peas are harvested while still flat and are used in salads and stir fries. Harvest snap beans when their pods are small and just as the seeds inside the pods are starting to form. Harvesting too early is better than harvesting too late. Harvest dried beans when the pods are completely dry and break open easily.

Cabbage, broccoli, and more

Cole crops include cabbage, broccoli, cauliflower, and Brussels sprouts. Kale is also in this group, but we covered that crop earlier in the section "Leafy greens." They all are related, but grow a little differently.

Choosing cole crop varieties

Broccoli varieties such as 'Premium Crop' produces a main head and, after it's harvested, smaller, multiple side heads that keeps you in broccoli all summer. Cole crops love the cool weather and fertile soils. Cabbage such as 'Red Acre' and 'Stonehead' and cauliflower such as 'Cheddar' and 'Snow Crown', form a single head; once it's harvested, the plant is finished for the season. Brussels sprouts, such as 'Bubbles', form small, round "sprouts" along the main stalk. You keep harvesting as long as they keep forming.

Growing cole crops

While it's easiest to buy started cole crop plants from a local garden center, you can start them from seed as well (see Chapter 6). The key is planting a few weeks before the last frost date in your area so they start growing and maturing before the heat of summer. The exception is Brussels sprouts, which take all summer long to form sprouts for fall harvest. Space plants following seed packet recommendations and, once established, mulch with hay or straw to keep the soil cool and moist. Side-dress your cole crops with fertilizer, following the recommendations in the section "Feeding" earlier in this chapter. Grow cabbage, broccoli, and cauliflower as fall crops as well, planting in mid- to late summer. In warm winter areas, these cole crops yield harvests throughout the winter and early spring.

The biggest pest of cole crops is the cabbageworm. This small, green worm eats holes in the cole crop leaves. If unchecked, it will decrease yields and may kill the plant. Cabbage maggots also can be a problem, attacking the roots. Check Chapter 20 for controls of these pests.

Harvest broccoli when the heads are full, but before the buds open into yellow flowers. Cut the stalk right below the head. Harvest cabbages when they are firm to the squeeze, cutting the heads at ground level. Harvest cauliflower when heads are full. Most modern cauliflower varieties either don't need *blanching* (blocking light so the texture stays white and mild) or are self-blanching. Brussels sprouts are harvested starting with the bottom sprouts, when they are firm to the touch. Allow Brussels sprout plants to be exposed to cool fall weather before harvesting to produce a sweeter-tasting sprout.

Easy herbs

Herbs are the perfect edibles for the urban gardener. They are mostly small plants that produce abundantly all season. They fit equally well in a container, flower garden, or vegetable garden. Many are perennials that will come back year after year. They grow best in full sun but some, such as parsley and chives, can tolerate part shade and still produce well. You can even grow some indoors under lights or on a windowsill to extend the growing season into winter in cold areas. (See Chapter 11 for more on indoor growing.)

Most culinary herbs such as basil, thyme, and oregano grow best in well-drained soil conditions. Although you can start most herbs from seed, it's easier to buy plants, especially for small plantings. Here are some of the easiest culinary herbs to grow in your urban yard.

- **Basil (*Ocimum basilicum*)**. The fragrant leaves of this annual plant are great for soups, salads, and, of course, pesto. Grow the 'Genovese' variety for pesto making. Try other flavors such as 'Lemon' basil and 'Thai' basil (licorice) for an added taste treat.

- **Chives (*Allium schoenoprasum*)**. This perennial herb likes cool weather, producing spikes of onion-flavored leaves in spring. By early summer purple flowers form that are attractive and also edible. Keep cutting the chives for cooking and the plant will continue to send up new, tender shoots. For a heat-tolerant herb with garlicky flavor, try garlic chives (*Allium tuberosum*) instead.

- **Cilantro (*Coriandrum sativum*)**. Cilantro is eaten for the flavorful leaves, but if you let the plant flower and go to seed, the edible seeds are called *coriander* and also used as a spice. Cilantro likes cool weather and goes to seed quickly when it gets hot, so sow seeds every few weeks in spring to keep a continuous supply of leaves coming and then again in late summer for a fall harvest. The flowers attract beneficial insects to the garden, so let some flower to feed the good bugs. Cilantro self-sows readily. Once you plant it and let it go to seed, you'll probably always have some growing in your garden.

- **Dill (*Anethum graveolens*)**. Used mostly for making pickles, breads, dressings, and sauces, dill is an annual herb that readily self-sows. It grows into a 2-foot-tall, narrow plant that produces tasty leaves, flowers, and seed. Grow 'Fernleaf' for a shorter variety with more leaves. Like cilantro, dill flowers attract beneficial insects to the garden.

- **Mint (*Mentha*)**. This aggressive and shade-tolerant perennial will trail all over the garden if not contained. There are many flavors of mint to grow including spearmint, apple mint, and chocolate peppermint. Plant it in containers to restrict its growth or in a garden area where it can roam freely. Use the leaves in teas, drinks, and cooking.

- **Parsley (*Petroselinum crispum*)**. This herb is a biennial that is mostly grown as an annual. It's more than a simple garnish; its green leaves are loaded with vitamins A and C and can be used in a variety of dishes. The plants tolerate part sun and, if kept well watered, will produce all summer into fall.

Garden safety

Handling fruits and vegetables safely doesn't just apply to preservation methods. It starts right when we harvest our fresh produce. Keeping food safe from garden to table is especially important if you use manure as a source of organic matter in your garden. This is because manure can be a source of the bacterium *E. coli* 0157:H7, a relatively new and especially virulent strain of this pathogen.

J.G. Davis, extension soil specialist, and P. Kendall, extension food safety specialist, both at Colorado State University (CSU), offer helpful advice on avoiding *E. coli* contamination on garden produce in the CSU Extension fact sheet "Preventing E.coli from Garden to Plate."

Some of their suggestions include locating your garden where there is the lowest possibility of contamination from fresh manure and manure-containing runoff, including runoff from uphill neighbors; keeping pets, livestock, and wildlife out of the garden with fencing; avoiding the use of fresh manure in the garden and never using aged manure on growing crops; composting manure correctly to minimize risks; making sure the water used to irrigate the garden is free from contamination; washing hands, clothing, shoes, and any garden tools that have been in contact with manure; and washing all produce well before preparing or eating it.

They also noted that recent studies have shown that soaking in vinegar is an effective way to reduce *E. coli* 0157:H7 on fresh produce such as lettuce and apples. Just soak the produce in distilled white vinegar for 3 to 5 minutes, stirring occasionally, then rinse well with clear tap water.

- ✔ **Rosemary (*Rosmarius officinalis*)**. This evergreen shrub is hardy to USDA zone 8 and makes a beautiful landscape plant as well as an edible herb. In colder areas, grow it in a well-drained container that can be taken indoors to overwinter in a bright window. Keep the plant trimmed and watered to survive indoors in winter.

- ✔ **Thyme (*Thymus*)**. This creeping herb has selections that are hardy to USDA zone 4. It is low growing and perfect as a scented groundcover in flower gardens, vegetable gardens, or even between stones in a walkway. Thyme fragrances range from lemon to coconut depending on the variety, and the small white, pink, or purple flowers attract beneficial insects. Plant in well-drained soil, keep well watered, and keep trimmed to encourage the tender young growth that is best for cooking.

Extending the Season

In most parts of the country the traditional growing season is pretty straightforward. Prepare the soil in spring, sow in April or May, harvest in summer and fall. In mild winter areas such as Florida, Texas, and Southern California, there's more planting in fall and winter and less in summer, with harvests year-round depending on the vegetable you're growing. However, by just planting once or twice a year, vegetable gardeners are missing out on opportunities to extend the harvest season and grow more in less space. That's our mantra in this book.

There are a few planting techniques any gardener can use to grow more vegetables and herbs in a small space. Two of the best are succession planting and intercropping.

Succession planting: Lettuce forever!

Succession planting is what truck farmers use to ensure they'll have a steady supply of certain vegetables over the whole growing season. It means planting small quantities of quick maturing vegetables, such as lettuce, radishes, and beets, throughout the growing season. By planting short rows every two to three weeks instead of long rows all at once you not only have a good supply of your favorite greens and roots, you avoid the classic dilemma of having too much lettuce ready all at once that will go bad if it's not eaten soon.

Here's an example of how succession planting works. If you have a 6-foot-long raised bed, plant the first 2 feet with lettuce in early spring. Two weeks later plant another 2-foot section. Two weeks later plant the final section. The key is to plant quick maturing vegetables. Plant cool season crops in spring or fall and warm season crops in summer.

Another way to succession plant is to follow a spring crop with a summer crop and then fall crop, all in the same bed. When one crop finishes, pull it out and plant the next one. Here are some possible combinations:

- Lettuce followed by bush beans followed by broccoli
- Peas followed by cucumbers followed by radishes
- Spinach followed by basil followed by kale

A key to succession planting is to be merciless in pulling out your spring or summer crop when it is mostly finished producing. Even if you have to sacrifice a few peas, beans, or radishes, it's important to have enough time to plant and harvest the next crop.

Intercropping: The space between

Another cool space-saving and production-increasing technique is *intercropping*. Intercropping is using the size and growth rates of different crops to your advantage. Large-sized veggies need to be spaced far enough apart at planting time to accommodate their eventual growth. But until they fill in, that's free space to use! Plant quick-maturing, small-sized veggies between these slower growing, large veggies (as shown in Figure 13-2). By the time the large veggies have gotten big enough to fill in the area between plants, the smaller veggies have matured and been harvested. So you've used space normally that would have gone to waste to produce a crop. Some good examples of intercropping matches are lettuce, mesclun greens, radishes, and spinach in between tomatoes, cabbage, broccoli, squash, and eggplant.

Figure 13-2:
Intercropping lettuce between tomato plants is a great way to maximize your garden space.

Illustration by Kathryn Born.

Protecting plants in cool weather

Certainly insects, diseases, and animals can cause damage to your garden. But weather is the ultimate culprit. Frost can bring a sudden ending to a productive garden. But gardeners have ways to cheat Mother Nature. Urban gardens tend to already be warmer than outlying areas because of microclimates (see Chapter 3), so often you can grow veggies and herbs earlier and later than everyone else. But there are some techniques that will help you extend the season even longer, making year-round growing a distinct possibility in many cities.

✔ **Cold Frames.** Cold frames are mini-greenhouses made of wood or metal boxes covered with glass or clear plastic (see Figure 13-3). Fill the box with compost and soil to create a planting area like a raised bed. The top lets light and heat in but protects the plants during cold nights. It's win-win! You can build a simple cold frame from scrap materials or buy a commercially manufactured one.

Getting too hot is as much a concern in a cold frame as getting too cold. During sunny, cool spring or autumn days, a sealed cold frame can overheat, frying the tender young plants. Use automatic vents or remember to prop open the cold frame in the morning on sunny days to keep the air moving.

Figure 13-3:
Cold frames are a good way to extend the growing season in spring and fall.

Illustration by Kathryn Born.

✔ **Floating Row Covers.** Made from white, cheesecloth-like material, row covers let air, light, and water penetrate but are thick enough to protect plants down into the mid-20 degrees F. Lay the floating row cover over young seedlings, loosely fastening it to the ground with boards or stones, and the plants will literally lift it up as they grow. You can grow greens, root crops, and cole crops to maturity under a floating row cover. There are also versions for insect control (we talk about those in Chapter 20). Other types of covers to use at night to temporarily protect your plants when frost threatens include bushel baskets, cloches, and plastic tarps. Just remember to remove these covers the next day so your plants can keep growing.

✔ **Microclimates.** Urban areas are loaded with microclimate nooks where you can tuck in some plants that will get enough sun to thrive but are protected from cold winds and low temperatures (see Chapter 3 for details). Look around your urban yard for planting areas along south-facing walls, buildings, and solid fences. Courtyards are great heat sinks, while a spot in front of evergreen shrubs can be another good protected place. Rooftops, balconies, and patios (that we discuss in Chapters 9 and 11) will be protected from cold temperatures if oriented correctly.

Putting veggies by

If you're growing more vegetables and herbs than you thought possible, you'll have to do something with the excess. Certainly friends and family will love to partake of your bounty, but you might want to save some vegetables and herbs for your own use in winter. That's where drying, canning, and freezing comes in.

✔ **Canning**. This is a great way to preserve excess tomatoes as a delicious sauce. Canning is an involved process requiring equipment, glass jars, and time. Getting the temperatures and processing correct is important, so can with a family member or friend who is experienced and check out canning resources such as the National Center of Home Food Preservation for the appropriate details on canning each crop.

✔ **Freezing**. This is the easiest and safest way for most urban gardeners to preserve their vegetables and herbs. Simply clean, process, and pop the veggies in a freezer bag and away they go into the cold to last for months. You can process your vegetables first by making tomato sauce or pesto to freeze, or freeze veggies whole. Many vegetables need to be *blanched* before freezing. Simply dip your vegetables in boiling water for a minute or two, then plunge them in ice water to preserve the color and texture. Pack them in bags and freeze. Easy breezy, lemon squeezy!

✔ **Drying**. You can dry vegetables in a dehydrator or oven to store them for winter. But the easiest plants to dry are herbs. Thyme, oregano, lavender, rosemary, parsley, and many other herbs lend themselves well to air drying. All you need is an airy, warm place to hang your herbs to until they are dry and brittle. Then store in airtight jars.

To dry herbs, cut the branches of herbs in the morning once the dew has dried. The leaves have the highest oil content right before they flower. Wash, pat dry, and bundle like herbs together and hang them in a well-ventilated place out of direct light. They should be dry and ready for storing in about one to two weeks. *Warning:* Don't dry herbs and vegetables outdoors in urban areas because air pollution can make the vegetables and herbs unpalatable and potentially harmful.

For more information on canning, pickling, fermenting, freezing, drying, cellaring, and otherwise making your food last, check out *Canning & Preserving All-In-One For Dummies* (Wiley).

Chapter 14

The Annual Flowering of the City

*I*f you're looking to create a splash of color, if you like combining colors and textures like an artist, if you have only a small space to make an impact on your deck and patio, then annual flowers are for you. Annual flowers are a city gardener's best friend. They grow quickly to flowering size, can bloom all summer long with care, and are easy to replace when the weather or your tastes change.

In this chapter, you discover the best annual flowers to grow in the city, how to combine them with other annuals and perennial flowers for a smashing display, and how to take care of your plants all season long.

Understanding Annuals

Annual flowers complete their life cycle in one season. Most grow from seed in spring, flower in summer, form seeds, and die in fall. Perennial flowers, on the other hand, come back each year from roots, bulbs, or stems. (We cover perennials in Chapter 15.)

The distinction between annual and perennial flower does get a little hazy in warmer climates. For example, geraniums and fuchsia are considered annuals in most areas of the U.S. because cold winter weather will kill them. However, in warm climates or if brought indoors, they really are perennial flowers that will grow for many years.

Some annual flowers drop seeds in the garden in summer, and those seeds will germinate on their own the next spring. These are called *self-sowing annual flowers*. They are handy if you want your annual flowers to fill in a large area, but beware — self-sowing annual flowers can become weeds in the garden if left to their own devices. To prevent this, cut off the fading flowers in the summer before they can set seeds or thin the self-sown seedlings out mercilessly in spring so they don't take over. Also, the new seedlings may not be the same color and size as the original plants you planted last year, so be discriminating about which ones you save.

Here is a list of annuals that tend to self-sow readily:

- Baby's breath
- Calendula
- California poppy
- Cleome
- Four o'clock
- Larkspur
- Morning glory
- Nicotiana
- Portulaca
- Salvia

Siting Your Annual Flower Garden

The beauty of annuals is their propensity to bloom. Annuals are often bursting with flowers when you buy them in the garden center and will continue flowering as long as the weather and fertility are right for the plants, and pests are kept at bay. They truly are the plants to grow for continuous color all summer long.

But before you go out and buy up all your favorite color combinations at the nursery, it's good to know a little about where annual flowers grow best and what will work best in your space.

Figuring out whether your garden can support sun- or shade-loving annuals

Most annual flowers need at least six hours of direct sun a day to bloom their best. Less sun won't kill the flowers, but they will be less floriferous and beautiful. In the city this can be problematic. Many urban gardens are surrounded by tall buildings or city trees that cast shade on your growing space during the day. However, this doesn't mean you can't grow sun-loving annual flowers. You just have to be observant of when and how long the sun is on your garden during the summer months. If you get a few hours of sun in the morning and a few hours in the late afternoon, that's enough to keep most sun-worshippers happy. In warm climates, this might work to your advantage, because often the midday sun is too intense even for sun-loving annuals because of the heat. If you don't get more than a few hours of sun all day, then consider shade-loving annuals such as impatiens and begonias. They shy away from direct sunlight and love shady conditions. We give examples of some sun- and shade-loving annuals to grow a little later in "Choosing Annual Flowers for All Seasons and Soils."

The amount of sun reaching your garden will change as the seasons progress from spring to fall. In spring, you may have lots of full sun because leaves aren't out on deciduous trees yet. Also, the sun's angle in the sky changes over the course of the growing season. By June, the sun is as high in the sky as it will go, providing lots of light to sun-loving annuals. However, by August and September, the sun's angle in the sky has dipped lower on the horizon, which may increase the amount of shade on your plants. If this is the case, you can replace your sun lovers with shade lovers (we'll cover that a little later on) or move the plants if they are in containers.

Prepping and planting

Besides the right amount of light, annual flowers love a fertile, well-drained soil. Take time to remove rocks, debris, and weeds from your annual flower garden before planting.

Most annual flowers are available as transplants at your local garden center. This is certainly the easiest way to plant annual flowers. However, if you're planting a garden bed or trying to save some money on your annual flower plantings, some annuals can be sown directly from seed into the garden. And some annuals, like poppies and larkspur, resent transplanting and do best if grown from seed where you want them to flower. Sunflowers, morning glories, sweet peas, and calendulas are just some of the annual flowers you can sow from seed in spring for summer flowering. Of course, these will flower later than nursery-started transplants, but if you're growing lots of one type of plant, it's an inexpensive way to go.

Considering color

If you're planting in a flower bed, consider planting annuals en masse or in groups of similarly colored flowers. We think annual flowers make the boldest statements when many of the same type are grouped together. This is particularly appealing if the garden will be viewed from a distance. The flowers will have more of a bang if many are grouped together and you choose varieties with hot colors such as red, orange, and yellow. They virtually jump out of the landscape. If your annual flowers will be viewed close up, you can still plant in same color groups, but select cool pastel-colored varieties featuring blues, pinks, and greens. These are easier to look at up close and won't overwhelm the viewer. Of course, annuals with large flowers, such as zinnias and sunflowers, add an additional "wow" effect, while those with smaller blossoms, such as violas and lobelia, draw the viewer in toward the planting.

If you're not going for a dramatic, one-color look, still consider grouping similarly colored or textured annual flowers together in a bed. I think groups of same-colored flowers look best when designing with annuals. You can complement the colors, using your own tastes or the *color wheel*. The color wheel is a circle of color divided like a pie into the same colors as the rainbow in the same order, with the primary colors — red, yellow, and blue — equidistant on the wheel. You can find examples of the color wheel online or in many gardening books, or you can purchase an actual wheel at an art supply store. Colors opposite each other on the wheel will complement each other. For example, orange and blue and purple and yellow are complementary color combinations that look soothing together in a bed. Or you can plant flowers in a gradual blend of similar hues between primary colors, such as yellow to orange, for a harmonious color effect. Of course, the beauty of annual flowers is you can do whatever you like. We've often been known to throw out the color wheel and plant clashing colors with amazing effects. The bottom line is to play with the colors to see what works for you.

Thinking about texture and fragrance

Because there is such a variety of annual flowers to choose from, and because they grow so readily, you can really play around with color, texture, and fragrance in your annual flower garden.

Don't just think of annuals for their flower colors and sizes. Their leaf textures can also add much to a garden. Many newer varieties of annuals have different-colored leaves that will contribute to a stunning display. Look for annuals with dark purple, white, or variegated (multicolored) leaves. Some annuals, such as coleus, dusty miller, and tricolor sage, are mainly grown just for their leaf colors.

It's also not only about looks in the annual garden. Many annual flowers have a magnificent fragrance. Heliotrope, four o'clocks, stock, sweet William, and sweet peas are just some of the annual flowers with a delicious fragrance. Often old-fashioned varieties of these annuals will have the most intense fragrance. Check information on the seed packets to choose the most fragrant varieties. Grow some of these scented beauties in a garden bed close to the house or in containers near a window. Imagine having the sweet smells of flowering nicotiana wafting into your house or apartment on a warm summer night. Ahhhh!

Harvesting cut flowers

To create the best cut flower bouquets, harvest your flowers in the morning before the heat of the day and when the flowers are partially open. Place the cut stems in a bucket of warm water immediately. Strip the lower leaves on the stems, cut the stems again under water at a 45-degree angle, and then place them in a clean vase with warm water and a floral preservative.

Growing flowers for cutting

Another way to use annual flowers in your yard is for cutting. While looking at your annual flowers in containers or beds through a window is pleasant, many annuals lend themselves to being cut and brought indoors. And you don't need acres of land to have an annual cut flower garden. The key is diversity. Plant many different types of annuals that are good for cutting in a variety of locations in containers and beds. As you go around and snip, you'll only need to take a few here and there to create a beautiful bouquet. You'll hardly notice the missing flower in the container and you'll have a bouquet indoors to enjoy.

Some great annuals for cutting include baby's breath, calendula, cosmos, larkspur, salvia, snapdragon, stock, sweet pea, sunflower, and zinnia. Include some everlasting flowers, too. These are annuals that dry quickly with papery petals and can be used for months as a cut flower in the home. Statice and strawflowers are two good everlastings to grow.

Growing Annuals in Containers

One the best ways to maximize color in a small urban yard is by growing annual flowers in containers. You can move most containers easily to take advantage of the best conditions for that particular flower. Growing in containers allows you to get creative with flower color and foliage texture combinations. Plus, if you don't like a particular combination or some plants start looking ratty, you can yank them out and start again. We often change out our containers two or three times during the growing season to suit the climate and our preferences.

Plant breeders have been creating new dwarf varieties of annuals that fit easily into a small window box, pot, or hanging basket. Not only does this allow you to grow annuals in any nook and cranny, it opens up a world of possibilities, letting you combine three, four, or even five different annuals in a pot with varying flower colors or leaf textures.

We cover how to grow flowers in containers in Chapter 8, but there's one concept that will help with designing your annual container flower garden. It's called the *thrillers, spillers, and fillers* plan. Michael Jackson would have been proud. By combining annuals of different sizes and shapes in one container (see Figure 14-1), you create more visual interest than if you had just one or two similarly shaped flowers.

✔ Thrillers are tall, eye-catching annuals that stand above the foliage and flowers of other annuals in your pot. Some good examples of thriller flowers include stock, cosmos, and nicotiana.

✔ Fillers are the medium-sized, bushy annuals that will fit around the thriller in your container. They fill in the space under the thriller. Some good examples of fillers include dusty miller, marigold, and sage.

✔ Spillers are annual flowers that love to trail. Planted along the lip of the container to cascade over the edge, they make the container seem larger than it is, maximizing the space below. Some good examples of spillers include petunia, calibrochoa, and lobelia.

Figure 14-1:
Thrillers,
fillers, and
spillers in a
container.

Illustration by Kathryn Born.

The concept of thrillers, fillers, and spillers works best in larger containers, but you can create mini versions in window boxes or small containers by choosing dwarf plants that are appropriate for that space.

Choosing Annual Flowers for All Seasons and Soils

Now the fun part! Choosing annual flowers for your container or yard is really a matter of horticulture and taste. As mentioned, getting the right plant for your conditions is important, but planning for flower colors and leaf textures allows you to be an artist in the garden.

Cool spring and fall flowers

These are some of the best annual flowers for the cool conditions in spring and fall. In areas with warm winter climates, such as Southern California and Florida, many of these annuals can be planted in fall to grow and flower all winter. However, for most everyone else, the annuals in this list are best planted in spring once the weather warms and again in late summer once the weather cools. Many of these flowers can even take a light frost.

- **Calendula.** Calendula, or pot marigold, produces yellow, white, or orange daisy-like flowers that are good for cutting and eating. The plants grow 1 to 2 feet tall and do best in full sun. Deadhead the old flowers to keep it blooming well. If you let some of the flowers go to seed, it will self-sow.

- **Dusty miller.** One of the most popular plants for providing contrast in the annual garden, dusty miller's grayish white leaves make a great backdrop to more colorful flowering plants. In warm climates it will survive as a perennial and produce yellow flowers. Grow dusty miller in containers or in the ground in full sun. It grows about 18 inches tall.

- **Flowering cabbage and kale.** Related to the common vegetables and also edible, flowering cabbages and kales are mostly grown for their hardy, colorful leaves. Many varieties feature frilly or ruffled, white, purple, or red leaves. They grow best in sun to a height of 12 to 18 inches tall.

- **Forget-me-not.** This shade-loving, low-growing annual produces delicate, powdery blue flowers. It grows well in a shady location and self-sows readily, eventually creating a mat of spring blooming flowers each year.

- **Larkspur.** This annual produces 1- to 4-foot-tall spikes of white, blue, purple, or pink flowers. This thriller plant grows best in light shade.

- **Lobelia.** A low-growing (4 to 6 inches tall), ground cover plant that features white, pink, or blue flowers. Lobelia grows well in containers cascading over the edge of the pot or planted as an edging flower around a border. It grows best in full sun, but will tolerate light shade.

✔ **Nasturtium**. This edible annual has either a bushy growth habit, like the variety 'Peach Melba' that grows well in containers, or as a 4- to 6-foot-long trailing vine, like the variety 'Jewel of Africa', which can be trained up a trellis. The yellow, orange, white, or red flowers and green leaves have a peppery flavor. Nasturtiums grow best in full sun but will take part shade, too. They are easily sown from seed planted directly into the garden.

✔ **Pansy and viola**. A sure sign of spring in many gardens is violas and pansies in bloom. Violas tend to have smaller, more numerous flowers than pansies, but both feature those cute "faces" that many gardeners love. These edible flowers come in a variety of colors including white, blue, yellow, orange, and many different multicolored combinations. They grow 8 to 10 inches tall and can take a light frost. Pansies and violas grow best in full sun when the weather is cool but part shade when it starts to warm up. Violas, in particular, will self-sow.

✔ **Poppies.** There are many different types of poppies including perennial, biennial, and annual species. California and Icelandic poppies are examples of annuals. These 1- to 2-foot-tall plants produce white, pink, yellow, or orange flowers, depending on the species and variety, and self-sow readily. They grow best in full sun.

✔ **Snapdragon**. Snapdragons are cold and part-shade tolerant annuals that produce spikes of flowers in colors including white, yellow, red, and purple. The flower spikes range in height from 12 to 36 inches tall, depending on the variety. Snapdragons are great flowers for kids, since their name is derived from the hinged blossom that you can squeeze to make move up and down. They're great for kid puppet shows.

✔ **Stock**. This spiky annual flower has spicy-scented, white, pink, or purple flower stalks that grow 12 to 30 inches tall. Stocks grow best in full sun and adapt well to growing in containers.

✔ **Sweet alyssum**. This low-growing annual makes a great flower edging around an herb or perennial flower garden, as well as a nice container plant. The plant grows 6 inches tall and has white or pink flowers, depending on the variety. It readily self-sows in the garden and is frost tolerant. It grows best in full sun.

✔ **Sweet peas.** This climbing vine is *not* related to edible peas and shouldn't be eaten, but grows in a similar way. Tall, old-fashioned varieties such as 'Old Spice' need a trellis and support when growing, while bushy dwarf varieties such as 'Cupid' grow well in small containers without support. The flowers include most colors of the rainbow, and many older varieties feature an intense fragrance. Plant in full sun.

✔ **Sweet William**. Although these old-fashioned flowers are biennials or short-lived perennials, varieties grown as annuals will bloom the first year from seed. The 6- to 18-inch-tall plants feature white, pink, red, or bicolor flowers. They grow best in full sun.

Summer flowers

Summertime should be drenched with color. Here are some annual flowers that love the heat and flower best under warm soil and air conditions in most areas.

- **Begonia.** There are many perennial species of begonias, but the wax leaf begonia is traditionally used as a shade-loving annual in the garden. The flowers range in color from white to red, and the waxy leaves may have a burgundy tinge to them. The plant grows to 12 inches tall.

- **Calibrochoa.** This trailing annual grows only 6 inches tall and has small leaves and petunia-like flowers. The flower colors include white, bronze, yellow, and red. Calibrochoa is also called *Million Bells* for its prolific flowers. It thrives in full sun but can tolerate some shade. It grows better in the heat of summer than petunias and tolerates drought.

- **Celosia.** There are two types of celosia: plume and crested. Both grow 2 to 4 feet tall and produce bright yellow, orange, or red flowers. The plume-type celosia has feather-like flowers, while the crested-type varieties have tight clusters of flowers shaped like cockscombs. Celosia can self-sow.

- **Cleome.** Cleome is also known as the spider flower for its open, spidery flower clusters. The plant grows 2 to 5 feet tall, depending on the variety, with white, pink, or purple flowers. It thrives in full sun and self-sows readily. One variety that doesn't self-sow is 'Senorita Rosalita'. Most varieties are drought tolerant. and some have thorny spikes on their branches.

- **Coleus.** Coleus is grown mostly for its intensely colored leaves and exotic leaf shapes. Leaves can be green, yellow, red, pink, or any number of combinations of these colors. The plants can grow quite large (up to 3 feet tall). Although traditional varieties are mostly shade loving, newer varieties, such as 'Bronze Pagoda', are more sun tolerant and don't fade in the bright light. Snip off flowers as they form to promote a bushier plant.

- **Cosmos.** These tall (up to 5 feet), airy plants produce white, pink, red, or striped daisy-like flowers in mid- to late summer. Some varieties, such as 'Sonata', produce dwarf plants. Cosmos grow best in full sun and look great as the backdrop for other lower-growing, bushy annuals.

- **Impatiens.** The quintessential shade flower, impatiens grow equally as well in containers as in the ground. The 1- to 2-inch-diameter white, red, pink, orange, or lavender flowers on 1- to 2-foot-tall plants brighten up a shady area. Taller New Guinea impatiens are more sun tolerant but still grow best in part shade.

- **Lantana.** This heat and drought tolerant tender perennial grown as an annual is a butterfly favorite. Flowers in shades of yellow, pink, or red form on the ends of airy branches, giving the plants a graceful growth habit. Depending on the variety, lantana grows from 3 to 5 feet tall, getting especially large in warm summer areas. It grows best in full sun.

✔ **Marigold.** Marigolds are one of the most popular, sun-loving annual flowers. The plants range from 1 to 4 feet tall, depending on the variety. The flowers range in size from diminutive to the size of a tennis ball and come in colors that include yellow, orange, and red. Marigolds can be directly sown in the garden but are best purchased as transplants for earlier flowering.

✔ **Morning Glory.** A great climbing annual that quickly grows into an 8-to10-foot-tall vine, it's great for planting on a fence or trellis. The flowers are white, blue, red, striped, or purple. and open, as advertized, in the morning, closing in the afternoon. So be sure to locate them where you can see the flowers in the morning for best enjoyment. Morning glories are easy to grow from seed and readily self-sow.

✔ **Nicotiana.** Also known as flowering tobacco, nicotiana produces tubular-shaped flowers in colors including white, pink, and purple. The plants can be 1 to 4 feet tall, depending on the species and variety. Some varieties have a sweet-scented flower. Nicotiana self-sows readily.

✔ **Petunia.** A widely grown, sun-loving flower grown as an annual, petunias grow 6 to 24 inches tall and wide, depending on the variety. The flowers can be single or double and come in colors such as white, pink, yellow, red, striped, or even black. Petunias are versatile, growing well in containers or the ground. If the stems get long and leggy by mid-summer, pinch them back to stimulate bushier new growth.

✔ **Portulaca.** Also called the moss rose, this sun-loving, heat and drought tolerant annual with succulent stems grows well in tough conditions. The small, rose-like flowers come in white, yellow, pink, orange, and red. A low-growing plant, portulaca can trail to 1 foot long and thrives in containers. Portulaca can self-sow.

✔ **Salvia.** Salvia is one of many types of sage plants. They produce 1- to 3-foot-tall flower spikes in colors such as white, blue, purple, and red. Deadhead or cut back spent flower spikes to encourage more flowering. Salvia grows best in full sun.

✔ **Scaevola.** Scaevola or fan flower is a low-growing (6 to 12 inches tall), trailing tender perennial grown as an annual that produces blue or white flowers, depending on the variety. It's a great cascading flower for containers and grows well as an annual groundcover, too. It grows best in full sun.

✔ **Sunflower.** No flower says summer quite like the sunflower. It used to be you could only buy sunflowers varieties that were tall with one large head. Now you can choose from dwarf varieties such as 'Teddy Bear' (2 feet tall) and multibranching varieties such as 'Soraya' (produces up to 20 heads). Sunflower flower colors range from the traditional yellow to red, white, and burnt orange. All grow best in full sun. Use sunflowers as a backdrop in the flower garden or planted en masse in a separate bed.

> The best varieties for seed eating are the large-headed varieties such as 'Mammoth Russian'.
>
> ✔ **Verbena.** A low-growing (6 to 12 inches tall), spreading plant, verbena flowers come in white, pink, red, or purple. This sun lover grows well in containers and in the ground. Like its relative, lantana, verbena thrives in heat and tolerates drought.
>
> ✔ **Zinnia.** Zinnias have a wide variety of plant and flower shapes and sizes. Some, such as the 'Profusion' series, are perfect low-growing annuals, while others such as 'State Fair' make great cut flowers. Variety is the name of the game with zinnias. Flowers can be single or double; shaped like daisies, dahlias, or globes; and in colors that include white, yellow, orange, salmon, red, and pink. Plants range from 1 to 5 feet tall, depending on the variety, and all thrive in full sun. If you have trouble with powdery mildew disease on your zinnias, try the disease-resistant 'Pinwheel' series.

If you live in the hottest parts of the Southeast or Southwest, you may have to protect even these summer warmth lovers from the harsh afternoon sun during the heat of summer.

Flowers for every soil

Besides heat and cold, special soil conditions can influence how well annual flowers grow. Here are a few lists to help you find the annuals best adapted to specific growing conditions in your garden.

If you have very poor soil conditions try growing...

✔ California poppy

✔ Celosia

✔ Cleome

✔ Four o'clocks

✔ Nasturtium

✔ Petunia

✔ Portulaca

If you have acidic soil, try growing...

✔ Nicotiana

✔ Marigold

✔ Verbena

If you have alkaline soil, try growing....

- ✔ Annual phlox
- ✔ Balsam
- ✔ Nasturtium
- ✔ Zinnia

Caring for Your Annuals to Keep a Continuous Flower Show

While an annual flower lives to bloom, if not taken care of properly, like any plant it will eventually stop flowering and perhaps die. Proper watering, fertilizing, and weeding are some of the keys to annual flower success. In this section, we talk about how to keep your annuals healthy and happy.

Along with watering, weeding, feeding, pinching, and supporting your annual flowers, always keep a look out for pests. Check the undersides of leaves for insects, look for diseased flowers, and watch for animal damage. We talk in great detail about pest controls in Chapter 20; however, keep in mind that the best form of pest control is you taking a moment each time you're in the garden to check for beginning problems.

Watering

Annual flowers need a consistent supply of water to keep flowering. Early in the season when plants are small, water frequently since young roots are small and close to the soil surface where they can dry out quickly. After a few weeks, your transplants and seedlings will have large enough root systems that you can start watering more deeply and less frequently. This encourages the roots to go deeper into the soil, where they will be less likely to dry out during drought periods in summer.

If Mother Nature is giving your plants about 1 to 2 inches of water a week, that will be adequate. But unless you have rain gauge, you won't be able to tell how much water your plants are actually receiving. A better way to gauge soil moisture is to do the *knuckle test*. Stick your finger in the soil up to the second knuckle (the one closest to your hand). If the soil feels dry at the depth of the tip of your finger, it's time to water.

When you water established plants, let the moisture soak down at least 6 inches into the soil. Dig around the plants to be sure it's sinking in and not running off. During hot dry periods you may have to check your in-ground flowers every few days. For container-grown annual flowers, watering may be a daily ritual, but plants will still grow fine if watered every other day as long as they have enough soil to hold the water.

Weeding

Weeding your annual flowers goes hand in hand with watering. Weeds not only compete with your annual flowers for space and nutrients, they like to steal water from plants as well. Weeds tend to be more aggressive than most annual flowers, so you'll have to be on your guard to keep them controlled. Many newer hybrid annual flowers are so intent on flowering up a storm, they don't put much energy into growing strong plants.

Weed your annual flower beds early and often. But be careful not to disturb the tender young roots of the annual flowers. After a few weeks, once the flowers are established, mulch the beds with a 2- to 3-inch-thick layer of organic mulch, such as untreated grass clippings, bark mulch, or pine straw. The mulch will prevent weeds from growing, preserve soil moisture, and give your garden a decorative look.

While we don't often think of weeding container gardens, weed seeds can blow in to large containers in particular, creating some unexpected visitors by summer. Be diligent at removing weeds in containers because there is even less soil mass, less water, and fewer nutrients for your annual flowers to share with these interlopers.

Fertilizing

Because most annual flowers burst with flowers all season long, they need lots of fuel to keep going. Think of them like active teenagers. They are moving so fast, it's hard to keep enough food in the house to keep them fueled. The same is true of your annual flowers. They are bred to bloom their hearts out, and flowering takes energy.

Young transplants and seedlings should be given a water-soluble, easily absorbed fertilizer such as fish fertilizer or worm juice (see Chapter 5 for more on these and other fertilizers). These are like energy drinks for plants. They absorb the nutrients through their roots and leaves, giving them a quick burst of energy to grow fast. Once they are established and cranking out the flowers, give your annual flower gardens a dose of a granular organic plant food every month to keep the show going. Container gardens should be fertilized every few weeks because there is less natural soil fertility to feed the annuals.

Deadheading

Deadheading your flowers means removing the spent flowers after they're finished blooming. This not only makes the plant look better, it prevents it from spending precious energy and time maturing seeds in the spent flowers. While some annual flowers such as calibrochoa and scaevola are called *self-cleaning*, meaning that they will naturally drop their dead flowers so you don't have to remove them, most other annuals need a little pinch.

To deadhead a spent flower, use your thumb and forefinger or a pair of scissors to pinch or cut off the flower just behind the petals and above a leaf on the stem. This stimulates new branching and eventually more flowers form.

Pruning

Sometimes your annual flowers will need more than a pinch. Some plants tend to grow wild, gangly, and unruly in your garden or container. They need more serious pruning. Floppy flowers such as cosmos or trailing annuals such as petunias often get larger than you want. Before the plant gets out of control, do a little constructive pruning to the stems. Prune back young cosmos plants when they are 1 to 2 feet tall to promote a bushier growth habit, causing more side branches to form and making the plant stem more manageable.

If your petunias, calibrochoa, scaevola, lobelia, or other trailing annuals are getting long and leggy, prune these back as well. Prune these trailers back to just above a set of leaves. You may sacrifice a few flowers, but eventually the plant will grow more branches and plenty more flowers. If you prune back annuals in midsummer, you will create a beautiful flower garden and containers for the remainder of the season, until cold weather shuts the plants down.

Here are some annuals that respond well to pruning:

- Ageratum
- Calendula
- Petunia
- Dianthus
- Salpiglossis
- Snapdragon
- Verbena
- Zinnia

Here are some annual flowers that shouldn't be pruned. If you prune, you'll will remove the flower stalk and deform the plant:

- Balsam impatiens
- Celosia
- Poppies
- Stocks

Keeping them up

Tall-growing annual flowers such as larkspur and cosmos and climbers such as sweet peas and morning glories need the proper supports to keep them up and off the ground. Tall annual flowers can easily flop over during a summer thunderstorm. Use bamboo, metal, or wooden stakes and gently tie the main plant stems to the stakes to keep them upright. You can also use plant supports and cages for groups of annuals that need help standing tall.

Climbing annuals need a fence or trellis to cling to. We sometimes use various branches found in the woods to create a rustic support for our sweet peas. The fence or trellis should have places where the climbers can grab. If you have a stockade-type wooden fence or a brick wall, consider draping mesh netting over it to give your climbers some material to grab on to.

Using Succession Planting to Maintain Your Annual Flowers

Yes, annual flowers are bred to bloom all season long and, yes, we know you're a budding gardener who will take good care of your annual flower plants from spring until fall. However, even with strong plants and an attentive gardener, things still can go wrong, and you may need to pull out plants. Weather is one of the main factors influencing your annual flowers. As we mentioned earlier, there are cool and warm season annuals. In some climates, such as the North, cool season annuals can last right through the summer and keep blooming well. However, in most areas, they tend to peter out from the heat by early summer.

You can take the damage from weather or pests as a sign of failure or as an opportunity to replant. We like the latter! In fact, annual flowers are perfect for succession planting.

Succession planting means removing a struggling plant before the end of the season and replacing it with the same or a different one to maximize the flowering space in your garden or container. Succession planting is a common concept in vegetable gardening (see Chapter 13 for more), but it works equally as well in the annual flower garden.

The first step is choosing the right flowers for the season. In winter in warm areas and spring everywhere else, grow cool weather-loving flowers such as pansies, violas, primroses, snap dragons, and forget-me-nots. These plants will thrive while it stays cool, but once the temperatures start reaching consistently into the 70- to 80-degree F range, they will suffer and even die.

Now it's time to succeed with a succession planting. Pull out those struggling cool weather lovers and replace them with heat-tolerant annuals such as petunias, verbena, zinnias, and sunflowers. These annuals will grow strong all summer into fall. Once the weather cools again in autumn, pull out the summer annuals and replace them with cool season annuals for fall. In warm winter areas, these plants will bloom right through into winter. In our northern garden, we even get violas and snapdragons to over-winter under the snow for an early spring flower show.

While weather certainly dictates which annual flowers you can grow, sometimes pests, diseases, or the plants themselves tell you it's time to switch. This is most evident in container annual flower gardens. If you have an insect- or disease-infested annual in a container, yank it! There are many other alternatives that you can use in its place. If one annual is shrinking from sight because others in that container are overly aggressive, yank it. Try to match annuals with similar growth habits so they stay in proportion throughout the growing season.

Chapter 15

Perennial Flowers, Roses, and Bulbs in the City

* *

In This Chapter

▶ Finding the right spots to grow perennial plants

▶ Growing perennial flowers in sun and shade

▶ Selecting and growing the right rose for the city

▶ Adding bulbs for perennial color

* *

*W*hile most annual flowers give you a constant show all summer long with their burst of blooms, perennial flowers, roses, and flowering bulbs bloom in waves. They require a little more thoughtful selection in order to have color all season. But the beauty of perennial flowers, roses, and bulbs is they are *perennial* (they grow back every year, either from the bulb, woody stems, or roots) and you can mix and match plants to have a cascade of flowers with different colors, textures, and shapes that ebb and flow from spring until fall.

Perennial gardening requires more experimentation than annual flower gardening, but the rewards are huge. You can create gardens with a mix of perennial flowers, annual flowers, roses, and bulbs or design plantings of only one kind of plant, such as a rose garden, bed of tulips, or a sea of daylilies. The combinations of perennials, bulbs, and roses you can come up with are expansive and the design options almost endless. This chapter walks you through what you need to know about perennial flowers, planting and maintenance considerations, as well as good plant choices for your particular urban setting.

Getting to Know Perennials, Roses, and Bulbs

First let's talk definitions. While perennials are any plant that regrows each year, we're using the term perennial flowers here as a flower that regrows from the stems or roots each spring. While roses are considered shrub, they have unique needs from other shrubs so that we've created a separate section for them here. And bulbs, well, yes, they are perennials, but like roses they have unique planting and growing needs, so they merit their own conversation.

Finding a Permanent Planting Spot

Like annual flowers, perennials can grow in full or part shade, depending on the variety. However, roses and most bulbs love to bask in the sun, so finding the right spot for them is most important. All three of these perennial kinds of plants love well-drained, fertile soil. Although it's not as common as with annual flowers, you can grow these perennials in containers, too. In cold climates they'll need protection, but in warm climates they can become permanent fixtures in your yard. The perennial flowers we mention here are *herbaceous perennials*. This means the tops die back to the ground each fall and the plant regrows from the roots in spring.

Finding a good spot to plant perennial flowers, roses, and bulbs is important because that's where they're going to stay year after year unless you dig them up. The following sections provide you with tips and guidance related to sunlight, soil conditions, and wind exposure. We also discuss how to utilize containers, if that's the way you decide to go.

Considering sun, soil, and exposure

Sunlight is probably the most important consideration for what and where to plant, but soil and wind also factor in. The follow sections provide more specifics in each of these areas.

Sun and shade

Perennial flowers tolerate a wide range of light conditions. Some perennial flowers, such as coneflowers, daisies, and tall phlox, thrive in as much sun as you can give them. Other perennials, such as foxglove, bell flowers, and dianthus, can tolerate filtered light or part shade. Others, such as hosta, fern, and lily-of-the-valley, grow best in mostly shady conditions. City gardens often have to deal with shade from trees, buildings, and the position of the sun in the sky, so having a good list of shade lovers makes sense.

Roses love sun. There's no two ways about it. Although some landscape and species roses can tolerate part shade and still flower, if you want a beautiful show of roses in early summer and throughout the growing season, find the sunniest, brightest spot you can in your yard. Some types of roses, such as the miniature roses, grow well in containers, so they may be an option if your urban yard just doesn't have much in-ground growing space in the sun. You can just move the container to where there is sun, perhaps a deck, front stoop, or driveway.

Flowering bulbs, such as tulips, daffodils, lilies, and gladiolus, also need full sun to flower their best, but the spring flowering bulbs have an extra advantage. Bulbs such as tulips, daffodils, hyacinths, crocus, and scilla usually bloom before the leaves of deciduous trees emerge. You may notice a lot more sun in your urban homestead in spring before the leaves come out. This allows the bulb to send up the beautiful flowers that we crave and to leaf out, thus producing food to rejuvenate the underground bulbs, all before shade creeps in by early summer. So look around your yard in late winter or early spring for spots that get full sun. These will be good candidates for planting spring flowering bulbs in fall. For summer flowering bulbs, such as lilies and gladiolus, treat these as sun-loving perennials and find a bright spot for them in the yard.

Soil

Whether your perennials are growing in sun or shade, they all need well-drained soil. The good thing about perennials in an urban setting is, since we aren't eating them, we don't have to be as concerned about the soil contaminants we mentioned in Chapter 4. Of course, you should be aware of any potentially harmful chemicals or debris in the soil, but adding some topsoil and compost so you can plant your perennial flowers, roses, and bulbs may be enough to turn an unused location in your yard into a flowering garden.

Wind

Another consideration on where to plant is wind. Cities are notorious for creating wind tunnels between buildings. Low-growing perennial flowers such as coral bells and salvia won't be too adversely affected by high winds, but tall perennials like delphiniums, climbing roses, and tall tulips can be harmed. Tall perennials and climbing roses will need support, and we talk about that later in this chapter. Although bulbs are low growing, once they flower, their petals are delicate and only last a few days. It would be a shame to plant a bed of tulips and wait six months for them to emerge and flower, only to have all the petals blow off after they open. Look for a protected spot to grow these, or use trees, shrubs, or structures to create a windbreak for your plants.

Going with containers

Annual flowers are a perfect fit for container gardening in the city, but perennial flowers, roses, and bulbs can also be grown in containers to provide color, texture, and fragrance. They just require a little more work to get them to survive from year to year and a realistic viewpoint on what's possible.

We've seen many an urban garden with rooftop plantings of perennial flowers, roses, shrubs, and trees growing successfully in containers. Here are some considerations that make this possible (for more on container gardening, go to Chapter 8):

- ✔ **The bigger the pot, the better.** Select large containers that can hold more soil. Bigger pots allow the roots to expand, hold more water and nutrients, and provide some insulation so plants will be more likely to survive the winter in appropriate climates. Make sure whatever container you use has adequate drainage holes in the bottom, and be sure to use high-quality potting soil.

- ✔ **Choose perennials wisely.** It's best to choose perennial flowers that are compact or have a mounding or clumping growth habit. These will be slower to outgrow their containers than perennials that like to spread. Choose plants that are very hardy for your area and tend to over-winter well in containers, such as bell flower, coral bells, coreopsis, daylily, dianthus, fern, hardy geranium, hosta, primrose, sedum, and yarrow. A rule of thumb for over-wintering plants in containers outdoors is to choose plants that are rated two zones hardier than your growing zone. For example, if you are in USDA hardiness zone 6, choose plants rated as winter hardy to zone 4 or lower.

  Perennial plants grown in containers will naturally grow smaller because of the limited soil mass and root growth. A perennial that normally grows 3 feet tall in the garden may only grow 1 or 2 feet tall in a container.

- ✔ **The right rose.** Select rose varieties that are low growing or compact. Hybrid tea, floribunda, and miniature roses fill the bill. Although you can grow larger roses such as climbers in containers, they will require more tending, especially in winter in cold climates.

- ✔ **Any bulb will do.** Since most bulbs are low growing, they often are perfect for containers. The only consideration is getting them to survive the winter in a cold climate. Also, they may eventually need to be replaced because they will get overcrowded or need more nutrients. We'll tackle bulbs a little later.

- ✔ **Feed them well.** Since there is a limited amount of soil in a container, you'll need to keep your perennial flowers, roses, and bulbs well fed so they flower well and are more likely to last for years in your container.

Choosing Perennials Fit for City Living

You can grow literally hundreds of different species of perennial flowers and choose from thousands of named varieties. Given the right soil, light, and exposure conditions, any perennial can grow in the city. But often the city isn't a perfect place for perennial flowers. Air pollution, foot traffic, and the ubiquitous pet waste can turn a flowering beauty into a ratty mess overnight. So we've culled through the vast list of perennial flowers to pick out some of the toughest, yet attractive ones to grow in your city garden.

We've included bloom times (so you can mix and match to have color all summer), hardiness zones (so you can select perennials adapted to your area), and growth habit (so you know how big the flower and plant might get) in the descriptions. We've also included any special features, such as fragrance or attractiveness to butterflies. This certainly isn't a definitive list, but is a great place to start.

Many perennial flowers only bloom for a few weeks during the growing season. So mix and match early, mid-, and late season flowering perennials in the same bed or container to have continuous flowering all summer.

Sun-loving perennial flowers

Here are some good choices for a sunny city setting. Remember, full sun means six to eight hours of direct light a day.

- ✔ **Aster.** *Aster species.* A favorite fall flowering perennial, asters produce daisy-like flowers in white, pink, red, or purple when most other perennials have finished flowering for the season. The plants grow 1 to 6 feet tall, depending on the variety. They grow best in areas with cool, moist summers, can grow in part shade, and the flowers attract butterflies. Hardy to zone 4.

- ✔ **Bee Balm.** *Monarda species.* A quick spreading, 2- to 4-foot-tall perennial with tube-shaped petals on rounded flower heads. Hummingbirds, butterflies, and bees love the midsummer blooming white, pink, or red flowers. The plant thrives in wet soils and can quickly spread, becoming a weed if you're not careful. Select powdery mildew-resistant varieties, such as 'Jacob Cline'. Hardy to zone 4.

- ✔ **Black-Eyed Susan.** *Rudbeckia species.* This native wildflower produces golden daisy-like flowers with dark centers in mid- to late summer on 2-to 4-foot-tall plants. Some newer varieties feature burgundy-colored petals and green centers. *Rudbeckia* self-sows readily and can spread in the garden. Hardy to zone 4.

- ✔ **Coneflower.** *Echinacea species.* This common native wildflower has become the darling of perennial flower breeders. The species have purple, white, or yellow flowers. Now there are varieties with orange, red, and golden flowers, too. All flowers have pincushion-like centers with daisy-like petals arranged around them. The plant grows 2 to 4 feet tall, is drought tolerant, and blooms midsummer until fall. Hardy to zones 3 to 5, depending on the variety.

- ✔ **Coreopsis.** *Coreopsis species.* This tough perennial grows 1 to 4 feet tall, depending on the variety, producing small yellow or red, daisy-like flowers in early summer for a number of weeks. Hardy to zone 4.

- ✔ **Daylily.** *Hemerocallis species.* If there's one flower you can plant and forget about, it's the daylily. This summer blooming perennial has 3- to

5-foot-tall flower stalks with trumpet-shaped flowers in yellow, orange, red, white, and many color variations. Depending on the variety, the flowers may be fragrant and the plant evergreen. Repeat blooming varieties such as 'Happy Returns' flower all summer long. Daylilies grow in full or part sun, tolerate adverse growing conditions and dry soil, and even are edible. Hardy to zone 3.

✔ **Geranium.** *Geranium species.* These low-growing perennials tend to stay under 2 feet tall, with a mounded growth habit, and produce white, blue, pink, or purple cup-shaped flowers in late spring and early summer. In hot climates, provide afternoon shade for the best flowering. Hardy to zone 4.

✔ **Russian Sage.** *Perovskia.* This 3- to 5-foot-tall, bushy perennial is known for its silver-green, thread-like foliage and pale purple flowers that bloom in late summer. The plant is drought tolerant and hardy to zone 5.

✔ **Salvia.** *Salvia species.* Related to the herb sage, salvia is a 2- to 4-foot-tall, clumping perennial with spikes of blue, pink, red, or white flowers in mid-summer. The plant tolerates heat and dry soils and is hardy to zone 4.

✔ **Sedum.** *Sedum.* This succulent can grow from 6 inches to 2 feet tall, depending on the variety. The clusters of pink, white, or burgundy flowers bloom in late summer and fall. Sedums do best in well-drained soil. Hardy to zone 4.

✔ **Shasta Daisy.** *Leucanthemum species.* This classic white daisy produces prolific blooms in early to mid-summer. Plants range in size from 1 to 4 feet tall, depending on the variety. The flowers are perfect for cutting and attract butterflies. Hardy to zone 4.

✔ **Siberian Iris.** *Iris siberica.* Although tall bearded irises are common in many perennial gardens for their stately flowers in spring, Siberian irises are easier to care for. They grow in 2- to 4-foot-tall clumps, producing white, purple, blue, or yellow flowers in late spring. They need dividing every few years to keep them flowering. See more about dividing perennials later in "Divide and Multiply." Hardy to zone 4.

✔ **Summer Phlox.** *Phlox paniculata.* This 2- to 4-foot-tall perennial features clusters of white, red, pink, or purple fragrant flowers loved by butterflies, hummingbirds, and bees. It blooms in mid- to late summer. Select powdery mildew-resistant varieties such as 'David'. Hardy to zone 3.

✔ **Yarrow.** *Achillea species.* This 1- to 4-foot-tall perennial is perfect for many city soils and climates. It tolerates drought and low-fertility soils, blooming from midsummer until fall. Varieties produce flowers in many colors, including red, pink, yellow, and white. The flowers are good for cutting, butterflies love them, and the plant spreads readily in the garden. Hardy to zone 3.

Shade-loving perennial flowers

Shadows are everywhere in the city, so choosing perennial flowers that tolerate shade is often important for city gardeners. The plants listed below will tolerate part or full shade. Many are grown as much for their striking leaf colors and textures as for their flowers. Give some of these a try in your urban garden.

- **Astilbe.** *Astilbe species.* This large group of shade-loving perennials includes 6-inch to 4-foot-tall plants. Many feature finely cut leaves and white, pink, or red flowers in mid-summer. Plants tolerate wet soil and are hardy to zone 4.

- **Bell Flower.** *Campanula species.* This variable perennial has species that grow only 6 inches tall and some that grow as high as 5 feet tall. Most fall in the 1- to 3-foot range and produce white, blue, or purple, bell-like flowers in summer. They grow well in light shade and are hardy to zone 3.

- **Bleeding Heart.** *Dicentra species.* This shrubby, 1- to 2-foot-tall perennial produces red, pink, or white heart-shaped flowers in spring in light shade. The top of the plant dies back in most areas by midsummer, so be ready to plant annuals or have other perennials growing nearby to fill in the space. Hardy to zone 3.

- **Coral Bells.** *Heuchera species.* This 1- to 2-foot-tall plant is known as much for its multicolored foliage as its white, pink, or red airy flower spikes. The foliage can be burgundy, variegated, yellow, or lime green, depending on the variety. It blooms in spring but, like hosta, the foliage adds color to the yard all summer. Hardy to zone 3.

- **Dead nettle.** *Lamium.* A low-growing groundcover, this perennial features silver-variegated foliage and white, red, or pink flowers in early summer. The plant spreads, but isn't invasive. Hardy to zone 4.

- **Ferns.** Many species. If you can't grow anything else in shade, try ferns. There are many different types growing from 1 to 5 feet tall. The Japanese Painted Fern has interesting green leaves with silver and red markings. Some ferns, such as the ostrich fern, produce edible shoots called fiddleheads. Ferns don't flower, but provide a green backdrop to other plants. They tolerate wet soils and are hardy to zone 4, depending on the species.

- **Foxglove.** *Digitalis.* This spiky perennial produces white, blue, red, yellow, or pink flowers in early summer in light shade. Plants do best in moist soils. Foxgloves are short-lived, but self-sow readily, so new plants emerge in late summer in the garden and flower the following spring and early summer. Hardy to zone 4.

- **Hosta.** *Hosta species.* Probably the best known shade perennial, hosta plants grow 6 inches to 3 feet tall, depending on the variety. Hostas are distinguished by their uniquely shaped leaves in colors such as blue-green, pale yellow, and yellow striped. Spikes of white or blushed pink flowers emerge in summer, and some varieties are fragrant. Hardy to zone 3.

- **Lily-of-the-valley.** *Convallaria.* A classic, low-growing groundcover that thrives in shade, it has broad green leaves and spikes of intensely fragrant, delicate white or pink flowers in spring. Hardy to zone 4.

Some groundcovers, such as lily-of-the-valley, can become invasive, so be sure to plant them where they can't spread into other plantings, public land, or your neighbor's yard. These are best grown in containers if you need to contain their spread.

- **Ornamental grasses.** Many species. While ornamental grasses love to grow in full sun, many can grow in part shade, so we included them here. Ornamental grasses display grass blades in a variety of forms and colors, along with attractive flower stalks in fall. Some types, such as Japanese blood grass, have burgundy-colored foliage, while zebra grass has striped colored leaves. Plants can be 1 foot tall and mounded to 8 feet tall and sprawling. Look for varieties that fit in your location. The flower heads not only adorn the garden in fall but can be used as cut flowers and remain on the plant all winter, adding interest in a season with little else flowering. Hardiness depends on the species; most are hardy to zones 4 to 9.

Growing and Maintaining Perennial Flowers

Give perennial flowers the sun, water, and room that they need and they will reward you with years of blooms. You just need to keep a few things in mind in order to get the most out of your perennials.

General care and maintenance

Adding some compost around the plants each spring is probably enough to fertilizer your perennials. If you have specific plants that are yellowing or growing slowly, consider adding a balanced organic fertilizer in spring as well. Keep plants weeded and mulched for optimum health. (We talk more about weeding and mulching in Chapter 18.) Deadheading spent blossoms not only makes perennials look better, it may encourage them to flower a second time later in the season.

Cut back herbaceous perennials to the ground in fall after the foliage yellows to clean up the garden and remove any pests, and you'll be ready to go next spring.

Providing a little extra support

Tall growing perennials may need some staking or caging to keep them upright, especially in windy locations (see Figure 15-1). Choose from growth supports, cages, and stakes to keep tall perennials such as peonies, delphiniums, and phlox vertical. Place the supports on the plants early in the season so as not to harm the foliage later on. When the foliage is about 1 foot tall, wrap chicken wire around bushy perennials such as peonies or place grow-through supports over tall stalky perennials such as delphiniums. The plants grow through the chicken wire and the supports disappear as the foliage covers, it but will support the heavy flowers that will come a few weeks later.

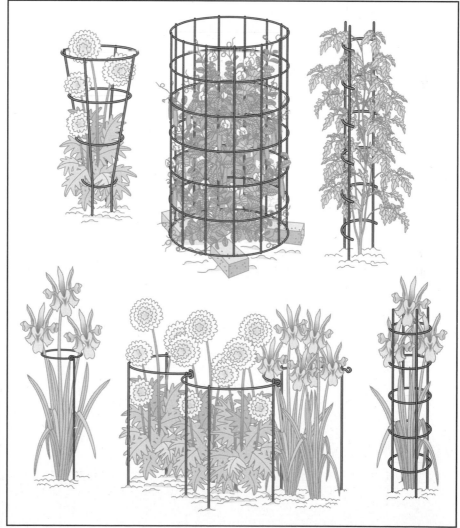

Figure 15-1: Support perennial flowers to keep stalk upright during windy weather.

Illustration by Ron Hildebrand.

Divide and multiply

One of the great things about growing perennial flowers is many of them grow so quickly you can make new plants from the old ones without skipping a flowering beat. The easiest way to do this with many perennials is to divide them. *Dividing* means to cut your clump of flowers into sections to replant them elsewhere in the garden or give them away. Some of the easiest perennial flowers to divide are daylilies, hosta, bee balm, ornamental grasses, Siberian iris, dead nettle, lily-of-the-valley, ferns, aster, sedum, and hardy geranium. Here's how to make the great divide.

1. **Choose the time.**

   In general, divide spring blooming flowers in late summer and fall blooming perennials in spring. Choose a cloudy, cool day, if possible, for dividing your plants to reduce transplant stress. Moisten the ground for easier digging if it hasn't rained lately.

2. **Cut back the tops.**

   If dividing in late summer, cut back the tops to 6 inches from the ground. The disturbed roots won't be able to support all that top growth, so this will bring the newly divided plant into balance. If dividing in spring, divide as soon as you see growth emerging from the soil.

3. **Dig it all up.**

   Dig up the entire clump with a sharp spade and place it on a tarp. Clean the soil off the roots with a stream of water from the hose, and look for where the clump can naturally be divided into new plants.

4. **Pull it apart.**

   Gently tease apart the new plants with your hands. For some thickly matted perennials that are hard to pull apart by hand, such as ornamental grasses and Siberian irises, simply cut through the clump with your spade to divide it into 1-foot-diameter pieces.

5. **Replant.**

   Discard insect-infested, diseased, small, or unusable pieces and replant the new divisions in compost-amended soil in a location with similar growing conditions as the mother plant. Pot up the extra divisions and give them away — a great way to make friends!

Enjoying La Vie en Rose

Everyone loves roses, but many gardeners are intimidated at the thought of growing them. They hear stories about roses being fussy about fertilizers, needing extra water, and having all kinds of pest problems. Don't let roses scare you off! By selecting the right types for your location and climate, and choosing varieties that are disease-resistant and fit in an urban setting, you can successfully incorporate roses into your city gardens and containers.

Selecting the best city roses

If you have adequate room, full sun, and well-drained fertile soil, you can grow most any rose that's adapted to your climate in your city yard. However, in most urban areas, space is often at a premium, so selecting roses that will stay small in stature, or that grow more up than out, is important.

Here's a rundown of some of the best roses to grow in a small-space urban environment. These are ever-blooming roses (they bloom all summer long), get few diseases, and generally require little care unless otherwise noted. Always check the rose varieties you're buying to be sure they are hardy for your area.

- ✔ **Old-fashioned roses.** Many types of old-fashioned roses are famous for their interesting flower shapes, fragrance, and plant sizes. Look for old-fashioned types that are hardy in your area. Also, some varieties, such as the Apothecary rose (*Rosa gallica*), *Alfred De Dalmas* moss rose, and some of David Austin's dwarf polyantha English roses, such as 'Baby Faurax', are naturally compact and perfect for a small-space garden.

- ✔ **Shrub roses.** A number of new lines of modern landscape or shrub roses feature ever-blooming flowers on 2- to 4-foot-tall wide plants that are tough, disease resistant, and hardy. Some of the best ones for small spaces include the Drift rose series such as 'Apricot Drift' and 'Coral Drift', the Town and Country series, such as 'Cambridge' and 'Cape Cod', and the Knockout series such as 'Pink Knockout'. There are groundcover-type shrub roses, such as the Flowering Carpet roses, that only grow 1 to 2 feet tall but spread like a groundcover, creating a mat of flowers.

- ✔ **Climbing roses.** When in doubt about space, grow vertically. We talk a lot about vertical gardening in Chapter 10. Climbing roses are a great way to have roses in a small-space garden. Some classic varieties include 'New Dawn', 'Cecile Brunner', and 'William Baffin'.

- ✔ **Tree roses.** Now here's a rose that looks like it was a Dr. Seuss invention. Tree or standard roses are grafted roses with a tall, thin stem and a clump of rose flowers on top. They look like the poodles of the rose world! Some varieties grow 4 to 6 feet tall while others only 1 foot tall. Their tall, narrow growth habit makes them perfect for small spaces or even containers. However, they are more sensitive to cold and wind in winter and require more care than the other rose types mentioned. Many popular hybrid rose varieties are grafted onto tree rose rootstocks.

- ✔ **Miniature roses.** Miniature roses were meant for city gardeners. They only grow a few feet tall and wide, and fit in the front of a flower border

or container. 'Sun Sprinkles' and 'Child's Play' are award-winning miniature rose varieties.

✔ **Hybrid Tea and Floribunda roses.** These are the most popular and
most abundant roses available. Hybrid tea roses can grow to 4 feet tall
and wide, while floribunda roses tend to produce clusters of flowers on
smaller bushes. 'Day Breaker' and 'Honey Perfume' are two shorter flori-
bundas to try.

Growing and caring for roses

Even if you select some of the more carefree rose types mentioned above,
you'll still need to do some basic care of your rose bushes. Roses do require
attention to planting, and we cover how to plant roses in Chapter 6. Once
they are in the ground, flowering their heads off and growing up a storm,
they'll need other care to keep them happy. If you live in a cold area or are
pushing the envelope by growing a rose variety that's marginally hardy for
your area, we'll talk about ways to protect your roses in winter.

Feeding and watering

Think of all but the hybrid tea, floribunda, tree, and miniature roses as small
shrubs. How you feed and water them is similar to growing a shrub. Each
spring remove any mulch left around the rose and add a 1- to 2-inch-thick
layer of compost. Then add a 2- to 3-inch-thick layer of mulch around the
plants, and they are generally set for the season.

With hybrid tea, floribunda, tree, and miniature roses, you'll need to be a
little more diligent in terms of fertilizing. These roses love food, so make
monthly applications of an all-purpose rose food. Organic gardeners may
choose products such as alfalfa meal, cottonseed meal, fish meal, and rock
phosphate to give their plants a boost.

Roses love coffee! Yes, roses love the high-octane, premium coffee. Actually
they like the dried coffee grounds, not for the caffeine but the nitrogen. Add
one cup of grounds around the drip line of the plant in spring and again one
month later to give your plants a boost.

Water roses as you would shrubs. It's better to water deeply and infrequently, rather than shallowly and frequently. Once or twice a week, soak the
rose roots to a depth of 8 inches to encourage vigorous growth.

Pruning

Pruning roses seems mysterious to many gardeners. For most roses, it's
really simple. Shrub, landscape, miniature, and old-fashioned roses just
need pruning in late winter to help shape the bush, remove dead or diseased
canes, crossing canes that are shading other canes, or thin, spindly growth.
It's best to remove canes to the ground, versus snipping the tips.

Hybrid tea and floribunda roses should be pruned in early spring once it's clear where any winter injury occurred. Prune to just below any injured sections on the canes. It's best to prune hybrid teas to three to five main canes coming off the crown or base of the plant. Remove thin and spindly growth. Cut back the remaining canes by one-third. This stimulates lots of new growth and flowers.

Tree roses should be pruned in early spring to remove any errant growing canes, suckers from the base of the plant, and shoots along the tall stem.

Climbing roses need a little different care. Prune these in spring, removing root suckers and training the main structural branches to fit the trellis. Once that's done, cut back the lateral branches growing off the main branches to 6 to 12 inches long. Climbing roses produce the most flowers off these lateral branches.

Providing winter protection

While most modern shrub and landscape roses are tough as nails and don't need any winter protection, hybrid tea, floribunda, miniatures, tree, and climbers do need extra protection, especially when growing in areas where the variety of rose is marginally hardy.

The easiest way to protect hybrid tea, floribunda, and miniature roses is to wait until after a few hard freezes in fall and then pour a 1-foot-deep mound of bark mulch over each plant. The bark mulch is a perfect winter insulator. It allows air to pass through around the rose crown so it doesn't rot, yet protects the plants from fierce, drying winter winds. If you wait until late fall, the mice and voles have found other homes, so they won't take up residence in your rose mound.

Tree roses should be wrapped in burlap in late fall to protect the stems and tops from winter cold. If they are in containers, move the entire container to a protected location.

Climbing roses should normally be fine without protection unless they are growing in a location where they are marginally hardy. Then they also need to be wrapped in burlap in late fall, gently bent down to the ground and anchored there with tent stakes and buried in mulch to protect them. If the canes die back on climbing roses, you'll get few flowers the next year.

Lighting Up Your Garden with Bulbs

Planting spring or summer flowering bulbs is an act of faith. You plant these months before they emerge and then you wait. Once the weather, soil, and temperature conditions are right, the bulbs emerge from the soil, much to the delight and often surprise of the gardener. We often forget where we've planted bulbs in fall; in spring, we're pleasantly surprised as they pop up and flower.

Bulbs add yet more color to the urban garden without taking up lots of space. They are considered perennials, but some, such as tulips and hyacinths, will eventually stop flowering and need to be replaced or replanted after a few years. Others, such as dahlias and gladiolus, should be treated like annual flowers and replanted each spring.

Finding a spot for bulbs

Bulbs grow best in full sun in well-drained, fertile soil. However, the beauty of the spring flowering bulbs is they will emerge early and often flower before the leaves of deciduous trees have emerged in spring. This allows you to plant them in areas that are shady all summer and still enjoy your tulip and daffodil flower show. Consider planting spring flowering bulbs in between existing trees and shrubs, in the perennial flower garden, in the annual flower garden, or even in containers. Bulbs in containers won't last multiple seasons, but they will be a bright spot in your yard for that year.

Consider planting summer flowering bulbs, such as Oriental and Asiatic lilies, in among other perennials, or create a stunning display of dahlias or gladiolus in a bed of their own. These summer bloomers also make great cut flowers, so consider planting them out of the way where you can harvest them for the table all summer.

Bulbs look their best when planted in groups. We cover bulb planting basics in Chapter 6.

Finding the best spring flowering bulbs for the city

From the smallest snowdrop to largest daffodil, there is a wide range of spring flowering bulbs that can grace your garden. Flowering bulbs are great for the space-starved urban garden because they can be tucked into small spaces, between plants or even around shrubs and flower. You can plant them close to perennial flowers without worrying about the plants being crowded. Often the bulbs will finish blooming before the perennial flowers get large sized. Look for varieties adapted to your area.

Widely adapted spring bloomers include snow drops (*Galanthus*), crocus scilla, grape hyacinth (*Muscari*), hyacinth, iris, daffodils, narcissus, species tulips, and regular tulips.

In warm winter areas (zones 9 and 10), try some more unusual bulbs, such as freesia, Persian buttercup, and lily of the Nile (*Agapanthus*).

Determining the best summer flowering bulbs for the city

These summer bloomers complement the perennial garden and provide cut flowers for arrangement. Some, such as the canna lily, are wildly colorful while others, like Oriental lilies, have a fragrance that's almost overpowering. They provide beauty and height to the perennial flower garden and some, such as callas and cannas, give your garden a tropical feel and look.

Widely adapted summer blooming bulbs include Oriental and Asiatic lilies, gladiolus, canna lilies, calla lilies, caladium, tuberous begonias, and dahlias.

 While bulbous lilies are hardy throughout most of the country, many of the other summer blooming bulbs are not. Some will only reliably return the next season in warm winter areas. In colder climates than those listed, dahlias (zone 9), gladiolus (zone 9), canna lilies (zone 7), calla lilies (zone 8), and begonias (zone 9) will need to be dug in fall before a hard frost and stored indoors in a protected location in winter. We'll talk more about the proper storage for bulbs in the next section. They can be replanted next spring in the garden. Of course, if you don't want to bother with digging and storing them, you can treat these bulbs as annuals, allow them to die in winter, and replant new ones in spring.

Caring for bulbs

Not all bulbs can be treated as perennials. Some, such as snow drops, scilla, daffodils, Oriental lilies, Asiatic lilies, and species tulips, will reliably return to flower and actually will slowly spread throughout your garden each year. Others, such as hybrid tulips, hyacinths, dahlias, canna lilies, and gladiolus, will either die out after a few years and need to be dug up and the bed replanted or will only last one season.

For those bulbs treated as perennials, maintenance couldn't be easier. Simply spread a thin layer of compost over the areas where they grow in early spring as they emerge, enjoy the flowers, and then cut back the foliage once it yellows in early summer. For summer flowering bulbs such as Oriental lilies, mulch them to prevent weed growth and conserve soil moisture.

You may notice that your tulips or hyacinths aren't flowering as strongly as in the past or have stopped flowering altogether. Some types of tulips, such as 'Darwin' and triumph hybrids just don't last long in the garden. When flowering declines after a few years, dig up and replace the bulbs. Other kinds of bulbs can be renewed when they decline due to overcrowding. Dig up the bulbs after the foliage has yellowed. Check the dug bulbs and remove any offsets or baby bulbs clinging to the main bulb. Redig the planting hole, add a handful of a bulb fertilizer, such as bulb booster, and replant.

Caging your bulbs

If you notice chewing damage on your bulbs, it might be from mice, rats, or voles. You can mix dried egg shells, diatomaceous earth, or sharp sand in the planting hole to deter them. But to really protect your prized bulbs, consider building a wire cage, sinking it into the planting hole, and planting your bulbs in the cage. Make sure the cage has small holes that these rodents can't squeeze through, but the top is open enough for the foliage to grow through.

When tender bulbs, such as dahlias, gladiolus, and canna lilies, are grown in a climate where they are hardy, treat them like a regular perennial flower, cutting back the foliage in fall and adding compost in spring. However, if you're growing these bulbs in a climate too cold for them to over-winter, dig the bulbs up and store them each fall. After frost has killed the foliage, dig up the bulbs, remove all but 6 inches of the foliage, knock off some of the soil from the roots, and let them dry in a well-ventilated garage, shed, or basement out of direct sun. After a few weeks, cut off the remaining foliage to just above the bulb, remove the remaining soil, and store them in a slatted container or basket filled with slightly moistened peat moss or sand. Place them in a dark location with 35- to 50-degree temperatures for the winter. In spring, plant them outdoors once all danger of frost has passed.

Some taller bulbs, such as Oriental lilies and gladiolus, will benefit from staking. Staking not only keeps the flower stalk upright so it's more beautiful, but the flowers stay off the soil where they can get damaged from splashing rain, insects, and disease.

Chapter 16

Growing a Tree . . . in Brooklyn

. . . .

In This Chapter

▶ Finding all the right reasons to grow a tree in the city

▶ Selecting a good deciduous and evergreen tree and shrub for your yard

▶ Planting, fertilizing, and caring for your trees and shrubs

▶ Selecting fruit trees and berry bushes in the city

▶ Maintaining the fruit patch

. . . .

You may think that a whole chapter on trees and shrubs is out of place in a book on urban gardening. After all, where are you going to fit that redwood in your postage-stamp-sized yard?

But trees and shrubs do have a critical place in an urban environment, and there are many that will fit in some pretty small spaces. Not only do they provide shade from the summer heat, but they help clean the air, reduce storm water runoff, and provide habitat for wildlife. And if you're going to grow trees and shrubs in the city you might as well look at growing some edible types, too. Fruit trees and berry bushes fulfill multiple roles in the city, providing beauty, functionality, and delicious fruits to eat.

In this chapter, we talk about the right tree and shrubs for your yard and give you the knowledge you need to keep them thriving under less than ideal conditions.

Selecting City-Friendly Trees

There are two main types of trees and shrubs: deciduous and evergreen.

Deciduous trees lose their leaves in fall. Some are strictly grown for their foliage, while other types have a dazzling flower season. Some deciduous trees have great fall foliage color, while some have exfoliating or colorful bark.

Evergreen trees can have needles like pines and spruce or broad leaves, like a rhododendron. They hold onto their foliage all season long. They are an unchanging feature of your yard, so place your evergreens before your deciduous trees in the yard and build from there.

The best deciduous trees

As you decide what kind of tree to plant, you'll need to keep a few things in mind before buying:

- ✔ **Check for the ultimate size of the tree.** Planting a tree that will outgrow its space, crowd a walkway, or interfere with power lines will just be a frustration down the road.

- ✔ **Check a tree's hardiness and heat zone ratings to make sure it's adapted to your area.** Use the USDA map we showed in Chapter 3 to find your area's zone ratings.

- ✔ **Check for any factors that may not make it the perfect tree or shrub in your yard.** Varieties of some trees, such as crabapples and horse chestnuts, drop lots of inedible fruit or nuts that can make a mess in the yard. Other trees have roots that can lift and crack pavement and sidewalks.

Deciduous trees (those that lose their leaves in fall) are perfect plants for balancing city temperatures. When planted on the south or west side of a building, a large deciduous tree provides shade in summer, reducing air-conditioning costs. However, in fall when its leaves drop, the same tree allows winter sunlight in to warm the building, reducing heating expenses. We should be paying the trees for their service!

Following are some of the best deciduous tree choices for a city environment. These trees have a better tolerance of poor soils, cramped growing conditions, windy corridors, and air pollution. Some are large, but most are shorter trees that do well in small spaces.

- ✔ **American Hornbeam** (*Carpinus caroliana*). Also called ironwood or musclewood for its long, sinewy trunk, this native tree tolerates shade and flooding while growing slowly to 30 feet tall in an upright, pyramidal shape. It's hardy in zones 3–9.

- ✔ **Chinese Pistache** (*Pistacia chinensis*). This spreading shade tree grows to 40 feet tall with stunning yellow, orange, or red autumn color. It's drought tolerant and hardy in zones 7–9.

- ✔ **Crabapples** (*Malus species*).There are hundreds of varieties of crabapples to choose from, with different flower colors (white, pink, or red), fruit sizes (mostly less than 2 inches in diameter), and tree shapes (round, upright, and squat). Many varieties only grow to 15 feet tall or less, making them great for small spaces. They are hardy in zones 4–8. Look for diseases-resistant varieties such as 'Prairie Fire' if powdery mildew or apple scab is a problem in your area.

✔ **Crape Myrtle** (*Lagerstromia indica*). This summer blooming, small (10–20 feet tall) tree is multi-trunked and hardy in zones 7–9. The trunk has colorful, exfoliating bark. It's adapted to hot, dry climates. Look for disease-resistant varieties such as 'Cherokee'.

✔ **Ginkgo** (*Ginkgo biloba*). This ancient trees is hardy in zones 4–9. It has interesting-shaped leaves and branches. Ginkgo has separate male and female trees. Always get a male tree because the female trees produce odorous fruit that drops and rots on the ground. It's well adapted to urban environments, grows 50 feet tall, has colorful fall foliage, and is usually pest free.

✔ **Japanese Tree Lilac** (*Syringa reticulata*). This carefree tree grows 25 feet tall with an oval crown. It fits perfectly into urban small spaces. It has few pests, tolerates part shade, and forms billowy white flowers in early summer. It's hardy in zones 3–7.

✔ **Japanese Zelkova** (*Zelkova serrata*). A good shade tree if you have the room, zelkova reaches to 40 feet tall and has a vase-like shape reminiscent of an American elm. It is fast growing and has colorful fall foliage. 'Green Vase' is a shorter selection. It's hardy in zones 5–8.

✔ **Maple** (*Acer species*). Maples are a huge group of trees, and many are large in stature. Some, such as sugar maples (*Acer saccharum*), have glorious fall foliage, while others, such as the Japanese maple (*Acer palmatum*), are beautiful small specimen trees in the yard. They are widely adapted, growing in USDA zones 4–9, depending on the selection. They don't like hot summers or mild winters. For city plantings, choose maples that are tolerant of city soil, water, and pollution conditions, such as hedge maple (*Acer campestre*), which grows to 20 feet tall and is hardy in zones 5–8.

✔ **Oaks** (*Quercus species*). There are many different types of oaks. Many are large trees growing to 40 to 50 feet tall and hardy to zones 3–8, such as red oak (*Q. rubra*). Others are evergreen, such as the southern live oak (*Q. virginiana*) and adapted to warmer climates (zones 7–9). The bur oak (*Q. macrocarpa*) was chosen urban tree of the year by the *Journal to The Society of Municipal Arborists*. It's tolerant of poor soils and urban stress, but it does need room to grow to a height of 50 feet. It's hardy in zones 3–8.

✔ **Serviceberry** (*Amelanchier species*). This single or multiple-trunked native tree has white flowers in spring; small black, edible berries in summer; orange leaves in fall; and interesting bark in winter. It grows 25 feet tall and is hardy in zones 3–8.

The giving tree: Enjoying the benefits of trees in your urban garden

Trees and shrubs are beautiful additions to a yard, forming the "bones" of the garden, the permanent structural plantings around which you add flowers and edibles. As attractive as many trees and shrubs are, especially when they are flowering, there are other benefits from growing them in the city.

✔ **Trees and shrubs are protectors.** Trees and shrubs can be used as screens from roads, neighbors, buildings, or just the outside world. They can create the perfect hidden nook for a retreat or for entertaining. They also protect your house from strong winds and the hot summer sun. They are like your personal bodyguard.

✔ **Trees and shrubs bring you money.** It's estimated that a well-landscaped yard can increase your property value by 10 percent to 15 percent. Mature trees and shrubs are definitely assets when it comes to the worth of your home.

✔ **Trees and shrubs add beauty.** Flowering magnolias, azaleas, hydrangeas, and lilacs are among the many trees and shrubs that add color and beauty to the yard. Even if they aren't blooming, the leaves and bark can offer interesting colors and textures.

✔ **Trees and shrubs make a cleaner environment.** Trees and shrubs clean the air of pollutants and dust. Their roots hold soil in place and reduce storm water runoff. Their branches and fruits house and feed wildlife. They truly are giving trees.

Evergreen tree options

If you're looking to block a view or create a more sheltered garden area, you can't beat an evergreen tree. Most evergreen trees grow huge, so you'll need some space to grow these to maturity. However, there are some dwarf selections that we highlight for the space-starved urban lot. Following are our top picks:

✔ **Arborvitae** (*Thuja species*). Most selections are hardy in zones 3–8. Although they can grow large, arborvitae are easy to prune into a hedge or narrow shape. Look for the tall-growing arborvitae, such as 'Green Giant,' for screening.

✔ **Fir** (*Abies species*). Thought of as the classic Christmas tree, fir trees can grow large in any environment and are hardy in zones 4–8. The best for a city is the white fir (*Abies concolor*) for its tolerance of poor soils and urban pollution. Look for dwarf selections.

✔ **Pine** (*Pinus species*). Most pines are large trees not adapted to small spaces. However, a few are good choices for larger yards in urban areas. A mugo pine tree (*Pinus mugo*) is a small tree or large shrub that can grow 15 to 20 feet tall. Its rounded shape fills in a screen well. There are dwarf versions that grow like a small shrub. It's hardy in zones 3–8.

✔ **Spruce** (*Picea species*). Many gardeners are familiar with Colorado Blue Spruce, Norway spruce, and other large-growing spruce selections. However, there are shorter versions for urban areas such as the Dwarf Alberta Spruce (*Picea glauca conica*), which grows slowly to 6 feet tall. It's hardy in zones 3–8, but may need protection from cold winter winds.

Growing Some Shrubbery

Trees take up space in the landscape, so the choices for city dwellers can be limited. However, shrubs are much more diverse. You can select shrubs as small as 1 foot tall to ones that grow more than 15 feet tall. There are colorful flowering shrubs and formidable evergreen shrubs. When selecting shrubs for your yard consider the function, ultimate size, and foliage and flower color and texture.

Looking at ways to use shrubs in your yard

Shrubs are great at filling in space, providing a backdrop, and adding a bold statement to a yard. Since shrubs are long-term propositions and can be expensive to purchase, considerable thought should go into what to buy and where to place it. First, think about the function of that shrub in the landscape. Here are some possible uses for your shrubs.

✔ **Show shrubs.** Some shrubs just live to bloom and put on a spectacular show. A planting of azaleas can be breathtaking when in full bloom in spring. If you're planting shrubs for their flower show remember their season of bloom, colors, and what else may be blooming near them at the same time. It's best to let them have the stage and then surround these show stoppers with other plants that bloom either earlier or later in the season. Consider repeating a favorite shrub in your yard as an accent plant and as a way to pull the landscape together as long as its growing in the right sun and soil conditions.

✔ **Foundation shrubs.** These are the functional shrubs. Foundation shrubs are planted around the foundation of buildings to hide their concrete underpinnings. Yews, junipers, and spirea are some common foundation shrubs. While their function it to cover up unsightly views, be creative about mixing and matching foundation shrubs that are easy to grow, yet provide some color and texture to the yard.

Weeping evergreens

If you really love your evergreens, want them for their beautiful needles and textures, but are not concerned about their functionality as a screen, try the weeping versions. Plant breeders have selected a number of weeping evergreen trees with a cascading habit that stay relatively small. They add a touch of evergreen to your yard or garden without taking up lots of vertical space, although some can grow quite wide with age. Some of the most noteworthy are weeping Norway spruce (*Picea abies pendula*), weeping white pine (*Pinus strobus pendula*), and weeping cedar (*Cedrus deodora pendula*). You can even try a deciduous weeping larch (*Larix pendula*), which loses its needles in winter.

For more ideas for good urban trees, check out the Urban Tree Foundation, `www.urbantree.org`.

✔ **Barrier shrubs.** Sometimes you'd just like to keep animals and people at bay. There are shrubs with thorns, such as barberries, that create a natural barrier to outsiders, protecting your yard while not seeming as imposing as a fence.

✔ **Hedge shrubs.** Certainly some of these shrubs, such as lilac and forsythia, can be used to build a hedge to define your yard, but they also can be used inside your yard to create garden rooms. This can make your yard feel larger and allow you to create different plantings in each room. Boxwood, euonymus, and privet are some of the shrubs that can be tightly trimmed to create these internal walls.

Discovering some great city shrubs

The key to selecting great city shrubs is to find ones adapted to your area, growing under the right sun and water conditions, and able to withstand the vagaries of urban living. It's best to visit your local garden center or check out what your neighbors are growing before slipping out to purchase a city shrub.

In the following list, we've selected some of the toughest shrubs for your yard and indicate which are sun or shade lovers, their hardiness, their size, and outstanding features.

✔ **Azaleas and Rhododendrons** (*Rhododendron species*). Rhododendrons and azaleas come in evergreen and deciduous species with hardiness ranging from zones 4–8, depending on the selection. This huge family of plants grows best in part shade on acidic soil. Azaleas tend to be smaller shrubs with spring flowers in colors such as white, pink, red, orange, yellow, and purple. Some rhododendrons can grow into small trees, with large spring flowers in colors such as white, red, and purple. They are not as well adapted to heat as azaleas.

- **Barberry** (*Berberis species*). Barberries can be evergreen or deciduous, depending on the species. Known for their thorny stems and bright red berries, barberries make a good low or medium-sized barrier hedge (4 to 6 feet tall) when grown together. Selections are hardy to zones 4–9. Barberries grow in part to full sun and are tough plants ready to adapt to urban conditions. 'Atropurpurea' is a variety that features reddish-purple-colored leaves. Japanese barberry (*Berberis thungbergii*) is considered invasive in many states.

- **Boxwood** (*Buxus species*). This evergreen is one the best shrubs to grow if you want to create a tightly clipped, manicured look. It is often grown as a low hedge dividing a garden into separate rooms. Boxwood's bright green leaves respond well to frequent trimming. Most selections are hardy in zones 5–8. 'Green Beauty' is a variety that stays bright green all winter.

- **Camellia** (*Camellia species*). These large, evergreen shrubs produce colorful red, pink, or white flowers in late winter in shady conditions. The plants have large glossy leaves and can grow up to 15 feet tall. Most species are hardy in zones 8–10, but *Camellia oleifera* is hardy to zone 6.

- **Cotoneaster** (*Cotoneaster species*). Cotoneaster has evergreen and deciduous selections ranging from low-growing ground covers to tall plants. These tough plants are widely adapted, with species hardy to zones 4–9. Most produce white flowers and classic red berries. Spreading cotoneaster (*C. divaricatus*) is a prolific berry producer.

- **Euonymus** (*Euonymus species*). There are evergreen and deciduous types of euonymus on the market. The evergreen types are mostly grown for their green, white and green, or yellow and green foliage. These creepers can climb walls and fences, making them useful as screening plants in the city. Deciduous types are hardy in zones 4–7, while evergreen types are hardy in zones 5–9. Evergreen types can be susceptible to powdery mildew and scale insects. Both evergreen and deciduous species are considered invasive in some parts of the country.

- **Flowering plum and cherry** (*Prunus species*). There are many selections of evergreen and deciduous shrubs and small trees in this group. They can grow 4 to 15 feet tall, depending on the selection. They are noted for their white flowers in spring, followed by red fruit in summer and fall. Evergreen types are hardy to zones 8–9, while deciduous selections are hardy to zones 3–7. These plants can be grown as part of a foundation planting, hedgerow, or as a specimen tree in the lawn. Some, such as 'Nanking' cherry (*P. tomentosa*), produce edible fruits good for making jams and jellies.

- **Fothergilla** (*Fothergilla species*). Fothergilla is a deciduous flowering shrub that offers three season of interest. It grows 3 to 8 feet tall, depending on the species, produces fragrant white flowers in spring, blue-green oval leaves in summer, and bright yellow, orange, and red foliage in fall. Give it moist, slightly acidic soil and dappled to full sun and it's happy. It can be grown as an informal hedge. It's hardy in zones 5–8.

✔ **Holly** (*Ilex species*). Hollies can be evergreen or deciduous, depending on the species. They are noted for their bright colorful berries in fall and winter. There are selections hardy to zones 5–9. Most have separate male and female plants; both sexes are need in order for the female plant to produce berries. Hollies grow well in part to full sun and like slightly acid soil. Compact selections grow only 3 to 5 feet tall while others can grow up to 15 feet tall and wide. 'China Boy' and 'China Girl' are two of the most cold-hardy evergreen hollies available.

✔ **Hydrangea** (*Hydrangea species*). There are a number of different species of this deciduous shrub with large leaves and late summer flowers. Most are hardy in zones 4–9. Low-growing big leaf hydrangea (*H. macrophylla*) features blue, white, or pink flowers; flower color often changes with the acidity of the soil. Panicle hydrangeas (*H. paniculata*) come in a range of sizes, from 2- to 3-foot-tall dwarf selections to 8- to 10-foot-tall shrubs, with white blushing to pink flowers in late summer. Oakleaf hydrangea (*H. quercifolia*) has large, pyramidal, white flower heads and attractive red fall foliage.

✔ **Junipers** (*Juniperus species*). This is perhaps the most versatile group of evergreen shrubs available. Selections range from ground covers such as 'Blue Rug' to small trees such as the Rocky Mountain juniper (*J. scopulorum*). They tolerate poor soil, drought, and adverse conditions, and the sharp needles come in colors ranging from blue green to gold. Junipers can take some pruning but look beautiful in their natural shape. There are species hardy from zones 3–9.

✔ **Lilac** (*Syringa species*). This group of deciduous shrubs is known for its amazingly fragrant spring blooms in colors ranging from white to purple. Hardy in zones 3 to 7, plants can grow 6 to 15 feet tall, depending on the species. Look for varieties that resist powdery mildew disease. *Ceanothus* or wild lilac is a group of evergreen lilacs with attractive lilac-like flowers, but they don't have the same fragrance. They are a good substitute for common lilacs in warm areas (zones 8–10).

✔ **Oleander** (*Nerium oleander*). This evergreen shrub can grow up to 20 feet tall but is easily trimmed to a shorter height. It flowers all summer in colors ranging from white to yellow to red. Oleander loves the heat and dry conditions and is tolerant of urban pollution. It is hardy in zones 8–10.

The stems, flowers, leaves, and roots of oleander are toxic if ingested. Avoid planting oleander where kids or pets might accidentally eat some of the leaves. Don't burn oleander trimmings because the smoke is toxic as well.

✔ **Photinia** (*Photinia species*). Photinias are warm-climate evergreens that grow up to 15 feet tall if not pruned regularly. They are hardy in zones 7–10. They have white flowers in spring and black berries in fall.

✔ **Potentilla** (*Potentilla species*). A great group of low-growing (1 to 4 feet tall), deciduous shrubs, their white, orange, yellow, or pink flowers bloom in early summer. Potentillas are hardy to zones 3–7 and tolerate poor, dry soils.

- ✔ **Spirea** (*Spirea species*). This deciduous shrub either has a dwarf mounding habit or tall fountain-like appearance, depending on the species. White, red, or pink flowers bloom in spring on this zone 3–7 hardy plant.

- ✔ **Viburnum** (*Viburnum species*). This large family of deciduous evergreen shrubs tends to grow large (10 to 15 feet tall and wide), with white flowers and attractive, red, blue, or white berries that birds love. Most grow best in zones 4–9, depending on the species. The American cranberry bush (*V. trilobum*) features red, edible berries good for making jams and jellies.

- ✔ **Yew** (*Taxus* species). These common, hardy (zones 4–7), dark green, needled evergreen shrubs can actually grow into large bushes or small trees if left unchecked. Luckily, yews respond well to pruning and make excellent foundation plants and hedges. Use them as backdrops to other plantings or to hide an unsightly view. Look for narrowly columnar yew varieties such as 'Hicksii' to fit in narrow areas.

 Some species and varieties of trees and shrubs we've listed are considered invasive in some parts of the country. For example, burning bush (*Euonymus alatus*), Japanese barberry (*Berberis thunbergii*), and amur maple (*Acer ginnala*) are now banned for sale in some states. Check with your local garden center or Master Gardener organization for a list of invasive trees and shrubs in your state.

Keeping Your Trees and Shrubs Fit

City trees, just by virtue of their location, often have lots of stresses to deal with. Air pollution, poor soil, wind, animals, vandals, and cramped spaces all can take a toll on a new planting and cause it to die prematurely. That's why it's important to treat your trees and shrubs well. Here are some tips to help upkeep the forest in your yard healthy.

Watering and fertilizing

Newly planted trees and shrubs need a lot of water, but not much fertilizer. After you've followed the steps we outlined in Chapter 6 on how to plant a tree or shrub, then you need to keep it healthy.

- ✔ **Water, water, and then water again.** Newly planted trees and shrubs are water hogs. Roots have been growing in a cramped space of a container for months for many plants. A large tree may have had up to 90 percent of its root system removed when it was dug from the nursery. When you plant it in the ground, there often aren't enough roots left to deliver adequate water to the leaves. This could result in branches dying back.

To help a tree in this situation, water well. If you have well-drained soil and it isn't raining, add about 5 gallons of water per tree or large shrub a few times a week during the first season. It's best to water infrequently, but deeply. Water all summer and into fall. This will keep your leaves looking green and help the tree and shrub roots grow. Consider placing tree gators, mentioned in Chapter 6, around new trees or shrubs to help slowly deliver water to your new plant. You can also use drip irrigation hoses on a timer as described in Chapter 19.

✔ **Weed and mulch.** Keep the areas around your new planting free of weeds that will compete for water and nutrients with your plant. Mulch with bark, straw, or grass clippings as described in Chapter 18.

✔ **Fertilize sparingly.** Only mix compost or soil amendments in the planting hole if your soil is of very poor quality as described in Chapter 6. Work in an annual layer of compost around the drip line of the tree or shrub and a balanced, granular organic fertilizer in spring for overall health. You'll know if your plant needs fertilizer by the amount and health of the new growth. Short stubby new growth or obviously deformed leaves could be a sign of poor nutrition.

✔ **Use amendments as needed.** Some trees and shrubs, such as rhododendrons and blueberries, need an acidic soil pH to grow their best. Consider adding sulfur or another acidifying amendment if your pH is too high.

Pruning 101

Even when you plant the right shrub or tree in the right location, you still have to occasionally prune it for proper health. Pruning is a mystery to many gardeners but in an urban setting shouldn't require a lot of work. You just need a little know-how to do it properly.

How to prune

The first step is understanding the different kinds of pruning cuts. How you prune your plant will determine how it grows in the future.

✔ **Thinning.** Thinning cuts (see Figure 16-1a) remove an entire branch back to a main branch or trunk. This creates better air circulation and reduces crowding within the shrub or the crown of the tree. Overcrowded branches can lead to more insect and disease problems. Make a clean cut just outside the branch collar (which extends from the bark ridge, a raised area on the upper surface where the branch meets the trunk, to the bulge that forms at the base of the branch where it intersects with the trunk) and it will heal the fastest.

✔ **Heading back.** This cut (shown in Figure 16-1b) shortens the branch and, unlike the thinning cut, doesn't remove it completely. When making a heading back cut, prune to just above a side branch or bud and at a

45-degree angle. This type of pruning stimulates new shoot and results in denser growth.

- ✔ **Pinching.** Pinch young branches as they emerge to thin them out and reduce crowding or head them back to stimulate new growth (see Figure 16-1c).

- ✔ **Shearing.** Speaking of dense growth, shearing is heading back taken to the extreme (see Figure 16-1c). It's used to keep hedges of boxwood and yews in line, creating green walls of growth.

a) Thinning

b) Heading

c) Pinching

d) Shearing

Figure 16-1: You can thin, head back, pinch, or shear your trees and shrubs, depending on the plant.

Illustration by Ron Hildebrand.

Now that you know the cuts, you'll need the right tools for the job. Hand pruners are probably the only essential tool you'll need in your small urban lot to keep the plants well pruned. We talk about those in Chapter 21. If you have a large tree that needs major limbs removed, it may be best to contact a local arborist to safely remove the branches without harming nearby buildings, power lines, or yourself.

When to prune

Remove any dead, diseased, or broken branches anytime you notice them. If branches are shading or rubbing against each other, remove one to prevent damage. Pruning in late winter stimulates new growth in spring. It's also easier to see the branch structure in winter on deciduous trees and shrubs because of the lack of leaves.

If you want to reduce the amount of new growth you get each spring, consider pruning in mid-summer. Mid-summer pruning doesn't stimulate as much new growth.

Prune out *suckers* and *water sprouts* in summer. Suckers are long, vertical shoots that arise from the base of the tree or shrub. Water sprouts are similar vertical shoots that arise from the branches. Both will crowd the tree and shrub, possibly leading to more disease and eventually dieback.

The timing of pruning also depends on the type of plant.

- ✔ **Spring-blooming shrubs.** Prune spring bloomers, such as lilac and rhododendron, just after the flowers fade. Generally, you have about 6 weeks after flowering to prune before the flower buds for next year set. If you wait too long after flowering to prune, you may be removing the flowers for next year.

- ✔ **Summer-blooming shrubs.** These shrubs, such as butterfly bush and crape myrtle, flower on new growth, so prune these in early spring to stimulate new growth and more flowers later in summer.

- ✔ **Formal hedges.** These shrubs, such as yews, boxwood, and photinia, need to be sheared to keep them in shape. Prune in spring and again during the growing season as needed.

- ✔ **Other ornamental trees and shrubs.** For most other ornamental trees and shrubs that aren't grown for their flowers, such as maples, junipers, and euonymus, prune in late winter or early spring.

Growing City Fruits

Growing fruit trees in the city may seem like a stretch to the budding urban gardener, but with new advances in dwarf varieties and container growing, fresh fruit salad may be closer than you think.

The key to growing urban fruit trees is having a site with at least 6 hours of sun a day, well-drained fertile soil, and enough room for the tree to grow. If you can fit a crabapple, Japanese maple, or dogwood in your yard, you have room for a fruit tree.

Finding the best fruit trees for the city

There are many different types of fruits that grow well across the country. But we're talking urban gardens in this book, so I'm going to focus on those fruit trees that are either naturally small in stature and perfect for an urban yard or have selections that can stay small, and are self-pollinating. Self-pollinating is important because many fruit trees require different variety to pollinate its flowers and produce fruit. In cities, there often isn't enough room for two trees or there aren't enough pollinating insects around to ensure pollination happens. Of course, if the tree is disease resistant and has few other pests, that's a bonus, too. While the fruits we mention are widely adapted across the county, look for specific varieties that will grow best in your area.

- ✔ **Apples** (*Malus sylvestris*). There are hundreds of varieties of apples available for purchase. Apples are widely adapted and tolerant of cold (zones 3–9). In fact, if you live in a warm climate, you'll have a harder time growing apples than in a cold one. In a small city lot, look for the dwarf trees that grow less than 10 feet tall and disease-resistant varieties, so you won't have to spray as much to get fruit. Some disease-resistant varieties to look for include 'Liberty', 'Jonafree', and 'Willams Pride'.

  If you're really pinched for room, try growing the *columnar apple* varieties. These apple trees grow only 6 feet tall, have small branches and produce a few dozen fruits. They can fit in a flower border or vegetable garden without any problems. 'Northpole' is a good variety.

- ✔ **Cherries** (*Prunus*). Sweet and sour cherries are truly a delight to eat fresh. For a small urban parcel, stick with tart cherries. They are hardy to zone 4, self pollinating, and dwarf varieties, such as 'Northstar' and 'Balaton', only grow 8 to 12 feet tall.

- ✔ **Citrus** (*Citrus*). This is a huge group of evergreen trees that generally grow best in zones 9–10. Many grow into large trees, but certain selections can be kept dwarf. Look for citrus grown on the dwarfing flying dragon rootstock. For small space yards look for 'Dwarf Meyer' lemons, kumquats, 'Bearss' lime, and 'Calamondin' orange. Some of these citrus can also be grown in containers. In cold climates, grow citrus in containers that you can move indoors when the weather turns cold. You'll enjoy the fragrant flowers, and maybe some fruits, inside in winter.

- ✔ **Peaches** (*Prunus persica*). There's nothing better than a tree-ripened, sun-warmed, fresh peach. Most varieties are self-pollinating and hardy to zone 5. Select varieties adapted to your area, such as 'Reliance' in cold climates, 'Desert Gold' in hot summer areas, and the disease-resistant 'Frost' in areas where peach leaf curl disease is a common problem.

✔ **Plums** (*Prunus*). You can grow Japanese or European type plums. Japanese plums, such as 'Shiro' and 'Santa Rosa', are round and need a second variety for proper pollination. They are hardy to zone 5, depending on the variety. European types, such as 'Green Gage' and 'Mount Royal', are oval, don't need a pollinating variety (but produce better with one), and are hardy to zone 4. Guess which one I'd recommend? Of course, since both of these trees only grow 15 feet tall, if you have room for two, go with either the Japanese or European types. If not, one European variety will provide you with plenty of fruit to share.

Many selections of fruit trees can be grown in large containers as described in Chapter 8. Look for dwarf varieties that fit well in a container such as 'El Dorado' peach, 'Northpole' apple, and 'Improved Meyer' lemon. In cold areas, protect the containers by bringing them indoors or wrapping them in winter.

Keeping those tree fruits growing

Many of the suggestions we made for growing trees and shrubs apply to tree fruits as well. Keep young plants well watered and mulched, protect their bark from mice and voles, feed the trees annually with a complete organic fertilizer, and prune regularly to promote strong branch growth.

Here are some other tips to keep in mind.

✔ **Location:** Most city gardeners don't have many choices where to locate their fruit tree. Heck, if they can find a spot with 6 hours of sun they are often lucky. But if you do have a choice, try to place your tree so its protected from cold winds in winter, away from the bottoms of slopes where frost may settle and kill spring blossoms, and where there is a constant air circulation (not strong wind) to keep leaves dry and reduce the likelihood of fungal diseases on your trees.

✔ **Pruning:** Follow the pruning guidelines for trees we outlined earlier in this chapter. Also, prune to open the center of trees to allow light to penetrate. Remove crossing or competing branches or branches with narrow crotch angles. The best branch angle is between 45 and 80 degrees. Prune in midsummer to remove suckers or water sprouts.

✔ **Pests:** There are many insects, diseases, and animals that will somehow find your city fruit orchard. Selecting resistant varieties is the first step to control. Using traps and barriers, such as baited red balls for apple maggots, described in Chapter 20, also helps. Always start with hand-picking or organic sprays, such as insecticidal soap and neem oil, for insect controls. Since you'll probably only be growing a few trees, to prevent damage by animals, try protecting individual fruits with fruit bags or covering the tops of trees with netting when fruiting begins. Use baffles along the trunk to keep squirrels and other rodents from climbing up into the tree's canopy.

Keeping Berry Bushes in the City

While growing tree fruits in the city may take some research and room, growing berries is a snap. Berry bushes tend to grow into small shrubs or vines, so they are a perfect fit for a space starved gardener. Many berries are widely adapted across the country. From Atlanta to Seattle you can grow your own fresh blueberries, raspberries, and strawberries. Of course, there are always regional differences, so it's a good idea to check out what friends and neighbors are growing and contact your local garden center and Master Gardener office for more ideas.

We're big proponents of edible landscaping. Edible landscaping means replacing ornamental trees and shrubs with edible versions without sacrificing beauty. As more and more homeowners grow food in their yards, it's only natural to want to include some berries. Nothing beats fresh raspberries sprinkled on your cereal in the morning, blueberry pies made from your bush, or strawberry muffins baked with homegrown berries. You'll know they're safe and fresh, and you'll save on your food bill as well.

Choosing the best city berries

You can grow berries that are in a bush, vine, or ground cover form to fit almost anywhere in your urban lot. Always check the hardiness of these perennials and find varieties that are suited for your location. Berries, like fruit trees, need full sun and well-drained soil to grow their best. They also benefit from high organic matter and mulch, so add compost and organic mulch each spring to the planting. Some need trellising to grow upright, while others need protection from animals. We'll tackle all these nuisances as we highlight the most popular berries for the city.

> ✔ **Blueberry** (*Vaccinium* species). Blueberries are one the easiest and most beautiful berry shrubs to grow. They are hardy in zones 3–10. You can select low bush varieties that grow like a ground cover, as described in Chapter 17. High bush blueberry varieties grow 5 to 6 feet tall and make an excellent hedge. Rabbiteye blueberries are a high bush type especially adapted to zones 7–9. Half-high varieties only grow 2 to 4 feet tall and make excellent foundation shrubs tucked around a building. If you have room, grow early, mid-, and late season varieties to extend the harvest season.
>
> Blueberries like full sun and well-drained soil. Their shallow roots dry out quickly, so mulching helps keep the plants healthy. Blueberries also need an acidic soil with the pH below 5.0 to grow best. See Chapter 4 for more on acidifying your soil. Using acidified mulch and soil amendments, such as pine needles and peat moss, will help keep the pH low. Purchase plants at your local garden center and plant as you would a small shrub. You should be picking fresh blueberries in a few years.

✓ **Grapes** (*Vitis* species). There are grape varieties adapted to zones 3–10. For cold areas look for American grapes such as *V. labrusca* and its hybrids. They are the most cold tolerant. For the southeast, look for muscadine grapes (*V. rotundifolia*). They grow well in zones 7–9. The European grape is commonly used for wine making and loves hot summer climates from New York to California. There are even new varieties that can rival the American types for hardiness.

Unless you have room for lots of vines to make wine, the best types to grow in a city lot are the table grapes for fresh eating and juice making. 'Concord', 'Reliance', and 'Centennial Seedless' are some examples of these grapes. It's best to look for seedless varieties for fresh eating. If you are primarily making juice, then seeded varieties are fine.

Grow your grapes on a fence, wire trellis, or pergola.

✓ **Raspberries and blackberries** (*Rubus* species). If you only have a partly sunny, narrow yard to grow fruits in, try these brambles. These highly perishable fruits come in colors ranging from black to red to yellow. They are expensive and hard to find fresh in the store, so it's a treat to be able to grow your own. There are varieties adapted to almost anywhere in the United States. They grow upright, fit in a small, raised bed easily, and can be prolific. Raspberries and blackberries come in two types: summer bearing and everbearing. Summer bearing brambles such as 'Latham' raspberry and 'Chester' blackberry produce a vegetative cane the first year that bears no fruit. The second year that cane produces berries in summer. Everbearing varieties, such as 'Autumn Bliss' and 'Anne' raspberries and 'Prime Jim' blackberries, produce fruit on the first-year canes in the fall the first year and again on those same canes the next summer. Then that cane dies.

These brambles like a well-drained soil loaded with organic matter. Add lots of compost to the planting area. Brambles also need a trellis to keep the row of canes upright. You can stake small plantings by tying canes to a post or create a 4-foot-tall, single-wire trellis on either side of the row to keep the canes upright. Prune out fruiting canes to the ground after they finish bearing in summer.

✓ **Strawberries** (*Fragaria* species). Strawberries are the perfect small space berry. These ground cover plants produce fruit the first or second year after planting, can fit in a container, hanging basket, or raised bed, and can produce fruit from summer until fall. The traditional June-bearing varieties, such as 'Sparkle', produce fruit the second year after planting. Day-neutral varieties, such as 'Tribute' and 'Tristar', produce fruit from summer until fall. Alpine strawberries produce small, wild-looking, sweet fruits all summer. For a small garden, I'd go with the day neutrals and alpine berries to maximize your production.

Plant in raised beds since they need well-drained soil. The June-bearing varieties will send out daughter plants attached to stolons (long stems) to colonize the bed all summer the first year of planting. Everbearing and alpine varieties are less likely to send out daughter plants. Let the daughter plants grow, moving them by hand to an open space to root themselves. The second year, pick away.

If growing strawberries in a pot, hanging basket, or other container, choose day neutral or alpine varieties, keep them well watered and fertilized, and in winter store them in a dark, cool location that stays above freezing. They should be able to last a few years before you'll have to replace the plants.

If you want to get a little exotic, try some other great berry bushes and vines in your yard. Currants and gooseberries produce small, white, pink, red, or black colored fruits that are great for pies, juices, and jams. (Growing currants and gooseberries is restricted in some areas because they can host a disease fatal to white pines. Check with your local Extension Service or state Department of Agriculture to see if there are restrictions in your area.) Elderberries are Native American fruits that grow well in part shade and wet areas. The small berries are great for making juice. Kiwi vines grow as strongly as grapes. In warm climates grow the fuzzy kiwi. In cold climates try the hardy kiwi that can withstand winter temperatures below -20 degrees F.

Pruning grape vines for shade

Grapes can grow rampantly and need annual pruning to fruit consistently. If you're growing them up a pergola or structure for shade, then follow these pruning guidelines.

1. **Plant the vines** at the base of the poles supporting the pergola. Two vines per small-sized pergola (6 to 8 feet long) should be plenty.

2. **Select the most vigorous vertical shoot** and prune off all other side shoots. Attach this shoot to the post with twine and train it to grow to the top of the pergola.

3. **Once it reaches the top of the pergola, top-prune the vine**, and allow it to branch. Depending on your pergola structure, it can have two to three branches that will be trained to cover the top of the pergola. Train a main branch along either end of the structure and one in the middle for larger pergolas.

4. **Each spring cut back any errant grape vines going off the pergola**. Cut back the lateral vines off the main branches on the top of the pergola to ten buds to stimulate new shoots that will produce fruit that year.

Staying berry healthy

Keeping berry shrubs such as currants, gooseberries, and blueberries healthy is simple. Select the right variety for your area and the right-sized bush for your space. Although berry shrubs grow best in full sun, currants and gooseberries can tolerant some shade and still produce a good crop. Keep plants well watered and feed with an organic fertilizer in spring each year. Mulch plants with bark mulch, sawdust, wood chips, or pine needles (for blueberries) to keep the soil evenly moist and weeds away. Organic mulch also decomposes into rich hummus that helps feed the plants. Prune only to remove dead, diseased, or broken branches and branches that are crowding or overlapping each other. Many of these shrubs don't require pruning for the first three to five years. Use bird netting to keep our feathered friends from enjoying the harvest. See Chapter 20 for more on bird controls.

For vining berry producers such as kiwi and grapes, grow these up structures to provide shade in summer or grow along a fence or in narrow alleyways to produce fruits in a small space. Construct a sturdy fence or pergola for them to grow on. These vines can live for many years and grow large, even after pruning. Feed them with compost in spring. Keep birds and insects such as Japanese beetles off the leaves following the techniques recommended in Chapter 20.

For low-growing berries, such as low bush blueberries and strawberries, grow in well-drained soil, keep weeds and other plants away so they have room to spread and fill in an area, and keep well watered and fertilized. Low-growing berry bushes may be troubled not only by birds but chipmunks and squirrels as well, so follow recommendation in Chapter 20 for controlling them.

Chapter 17

Lawns and Ground Covers

· ·

In This Chapter

▶ Selecting the right kind of grass for your city lawn

▶ Sowing seed versus laying sod

▶ Watering, mowing, and caring for your lawn

▶ Growing ground covers as an alternative to lawn

· ·

*L*awns are probably not the first thing you think of when we say "gardening in the city." Most urban gardeners are hard-pressed as it is to fit all the flowers, vegetables, shrubs, and trees they want into their yards. Lawns are often last on the list. In some areas, such as the Southwest, lawns just aren't part of the natural environment. Planting these water and fertilizer hogs doesn't make sense if you're trying to garden in a more environmentally friendly fashion.

So admittedly, we're not big lawn fans, but lawns have their place in the urban landscape. Lawns and ground covers serve a number of functions in a yard and garden. They provide green space for entertaining, playing, and walking around your yard. Lawns and some ground covers make excellent pathways between gardens and plantings. They also reduce soil erosion and most importantly, decorate your yard to make it more attractive. Plus, there's something attractive about having a patch of lawn on the ground or on the roof (see Chapter 9) to relax and lounge around on. In a small way it keeps us connected to our rural roots.

So, in this chapter, we're embracing these low growers. We're talking about the best lawn grasses and ground covers to use in an urban environment and ways to keep them growing great.

Selecting the Right Grass

When we talk about selecting the right flowers, vegetables, shrubs, and trees for your yard, it all starts with varieties. Choosing the right variety for your area and landscape will eliminate many problems before they even occur. The same is true when selecting a lawn grass. Growing a grass that can tolerate your specific conditions such as sun, shade, drought, cold, and heat will help ensure that it stays green and lush all summer long.

Lawn grasses are broadly grouped into *cool-season* and *warm-season* types. Cool-season grasses grow best between 60 degrees F and 75 degrees F. They grow well in cold winter areas and are generally planted in USDA zones 6 and colder. Warm-season grasses grow best in the heat. They like temperatures above 80°F, are planted mostly in USDA zones 8 and warmer, and don't tolerate cold winters. There is a transitional zone in USDA zones 6 and 7 where you can grow either warm- or cool-season grasses. It's best to consult with your local garden centers or Master Gardeners to see which grass types are best if you live in these areas. The first step to growing grass in the city is finding your hardiness zone to decide which type of grass is best. Then find the grass that fits your growing conditions.

 Most grasses are sold as seed and in a seed mix. It's uncommon to find just one type of grass seed sold in bags, so it's best to look at the mix of grasses on the label and select a type that has the grass type you need as the dominant one in the mixture.

Cool-season grasses

Cool-season grasses grow most actively in spring and fall. During the summer, they often will slow down and can become brown and go dormant if the temperatures stay hot and the conditions dry for a period of time. But with moisture and cooler conditions, they'll be green and growing again in fall.

 Cool-season grasses can be grown in hot summer areas and stay green, if you keep them well watered. Some gardeners in warm-season grass areas seed cool-season grasses, such as annual ryegrass, in the fall right into their warm-season grass lawns. The cool-season grasses grow all winter, keeping the lawn green while the warm-season grasses are brown and dormant. Annual ryegrass then dies off in spring as the warm-season grasses start to grow actively again. We'll talk more about *overseeding* later in this chapter.

The big three cool-season grass types are Kentucky bluegrass, fescues, and ryegrass.

Kentucky bluegrass

This is the most popular lawn grass for cool areas. It has a soft, fine-textured grass blades and a blue-green color. It's the kind of lawn you want to walk barefoot across. It's relatively slow to get established, but once it does, it forms a solid mat of turf. Kentucky bluegrass, though, is like the hybrid tea roses of the grass world. It requires full sun and consistent moisture, fertilizer, and care to keep it healthy. If you have suitable conditions in your small urban lawn and are willing to put in the time and effort, Kentucky bluegrass will reward you with a soft carpet of green.

The fescues

Fescue grass is grouped into fine and tall types. Fescue grasses, in general, are tougher and more tolerant of adverse conditions compared to bluegrass. They require less water, fertilizer, and care. However, they aren't as soft and beautiful as bluegrass, so there's a compromise.

Fine fescue is the most shade tolerant of the cool-season grasses. It's the grass type for many northern urban gardeners. As we mentioned with flowers and other plants, shade is a limiting factor in many cities, so growing a grass type that will tolerate some shade is often the best choice. Fine fescue also grows better around tree roots, which can be another limiting factor in the city.

Tall fescues have larger grass blades than the fine fescues. The newest versions of tall fescue are the turf-type tall fescue varieties, such as 'Shenandoah'. These are drought and traffic tolerant and more attractive than older varieties. Tall fescue grasses are often used on sports fields. They aren't as shade tolerant as fine fescues, but tolerate heat better and are a good grass type in the transitional USDA zones 6 and 7.

Ryegrass

There are two types of ryegrass: annual and perennial. Annual ryegrass is often used as a winter cover crop in the north or overseeded in warm-season lawns to provide green grass during the winter when the warm-season grasses are dormant. Perennial ryegrass is fine-textured and has a deep green leaf blade. It is a tough grass that tolerates traffic well, is disease resistant, and cold hardy. It grows quickly, so it's often blended with Kentucky bluegrass to establish the lawn faster. Like bluegrass, it grows best in full sun.

Some grasses contain *endophytic* fungi. This fungi naturally repels some lawn grass pests such as sod webworm. Look for grass seeds treated with endophytic fungi if you're dealing with lawn pests in your yard.

Warm-season grasses

Some like it hot, and their names are the warm-season grasses. These grass types need temperatures in the 80 degrees F to green up and grow their best. In subtropical and tropical areas they stay green year-round. However, in cool winter areas, as soon as the temperatures drop in fall, they stop growing and may turn brown. If you live in a warm-climate city, look to grow some of these grasses in your yard.

Bermudagrass

This is the most common warm-season grass type. Varieties of Bermudagrass feature drought and disease resistance, are quick growing, and can withstand traffic. They do require full sun to grow their best. New improved varieties have a soft leaf texture. Bermudagrass is grown all across the South and even up both as far north as the Mid-Atlantic states and Central California.

Bermudagrass is great when you need a grass that grows fast and can fill in a yard quickly. However, it can also become a weed when it gets into flower gardens, so use edging to keep it contained to the area you want.

Buffalograss

This native grass with fine-textured, gray-green leaf blades is often planted in the southern section of the Midwest. It's a heat, cold, and drought tolerant grass that withstands insect and disease attacks and requires little fertilization and mowing. Perfect, right? Well, maybe not. It has some downsides. Buffalograss doesn't tolerate shade or poorly drained soils.

Centipedegrass

This southern grass grows slowly, is disease tolerant, grows well in acidic soils, and needs little fertilization. It spreads by stolons (stems that root along the soil surface), hence the name centipede. The grass blades are blunt and coarse, so it's not the most attractive grass type. It tolerates shade, but is one of the first warm season grasses to brown up with cold weather.

St. Augustinegrass

This coarse textured green grass tolerates part shade, salt sprays, heat, and alkaline soils. However, it is susceptible to diseases and insects, needs a good deal of water to grow well, and doesn't tolerate freezing temperatures so is limited to the far south.

Zoysiagrass

Another coarse-textured grass, zoysiagrass is slow to get established in a lawn, but once growing well, it is a tough warm-season type. Once established it tolerates traffic, drought, pests, and salt spray and can grow in shade. Newer varieties, such as 'Zenith', are more cold tolerant and green up faster in spring than older types.

Seed versus sod

Once you've decided which grass type would work best in your city lawn, you'll have to decide how to plant it. There are two ways to plant a lawn; sowing seeds or laying sod. Sow seeds like you would broadcast flower or vegetable seeds. Sod is basically lawn grass already growing that is dug up and then rolled out on your ground. Each planting style has advantages and disadvantages.

Sowing seed

Most of the lawn grass types mentioned earlier are available in lawn seed mixes. Sowing a lawn from seed is less expensive than planting sod and more grass types are available to use. However, seeds require more steps to get established and it takes time for the grass to fill in. This may be a problem in crowded urban areas where everything from animals to neighbors to delivery people may be walking on your newly sown grass area. The best time to sow grass seed in cool season areas is fall or early spring. The best in warm season areas is late spring.

Here are some steps for sowing your green patch of heaven in your yard.

1. **Remove weeds, concrete, stones, debris, and old grass from the area to be planted.** Do a soil test to determine any fertilizer or amendment needs. Spread these amendments on the soil before tilling. If your soil is hard packed or very poor quality, consider bringing in topsoil. Ideally, grass will have a 6-inch-deep layer of fertilized soil to grow in, but 3 to 4 inches should be enough to establish a healthy lawn.

2. **Till under the topsoil and amendments.** Turn the soil by hand in a very small yard or rototill just enough to mix the amendments and loosen the soil. It's best not to have too smooth a seed bed so the small grass seeds will have nooks to settle in to germinate.

3. **Level the soil with an iron rake.** Then pack it down lightly with a roller or the back of a hoe or shovel.

4. **Sow seeds.** Sow the mixture based on the rate indicated on the grass seed bag. Use a lawn spreader (see Figure 17-1) to sow seeds in a big yard. If you have a small yard simply sprinkle the seeds by hand. Break the amount of seed in half and sprinkle one half of the seed in one direction over the entire area. Then come back and sprinkle the other half walking in the opposite direction over the entire area.

Figure 17-1:
Use a lawn seed spreader to sow seeds on a large yard.

Illustration by Wiley, Composition Services Graphics.

5. **Rake the seed lightly to barely cover it with soil.** Pack it again with a roller (or for a small space, use the back of a shovel), especially if the ground still seems soft.

6. **Mulch the grass seed with a 1- to 2-inch-thick layer of straw or untreated grass clippings.** This will protect the seeds from washing away during storms, keep it from being eaten by birds, and keep the soil moist until the seed germinates. Water the area well and keep the soil moist until the seed starts growing. Keep people and animals off the seed bed until the grass is well established.

Laying sod

The advantages of laying sod are obvious. Sod is an instant lawn. Simply roll it out like a carpet in spring, summer, or fall, water well, and you have a lawn. For small city lawns that may have a hard time growing from seed, sod makes sense, especially if you're only growing a little patch in a rooftop garden. However, sod may not be readily available in cities, you'll have fewer grass type choices, it's more expensive, and is heavy to work with. Unless you have some strong backs to pitch in, it may be hard work establishing a sod lawn. If you're sold on sod, here's how to install it.

Springing for sprigs and plugs

Sprigs and plugs (small plants) are another option. They're mostly sold for warm season grasses and are planted like a ground cover.

Prepare your lawn for sprigs and plugs as you would for seed. Buy the plugs or small plants in trays and plant then as you would a ground cover (see "Planting and caring for your cover" later in this chapter). Like a ground cover, sprigs and plugs take time to grow and fill in. They fill in faster than seed but obviously slower than sod.

1. **Level the ground and add topsoil and soil amendments as you did for sowing seeds.**

2. **Water the area well, then roll out the sod.** Lay pieces so the edges slightly overlap. Use boards laid on the sod to walk across the laid pieces as you work.

3. **With a sharp knife, trim the sod.** Trim sod pieces to fit together like a jigsaw puzzle. Fill in the edges between pieces with topsoil.

4. **Roll the sod with a roller so it's level and flat and the roots make good contact with the soil.**

5. **Water the sod well.** Rake the sod to lift up flattened grass and water heavily until the sod is established. Once the sod starts actively growing, keep it moist for the rest of the growing season, and mow regularly.

Caring for Your Lawn

Now that you've chosen the right lawn grass for your climate and situation and have planted it to perfection, it's time to care for your lawn. Lawns have a reputation for being water hogs and fertilizer guzzlers, but some types of grasses are less demanding than others. Plus, how you care for your lawn can go a long way toward making it a low maintenance part of your landscape. Mowing it properly, watering and fertilizing in a timely fashion, and controlling pests can keep your grass green without spending a lot of greenbacks to do it.

Looking at city mowers

Since most urban lawns are postage stamp sized, buying a riding lawn tractor or large mower isn't practical. Not only is it overkill, where are you going to store that beast? The more practical choices are gas- or electric-powered rotary mowers, reel mowers, or even just a string trimmer.

✔ **Rotary mowers.** This is the most common type of mower. Gas-powered versions are more powerful than battery or corded electric-powered versions, but they require gasoline, are noisy, and pollute the atmosphere. Corded electric mowers are more powerful than battery-powered mowers, but you have to contend with the electrical cord. Battery powered versions have a battery that needs recharging, but are versatile. If you have a sloping yard, consider a self-propelled rotary mower, where the engine turns the front two wheels for you, helping push it up hills.

✔ **Reel mowers.** For a small grassy yard, consider the old-fashioned reel mowers. Reel mowers have spinning blades that cut the grass like a scissors. The harder you push, the faster they cut. They rely totally on people power, so are great for the environment and giving you a little workout. But the blades need frequent sharpening and don't cut tall grass well.

✔ **String trimmers.** If you have a very small lawn, consider simply getting an electric- or gas-powered string trimmer, although you won't get as clean a cut as a mower. String trimmers are the most practical tool for cutting grass and weeds along fence lines, buildings, and walkways.

Mowing correctly

One of the simplest ways to keep your lawn fed and healthy is to mow it properly. Mowing is one of those lawn-care chores people either love or hate. You can tell which side of the aisle you're on by the lawn itself. If your lawn gets shaggy and you end up cutting it only after your lose the dog in the high grass, you're probably a mowing hater. If, however, your lawn looks like a GQ model's finely trimmed hair at every turn, you're a lawn-mowing lover. Whichever camp you fall in, mowing properly and at the right time is the most important part.

Here are some pointers for lawn mowing.

✔ **When mowing your lawn you should never take off more than one-third of the grass blade height in any one mowing.** Mowing lower than that will weaken the grass and make it look unsightly. For example, if your lawn is 6 inches tall, don't take off more than 2 inches at any one mowing. Adjust the settings on your mower to fit the lawn type you're growing.

✔ **Mow grasses generally to a height of 2 to 3 inches tall.** Mowing too short will "scalp" the lawn, making it hard for the grass plants to recover and opening up the lawn to weed invasions. Generally, the thicker and lusher the lawn, the fewer problems with weeds.

✔ **Mow the grass when dry to avoid spreading diseases.** Mow in different patterns on the lawn each time to help keep the grass blades standing upright.

> ✔ **Keep the mower deck cleaned of dead grass after every mowing, sharpen the mower blades at least once a year, and leave the grass clippings on the lawn as a fertilizer.** Only clean up grass clippings if you waited too long to mow and you have clumps of clippings on the lawn. Clumps will create dead spots on the lawn and should be raked up and composted.

Use mulching mowers or a mulching mower blade on your rotary mower to finely chop up the grass clippings and drop them back on the lawn. It's estimated that up to one-third of the nitrogen needs of your lawn can be met just by leaving the grass clippings.

Maintaining your lawn

Plants need proper watering, fertilizing, and pest control to grow their best, and lawn grasses are no exception. Watering properly and fertilizing with the right products at the right time will help you grow a lawn that will be much less likely to need pest controls.

Providing plenty of water

City lawns need a good supply of water to stay green all summer. If you skimp on watering, you'll notice grass blades browning and dying back. In general, water deeply by applying at least 1 inch of water a week in the morning. This allows the grass to dry by nightfall, reducing the chances of diseases. If you have a small grassy lawn patch, simply sprinkling the lawn with a hose-end nozzle will probably be easiest. Water until the soil is moist 8 inches deep. Use a metal probe to see how deep your water is penetrating, and adjust the amount of time you water accordingly. For larger urban lawns, consider watering devices such as overhead sprinklers. We talk more about sprinklers in Chapter 19.

Water in short intervals instead of one long stretch. Water for 5 to 10 minutes, then stop and let it sink in. This avoids the water running off the lawn and being wasted. Water, take a break and go pull some weeds, then return in 10 minutes to water some more.

Fertilizing your lawn

Fertilizing the lawn can get complicated. But remember, you aren't growing a putting green. If you only fertilize once a year, do so in the fall for cool-season grasses and spring to early fall for warm-season grasses. This allows the plants to take up the nutrients best, feeding the roots, which in turn creates a thicker, lusher lawn.

The best type of fertilizer to use would be a slow-release organic fertilizer with a ratio of 3-1-2. This applies enough nitrogen for green growth but helps feed roots and toughens the grass as well. Follow the fertilizer bag instructions for applying the correct quantity. For more on fertilizers go to Chapter 5.

Fertilizing your lawn is like Goldilocks looking for the perfect bowl of porridge. The grasses need just the right amount of fertilizer to thrive. Too little and they won't grow as well as they could. But too much and those extra nutrients, like phosphorus, will run off to pollute waterways. If your soil naturally has adequate amounts of phosphorus or there is plenty in the soil from previous additions of fertilizer, don't just add more indiscriminately. Unless a soil test shows a deficiency, use a fertilizer that doesn't contain phosphorus (one with zero as the middle number of the analysis). Check with your local garden center or Master Gardeners about lawn fertilizer recommendations for your area.

If you grow the right grass for your area, water well, fertilize annually, then you shouldn't have many disease and insect problems. However, even the best lawn may have problems. Grubs will eat lawn grass roots. Skunks will dig in lawns looking for food. Moles will tunnel to their heart's content in your green patch. Luckily, there are organic controls for all these problems, and you'll find them in Chapter 20.

Tending to other maintenance tasks

Two gardening practices that help make for a healthier lawn are *overseeding* and *topdressing*. Overseeding means spreading seed on top of the existing lawn. This can be done in spring or fall to help a sparse lawn fill in. The grass seed germinates and helps fill in bare spots. Lawns of warm-season grasses that go dormant in cold weather are also often overseeded with cold tolerant annual ryegrass to keep them green all winter.

Topdressing is spreading a ¼-inch-thick layer of compost over your whole lawn. Rake it in so it doesn't cover grass blades. The compost will feed the grass roots, help maintain soil moisture, and create a healthy environment for microbes in the soil.

Weeds can get the best of any lawn. Weed tolerance is a personal affair. Some urbanites are content with just a green patch, no matter what it is. Others insist on purity. If you are mowing high, watering, and fertilizing well, you shouldn't have too many weeds to deal with. There are certainly many chemical herbicides on the market that claim to keep your lawn weed free. Considering the concerns for the environment, we tend to steer gardeners towards organic herbicide solutions such as acetic acid and corn gluten. *Acetic acid* is the active ingredient in vinegar. Commercial products have concentrated forms of vinegar that, when sprayed on weeds, kills them. But be careful; these types of herbicides are nonselective. If you accidentally spray your flowers, veggies, or lawn grass, they will die too. *Corn gluten* is a by-product of the corn industry that kills weed seeds as they germinate. For example, it can be spread in spring to prevent crabgrass in established lawns. Be careful not to spread corn gluten where you have recently sown vegetable, grass, or flower seeds, as it will kill these as they germinate as well.

Patching up paradise

If you inherit some trashed turf or your lawn gets out of control, there are ways to reclaim it. If the lawn has more than 50 percent weeds, it may be time to till it up and start over. However, if it looks salvageable, try these steps to bring it back to life.

1. **Mow your lawn close to the ground and rake off all the cuttings.**

2. **With an iron rake, rough up the soil and remaining grass.**

   Don't worry if you pull some of it out. It's important that the soil is loose so seeds can grow and water drain. You can even lightly run a rototiller over the area if the soil is very compacted.

3. **Add soil amendments, such as lime, if needed, based on a soil test.**

4. **Add a thin layer of topsoil or compost to provide a healthy seed bed for your new grass seed.**

5. **Sow the right grass variety for your area**.

   Press the seed down with the back of a shovel or roller so it makes good contact with the soil.

6. **Cover the seeded area with hay or straw mulch and water well.**

   The existing grass will grow through the topsoil and mulch and the new grass should fill in the vacant spots.

Ground Cover Alternatives

If you aren't a lawn lover but still want something green under foot or have an area too shady for grass to grow, there are alternatives. Ground covers do just what they sound like — low-growing, spreading, evergreen, or deciduous perennial plants or shrubs. These ground-hugging plants range from a few inches to a foot or so tall, and once established, they create a green mat that doesn't yield to weeds and is easy to care for. Ground covers are not only a good alternative to lawns in flat areas but are often the perfect choice for hard-to-mow slopes.

Lawns versus ground covers

Ground covers are easier to care for than lawns but can't take foot traffic as well. Here are some other advantages of ground covers in your landscape.

✓ **Ground covers need less care.** Ground covers need less water, little mowing or shearing, and once established, little weeding.

- ✔ **Ground covers are adaptable.** Ground covers fit in diverse spaces such as on a slope, in a small area, or in an area too shady to grow grass.

- ✔ **Ground covers are beautiful.** Although green is the most common color of ground cover foliage, there are hundreds of different plants you can use as ground covers, offering a variety of colorful foliage and flowers. Some have excellent fall foliage and even produce colorful berries.

Cityside ground covers

There are so many ground covers to choose from, it's hard to narrow the list to a few favorites. As with any perennial or small shrub, each has its unique needs for sun, water, and soil. Certainly check your local garden center for the best varieties in your area. Here are some evergreen types to try (most are adapted to partial or full sun):

- ✔ **Barberries** (*Berberis*). There are many low-growing varieties of the green- or red-leaved barberry such as 'Crimson Pygmy'. They grow only 18 inches tall and have red berries in fall. Barberries are hardy in zones 4–8.

- ✔ **Carpet Bugle** (*Ajuga reptans*). Ajuga has broad, deep green or reddish-colored leaves with low spikes of blue flowers in late spring. It only grows 6 inches tall. It's hardy in zones 4–9.

- ✔ **Cotoneaster** (*Cotoneaster*). These low shrubs can be deciduous or evergreen, depending on the species. They often sport white flowers and red berries along with attractive foliage. Hardiness varies depending on the variety.

- ✔ **Creeping Thyme** (*Thymus praecox arcticus*). This creeping herb grows 3 to 5 inches tall with pink or white flowers. It grows well in small spaces such as between stepping stones. It can withstand some foot traffic, so it makes a great ground cover near flower beds. It's hardy in zones 4–9.

- ✔ **Dwarf Periwinkle** (*Vinca minor*). The small, dark green laves of this ground cover grow 6- to 12-inches tall. It produces beautiful violet-blue flowers in spring and early summer and grows best in partial shade. Vinca is hardy in zones 4–9.

- ✔ **English Ivy** (*Hedera helix*). English ivy has attractive green, lobed greens. It trails about 1 foot above the ground but can also climb up trees and structures if you let it. It's hardy in zones 6–10. It can become invasive, so plant it in an area where it can safely spread or keep it contained.

- ✔ **Ice plants.** This large group of low-growing, succulent perennials are popular in warm climate areas. They grow 6 to 12 inches off the ground, with fleshy green or red-tinged leaves and colorful flowers. They are hardy in zones 9–10.

- **Japanese Spurge** (*Pachysandra terminalis*). The large, bright green leaves grow 10 inches tall and cover this low-growing perennial. It produces white, fragrant flowers in summer and grows best in partly shaded, moist conditions. It is hardy in zones 4–9.

- **Junipers** (*Juniperus*). There are many types of this evergreen shrub. The low growing varieties such as Bar Harbor and Blue Rug grow only 1 to 2 feet tall. They grow best in full sun and in zones 4–8.

- **Meehan's Mint** (*Meehania cordata*). This 6-inch-tall ground cover has showy lavender-blue flowers in spring. This isn't technically in the mint family, but spreads quickly and can grow and flower in moist, deep shade. Meehan's mint is hardy in zones 4–9.

- **Winter Creeper** (*Euonymus fortunei*). This tough plant comes in varieties with green or yellow and green and white and green variegated leaves. Most grow only a few feet off the ground and spread vigorously. They can be trained up a fence as well. Most types are hardy in zones 5–9.

The nature of many non-woody, perennial ground covers is to spread and root their stems along the ground. This makes them excellent ground covers, but if they get into areas you don't want such as your vegetable, flower, or herb garden, they become a tough-to-eradicate weed. Consider edging around a ground cover area or annually weed out errant branches to keep your ground cover in bounds.

Also, some species of these ground covers, such as the barberries, English ivy, and euonymus, are considered invasive plants in some areas and may be banned. Check local garden centers and Master Gardeners for lists of invasives in your area and always choose noninvasive species or varieties.

Planting and caring for your cover

Plant ground covers as you would any perennial flower or shrub. See Chapters 14 and 15 for more on planting. Because you often are growing a number of these plants in a single area to cover the ground, you'll sometimes find ground covers sold as small plants in a flat or tray. Although the plants are small, it is a more economical way to buy a large number of plants.

Spacing is critical with ground covers. If you plant the ground covers too far apart for that type they will take forever to fill in and you'll be weeding between the plants for years. If you plant them too close together, they will quickly fill in but may overrun each other, becoming too crowded to grow properly. Measure the space you want to cover and check the spacing recommendations of those ground covers before buying or planting them. That will help you determine how many plants to purchase.

If you're planting many small plants, such as vinca, prepare the area as you would a seed bed and space and plant accordingly. For larger shrubby ground covers, such as junipers, simply dig individual holes for each plant. On slopes, terrace the planting hole to create a flat basin around the plant so the soil doesn't erode away when watering.

If your non-woody, perennial ground cover turns brown from winter injury or damage, simply give it a haircut. Shearing ground covers removes dead and damaged leaves and allows new leaves to take their place, creating a more attractive plant. Woody ground covers can't be sheared in the same way, but certainly removing any dead or damaged branches is always a good idea.

Whichever ground cover you choose, you should be prepared to weed for the first few years. For spreading perennial ground covers, such as English ivy, lightly mulch between plants, allowing the ivy to root along its stems as it grows to fill in the spaces. For shrubs, such as barberries, apply a thicker mulch or use landscape fabric to control weeds. These ground covers spread as their branches grow outward, but the branches don't tend to root along the ground as they grow.

Part V
Growing to Perfection

The 5th Wave
By Rich Tennant

"I'll be right in! I'm just sprinkling the garden with salty bar snacks to attract the slugs to the beer traps."

In this part. . .

Once all your gardens are planted and you're happy with your choices, the ongoing maintenance begins. In this part, we describe the best ways to weed your gardens and the advantages of using mulches to keep weeds at bay and retain soil moisture. Water is a critical element to any garden, and urban gardens are no exception. We talk about the best ways to water your plants to save this precious resource, as well as time and money. And yes, even the best gardeners can have trouble with insects, diseases, and animals in their urban garden. We describe some of the worst offenders and give you organic solutions for each.

Chapter 18

Weeding and Mulching Your Plants

*W*eeds are one thing that can quickly get under a gardener's skin. We spend hours preparing the soil, planting, fertilizing, and watering, only to see as many weeds pop up in our vegetable, flower, and herb garden as plants. Weeds also have this uncanny ability to outgrow our favorite veggies and flowers. What starts as just a few weeds here and there can quickly become a jungle in a few weeks.

But weeds don't have to be a garden deal breaker. With some planning, timely weeding, and the right techniques, weeds can become a passing concern that gets dealt with quickly. One of those techniques is mulching. Mulches not only prevent weeds from growing, but they also help plants grow faster, conserve water, and can look great in the landscape. Weeding and mulching are linked on your path to creating a beautiful garden, lawn, and landscape.

Winning the War on Weeds

Weeds are really just plants growing in a place you don't want them. Most can be controlled with proper attention and by using the techniques we mention later in this chapter. However, some perennial weeds are so invasive they can not only take over your garden and lawn, but can actually harm natural habitats and alter wildlife patterns. So, it's good to know what kind of weed you're dealing with before you get started.

Like all plants, there are annual and perennial weeds. Some weeds spread by self-sowing seeds, while others spread by underground roots. The trick is to properly identify your weeds in the edible and flower garden before they become problems. Then you can use organic gardening techniques to thwart their growth.

Identifying weeds and knowing why you should care

Weeds are just a plant in the wrong place, and some are actually quite beautiful, while others are even edible. So what's the problem? Well, weeds compete with your plants for water, sun, and nutrients. A sure way to have a stunted flower or a yellowing shrub is to let weeds grow up around it.

Luckily, weeds are predictable and if caught early, controllable. Give weeds the same conditions your plants like, sun, water and the right temperatures, and they grow. In urban settings, certain weeds seem to have a leg up on other plants. These are perennial weeds, such as dandelions, with strong taproots that can grow in the smallest crack in the pavement, or annual weeds, such as crabgrass, that are prolific self-sowers. Many weeds thrive in the less-than-ideal setting of an urban environment.

Here's a rundown of some common weeds you'll find in your gardens and lawns. The controls for each are explained in detail later in this chapter.

- **Crabgrass** (*Digitaria*). In a dry, sparse urban lawn, crabgrass is quick to invade. The narrow, bluish-colored grass blades grow in clumps that can be hand-pulled. On lawns, use corn gluten herbicide in spring to control crabgrass before it starts to grow

- **Curly Dock** (*Rumex crispus*). This perennial is known for its deep taproot, making it very adaptable to growing in tough city conditions. It can grow 4 feet tall and sows seed readily. Repeatedly cut off the tap root to kill this weed.

- **Dandelion** (*Taraxacum officinale*). This Italian delicacy is a desirable "weed" in some gardens because the tender young greens are tasty to eat. Other gardeners don't share this love of dandelion greens, and the yellow flower that follows quickly can sow seeds around your landscape. Dandelion is a perennial with a strong taproot and grows in small cracks and crevices, so dig it out thoroughly to remove the entire root.

- **Ground Ivy** (*Glechoma hederacea*). This common garden and lawn weed has beautiful, round leaves with scalloped edges and purple flowers in spring. Unfortunately, it spreads quickly, invading flower gardens and lawns, especially in shady sections, rooting along its stem as it grows. Hand-pull this one as soon as it's noticed.

✔ **Lamb's Quarters** (*Chenopodium album*). This is an edible weed when harvested as a young green, but self-sows readily in the garden. It grows 3 feet tall with leaves that have characteristic dusty white coloring on the undersides. Cultivate the garden often to control it.

✔ **Mallow** (*Malva neglecta*). Common mallow is often found growing near foundations of buildings and along roadsides. The plant has a taproot and is an annual in cold climates and perennial in warm climates. It has a whorl of leaves and white or lavender flowers. It spreads by seed but can be controlled by frequent weeding or mowing.

✔ **Oxalis** (*Oxalis species*). A widespread perennial weed known for its yellow flowers and low-growing, clover-like leaves, oxalis is found in lawns and disturbed areas. Spread corn gluten herbicide to kill the weed seeds and cultivate frequently to kill existing plants.

✔ **Pigweed** (*Amaranth retroflexus*). Pigweed is a poor name for this nutritious, tasty, yet aggressive annual weed. It's a good salad green when picked young, but can overwhelm a garden when it grows larger. Looks for the reddish-stems and pointed leaves and cultivate and pull this weed when young to control it.

✔ **Plantain** (*Plantago major*). This broadleaf, perennial weed thrives in compacted soil, which is common in cities. It spreads by seed, so if you can't pull it out, at least cut off the flower heads when they form so more seed doesn't spread.

✔ **Wild Morning Glory or Bindweed** (*Convolvulus arvensis*). This vining perennial weed looks beautiful when flowering, but watch out. It spreads quickly, taking over gardens, shrubs, and trees. It can grow in any small crack in pavement. Hand-pull it as soon as you identify bindweed in your yard.

Stopping weeds before they're a problem

Clearly, the best way to avoid having a weed-infested garden or lawn is to stop these buggers before they get established. Here are ways to stop the weed seeds and young plants before they take over.

✔ **Get them while they're young.** Annual weeds grow from seeds lying dormant in the soil. As soon as you turn the soil, exposing them to the right sun, temperature, and moisture conditions — boom — they grow. Removing weeds, such as pigweed and lamb's quarters, while the plants are young is the best way to control these weeds. Hand-pull the young weeds or simply cut off the weeds with a sharp hoe or cultivator right below the soil line (see Figure 18-1). Don't dig deep or you'll be bringing more weeds seeds to the surface to grow.

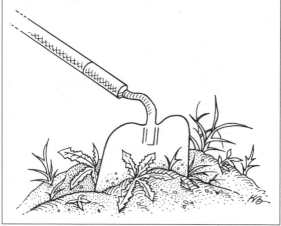

Figure 18-1:
Cut young
weeds
with a hoe
early in the
season to
keep them
controlled.

Illustration by Kathryn Born.

Another way to use weeds' propensity for growth to your advantage is to sprout them before planting. One week before planting, turn the soil, water it well, and let the weeds grow. Then hoe the weeds down, and you have eliminated a big batch of potential problems.

✔ **Glutenize them.** For crabgrass and dandelions in lawns or perennial gardens, consider spreading corn gluten organic herbicide on those areas as the seeds are starting to germinate. This is a safe herbicide that kills weeds as they sprout. It also contains nitrogen fertilizer that helps your existing plants grow.

Corn gluten herbicide kills *all* seeds as they sprout, so be careful using it near newly seeded lawns or around newly sown annual flowers and vegetables.

✔ **Cover them.** If you cover the soil, then the seeds in the soil won't get the light and conditions they need to germinate. No sun, no growth. Cover the soil around trees and shrubs, perennial gardens, and vegetable gardens with landscape fabric or mulch (We'll get into types of mulches and how to use them next.)

✔ **Burn them out.** You can literally heat up the soil to temperatures high enough to cook the weed seeds. This technique is called soil solarization, and it works best in sunny, hot climates. In summer use clear plastic sealed over a bed to solarize your soil. Unfortunately, you'll have to sacrifice planting that bed for a few months while it cooks. But for really weedy beds, this might be the best long-term solution.

Controlling weeds once they're large

Cultivating young plants, mulching, and using organic products like corn gluten herbicide are good ways to stop weeds from becoming a problem. But what do you do if the weeds are already there? Here are some tips on controlling weeds once they already have started growing in your landscape.

- ✓ **Mow them down.** One technique that works to eventually get a leg up on tenacious weeds (especially those with big roots like dandelions and bindweed) is to continually mow or cut them down. This will eventually exhaust the weed root reserves and they will die.

- ✓ **Juice them with vinegar.** A home remedy that works on many annual weeds, and to a lesser degree on perennial weeds, is to spray vinegar (acetic acid) on leaves on a hot sunny day. The vinegar changes the leaf pH and kills it. This works best on weeds in pavement cracks or walkways where you can easily identify what's a weed. It is non-selective, meaning if you accidentally get some spray on a flower or vegetable in a garden it will kill that leaf as well. While vinegar is good, commercial organic herbicide products have a higher concentration of acetic acid and are more effective. Other similar products use liquid soap and clove oil for the same purpose.

- ✓ **Keep them from flowering.** If all else fails, at least don't let weeds in your garden, yard, or nearby area flower and go to seed. That's just creating years more work for you in the garden. Cut down the tops of weeds at the flowering stage. Sure, some seeds, like dandelion puffs, will still blow in on the breeze, but by stopping weeds nearby from flowering, you'll get a leg up on weeding.

- ✓ **Burn them.** Where appropriate consider using a propane-fueled weed flamer to repeatedly scorch weed tops. This tool is custom designed for controlling weeds, directing the flame down and focusing it on the plant. You may have to flame perennial weeds a number of times to kill them outright.

- ✓ **Pull them**. Sometimes the simplest solution is the best. After a good rain while the ground is wet, hand-pull weeds. They will pop out, roots and all, easier than on dry ground.

Mulching 101

One of the best ways to keep weeds from taking over is to mulch your plantings. There are a variety of mulch materials you can use to keep your garden healthy. In a city garden, mulches can be critical to a garden's health. Which mulch you use depends on the plants you're growing, where you live, and what's available.

Mulch is more than just a weed barrier, though. A good mulch keeps soils cool in warm climate areas, or heats them up in cool climates. A good mulch conserves precious soil moisture so you don't have to water as much. This saves you money and helps the environment. A good mulch can add precious organic matter to the soil, helping your plants grow strong. Check Chapter 4 for more on the benefits of organic matter to the soil. A good mulch also can look beautiful, highlighting your flower colors or the color of tree and shrub bark.

So, yes, it's good to mulch. But how you mulch and the materials you use can go a long way toward determining if your mulching is really helping your garden.

Types of mulch

While anything that covers the soil can be considered a mulch, here are some specific items that are best to use in your garden as mulches. Mulches are generally grouped as organic (once was living material) and inorganic (never was alive). Organic mulches slowly add nutrients to the soil as they decompose and help to keep the soil cool. Most inorganic mulches heat up the soil and don't have any nutritive benefits. Choose the best ones for your climate and your aesthetic taste.

Following are some good organic mulches to consider:

✔ **Hay and straw.** This is one of the most common organic mulches used in vegetable gardens, but may be hard to find and pricey in the city. Straw doesn't have weed seeds, while hay may have lots. Add a 2- to 3-inch-thick layer around your plants and in pathways. Use straw or hay around cool-weather-loving annuals, such as snapdragons and broccoli, after planting, but wait to apply it around heat-loving annuals, such as squash and zinnias, until after the soil has warmed.

✔ **Bark.** Often sold in bags in the city, some garden centers may also sell it in bulk. This is one of the most commonly used forms of mulch in the city. Tree bark can be in shredded, chipped, or nugget form. It can be made from hardwoods or evergreen trees, and its color depends on the type of tree used or colorant added. Some, such as cedar and redwood, have a pleasant fragrance, and cedar mulch can repel insects. Spread bark mulch around perennial flower gardens, shrubs, and trees, using about a 2-inch-thick layer. Wood chips and sawdust are also sometimes used. See Table 18-1 for more details on the different types of bark mulch products.

Bark, wood chips, and sawdust are high in carbon and can temporarily deplete the soil of nitrogen, creating a deficiency in your plants. This effect is most notable in annual flowers, herbs, and vegetables. Add a form of nitrogen fertilizer, such as alfalfa meal, to your plantings before you use these mulches to counteract this effect.

Table 18-1	Different Kinds of Bark
Bark Type	*Characteristics*
Evergreen bark	Pine, cedar, cypress, redwood, and other evergreen bark is a good all-purpose mulch in the landscape. It's especially good for mulching around acid-loving plants, such as blueberries and rhododendrons.
Hardwood bark	Hardwood bark from deciduous trees is not as decorative as evergreen mulch, but less expensive and quicker to decompose than evergreen mulch.
Colored mulch	This is a wood mulch that is artificially colored. It's becoming more popular in certain areas of the country. However, there are some concerns about the chemicals used to color the mulch leaching into the soil.
Shredded bark	Probably the least expensive bark mulch type and one that gives the best coverage. It's good for pathways since it compresses, making it easy to walk on.
Bark chips	Smaller and more delicate than nuggets, but more durable and longer lasting than shredded bark, bark chips are best used around perennial flowers, shrubs, and trees. They will eventually flatten so can also be used in walkways.
Bark nuggets	Large nuggets are decorative but best used around foundation plants or in areas where you don't have to walk on them. They create an uneven walking surface and can float away in heavy rains. They do last many years in most areas.

✔ **Grass clippings, leaves, and needles.** These organic mulches are great for using around vegetables and flowers and probably the cheapest types to find in the city. Fresh grass clippings add nitrogen to the soil. Use dried leaves in fall to mulch around trees and shrubs, but shred them first so they don't mat near the plant trunk and cause it to rot. Pine needles are acidic and great mulch for acid-loving plants such as blueberries, camellias, and rhododendron. Use a 1- to 2-inch-thick layer of grass, leaves, or needles around plants.

Only use grass clippings from untreated lawns. Clippings from lawns treated with chemical herbicides can kill the plants you are mulching around.

✔ **Newspaper and cardboard.** These organic mulches are great for mulching pathways or smothering grass or weeds in anticipation of creating a new garden. Use black-and-white or colored newsprint only and cardboard that doesn't have any glossy covering on it. Glossy newsprint and cardboard covering can container harmful chemicals that can leach into the soil.

✔ **Compost.** Compost not only is the great soil additive we raved about in Chapter 5, it can be used as a mulch. It feeds the soil and helps retain water, but it doesn't work well to keep out weeds.

Some mulches such as peat moss, shredded leaves, and grass can form a mat that sheds water, creating a drought conditions in the soil. Don't let your organic mulch become matted. Gently stir the mulch with an iron rake or hoe occasionally so water can penetrate when it rains and reach the plant roots.

Following are some inorganic mulches you may want to consider:

✔ **Plastic.** This common inorganic mulch is used around vegetables primarily. It heats up the soil, making for faster growth on warm season vegetables. Different colored versions are now available that help specific vegetables grow better such as red mulch for tomatoes and strawberries and dark green mulch for melons. White plastic is a good mulch in hot climates because it doesn't overheat the soil, yet still prevents weed growth.

✔ **Stone.** Crushed or small-sized stone is an attractive inorganic mulch that keeps the soil cool and moist. It's often used in hot, dry climates, such as the Southwest, as a general landscape mulch or in locations where wildfires are a concern. It's often a good mulch to use against your house if ants and other insects are a problem. These pests are not as attracted to this mulch compared to bark. Because there is space between the individual rocks, consider using landscape fabric under the stones to help prevent weed growth. Different types of crushed stone, such as volcanic and river stone, are available for different looks.

✔ **Landscape fabric or even old rugs.** This inorganic mulch is often used around shrubs and trees to prevent weed growth. It's long lasting, lets air and water through, and is effective as a weed barrier. However, it's not very attractive on its own, and when covered with a more attractive mulch such as tree bark, weeds can start growing on top of the landscape fabric. Old rugs probably should be used in pathways only since they will take many years to decompose. Cover these mulches with bark or another mulch to make it more attractive.

The dark side of some mulches

Not all mulch is good for the soil, you, or your pets. Use certain mulches carefully. Cocoa bean hull mulch is a by-product of the chocolate industry. This finely textured mulch adds a dark look and chocolate fragrance when applied around plants. However, it blows away easily, can get moldy during rainy weather, and is toxic to dogs if they eat it. Not a good choice if a pooch lives close by. Never use wood mulch made from pressure-treated lumber or pallets because these have chemicals that can leach into the soil. Mulch made from shredded car tires is getting more popular in playgrounds, but there are concerns about chemicals leaching into the soil and the rubber smell. Leaves from certain trees, such as black walnut, may have natural chemicals in them that will inhibit plant growth if used as a mulch.

Mulching correctly

While what you decide to use for mulch is important, how you apply it is even more so. Mulch applied too deeply can lead to plants rotting. Mulch applied too lightly won't stop weed growth.

- **Mulching annual flowers, herbs, and cool-season vegetables.** Apply a 2- to 3-inch-thick layer of hay, straw, grass clippings, shredded leaves, pine needles, or bark around these plantings.

- **Mulching warm-season vegetables.** Use a plastic mulch laid over the bed two weeks before the scheduled planting time. If using drip irrigation or soaker hoses, lay these on the bed before laying down the plastic mulch. Tuck in the edges of the mulch so it heats the soil. At planting time, make cuts in the plastic mulch with a sharp knife and plant your seedlings or seeds. If not using drip irrigation, water the young seedlings through the holes in the plastic until they get established.

- **Mulching trees and shrubs.** Use a 2- to 4-inch-thick layer of shredded leaves, hay, straw, wood chips, or bark mulch around these plants. Create a mulch ring out to the drip line of the tree or shrub, removing all the grass and other plants inside that ring. Create a basin in the mulch so water penetrates the soil better when watering. (For more on watering trees and shrubs go to Chapter 19.)

Don't pile the mulch against the trunk or you'll create volcano mulching. Volcano mulching is when the bark mulch is piled too deeply around a tree or shrub. It causes the roots to suffocate and can kill a tree. It often happens when new mulch is piled on top of old mulch. In spring when mulching, remove and compost the old mulch before applying a fresh layer.

✔ **Mulching perennial flowers.** Apply a 2- to 3-inch-thick layer of bark mulch, wood chips, hay, straw, grass clippings, or shredded leaves around flowers in spring after a good weeding and replenish the mulch in summer in warm climate areas.

Chapter 19

Watering Your Garden

. . . .

In This Chapter

▶ Discovering the importance of water to your plants

▶ Following some basic water conservation procedures

▶ Finding out about rainwater harvesting

▶ Using hoses, sprinklers, and drip irrigation efficiently

. . . .

*W*ater is an essential building block for plants. Plants need adequate water throughout the growing season to germinate, grow, flower, and fruit. But water is becoming a big issue in many parts of the country, especially in urban areas. Periodic droughts, depleted ground water resources, and pollution are making water a top issue of the 21st century.

Americans use, on average, about 180 gallons of water a day. According to the American Water Works Association, more than 50 percent of urban water use in the United States goes into the landscape. However, gardening is often one of the first areas to get curtailed when drought threatens. When water restrictions are put into place during dry periods, using municipal water for watering lawns, landscapes, and gardens is often limited or banned. That's understandable because, unfortunately, it's also estimated that 50 percent of that landscape water is wasted.

So conserving this vital resource is not just a good idea, it will become more and more of a necessity. In this chapter, we not only tackle the hows and whys of watering but also offer solutions for reducing water usage so your city yard can thrive. You can still garden in the city with reduced water availability, especially if you're smart about water usage and conservation.

Conserving Water

You can conserve water in many different ways. But, you first need to understand how much water your plants will need. Then you can apply tips and techniques to save water without sacrificing plant performance. One key term that's important to understand is *evapotranspiration*. This is the loss of water due to evaporation from the soil plus through transpiration from plant leaves. Hot, dry, windy days increase the amount of water loss from both. Mulching helps reduce evaporation from the soil, and growing the right plants for your location helps reduce transpiration from the leaves. But let's get more in depth about how much water your plants need.

Knowing how much you need to water

Water is critical for plant growth. In general, plants need 1 to 2 inches of water a week for adequate growth. But that can vary, depending on a variety of factors such as where you live, the time of year, your soil, and what you're growing. By understanding these factors, you can easily be smart about applying the right amount of water at the right time for your plants. This will reduce your water usage, save you money, and keep you from wasting this resource.

As you determine the right amount of water for your garden, keep the following in mind:

- **Right plants.** We've said this a bazzilion times throughout this book, but planting the right plant in the right place in the right climate is critical for success. Some plants have higher water needs than others. Knowing your soil and climate will help you determine which selections are best for your yard. Choosing a drought-tolerant lawn grass, perennial flower, shrub, or tree may save you time and money and save your garden. Young perennial flowers, trees, and shrubs will need more supplemental water than older ones. In general, after the third year, your perennial plants should have sufficient roots to survive without lots of additional watering. Newly planted lawns, annual flowers, and vegetables require more frequent watering than established versions of these plants. Plants that are flowering or fruiting have higher water requirements.

- **Soil.** Knowing what type of soil you have and working to improve it can help reduce water usage. That's why we spent all of Chapter 4 on soil health. Sandy soils don't hold as much water as clay soils. Soils high in organic matter hold more moisture than soils low in organic matter.

- **Time of year.** The time of year affects the water needs of your plants. Those that are growing actively in spring and summer need more water than plants going dormant in fall or winter. Some areas of the country, such as the Southwest, experience seasonal rains during the growing season that replenish water supplies. They also have periods of hot, dry, windy weather when plants require extra watering. Knowing what Mother Nature is up to helps you determine an appropriate watering schedule.

✔ **Where you live.** In some areas of the country, such as the Pacific Northwest and Northeast, lack of water for the garden isn't often an issue. Rains usually come on a regular basis, and you can often go weeks without having to supplement what the rain clouds bring. (However, with climate change occurring, rainfall is becoming more irregular in some areas.) In other areas, such as Southern California, long stretches of dry weather require constant watering to keep young plants alive.

Using less water

Knowing how much water plants need and the environmental factors that affect those needs is important, but how you actually deliver water to the garden can play a big role in how much water you actually use. Regardless of whether you are watering vegetables, trees, or a lawn, some basic watering practices that are most efficient will save you water. Here are some tips.

✔ **Time your watering right.** There's a reason those sprinklers go on at hotels and golf courses at 5 a.m., besides not to annoy the guests. Watering in the early morning is a good way to make moisture available to plants before the heat of the day increases water loss through evaporation. Generally, the warmer the temperature, the more water evaporates into the atmosphere. Evening is another good time to water to reduce moisture loss, but having wet leaves going into the night contributes to disease build-up, so avoid watering at night.

✔ **Water deeply and infrequently.** It's best to water deeply when you irrigate established lawns, shrubs, flowers, and trees. This means allowing water to soak into the soil at least 8 inches deep. Applying water a few times a week this way is better than watering a little each day and wetting only the top few inches of soil. Deep watering encourages roots to grow down into the soil, where they can take advantage of stored moisture. Shallow watering results in root growth only in the top several inches of soil, where they are much more vulnerable to heat and drought. The exception is watering containers and young seedlings. These plants may need daily watering. We talk more about watering containers in Chapter 8.

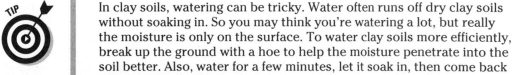

In clay soils, watering can be tricky. Water often runs off dry clay soils without soaking in. So you may think you're watering a lot, but really the moisture is only on the surface. To water clay soils more efficiently, break up the ground with a hoe to help the moisture penetrate into the soil better. Also, water for a few minutes, let it soak in, then come back and water again. This allows the water to sink into the soil instead of running off.

Xeriscaping

Xeriscaping is a term that has been used frequently in low rainfall areas, such as the desert Southwest. It means using gardening practices that reduce or eliminate the need for supplemental watering. Step one is choosing drought-tolerant plants. Throughout this book we've tried to highlight those plants and varieties that are the most drought tolerant. These often are native plants that have adapted to the regional climate and soil in a particular area. It's best to check with your local Master Gardener Program or Extension Service office for lists of native and drought-tolerant plants in your region. Here are some suggestions for drought tolerant plants to try.

✔ **Common drought-tolerant perennial flowers.** Artemisia, echinacea, Russian sage, lamb's ears, penstemon, lavender, sedum, and yarrow.

✔ **Common drought-tolerant trees and shrubs.** Barberry, crape myrtle, cactus, cotoneaster, hawthorn, common juniper, sumac, and viburnum,

✔ **Common drought-tolerant edibles.** Thyme, rosemary, hot peppers, dried beans, pomegranate, fig, mulberry, and persimmon.

✔ **Reduce water competition.** Keep your gardens well weeded, apply compost each year, and mulch with organic matter to conserve water. In urban areas, street trees are usually searching for any place to suck up water and nutrients, due to the amount of paving in a city. If you create an oasis of healthy soil and plants, the nearby tree roots may find it and compete with your plants for water. You certainly don't want to harm city trees. They are your friends. But you may have to add extra water to account for their thievery.

✔ **Keeping track of water.** Using a rain gauge or an automatic water timer on your faucet, you'll be able to keep track of how much rain has fallen and how much water you've applied to your plants.

Harvesting Water

There's only so much that conserving water can do for your garden. If Mother Nature isn't providing regular rains, you'll have to get creative about ways to collect and store water when it's available. One way to harvest water is to use rain barrels and cisterns. Rain barrels and cisterns are positioned under roofs and buildings. Rain water is funneled to these catchment basins to be collected and saved for use during dry periods. This ancient technology has seen a revival of late, especially in urban areas. With climate change and the resulting increase in weather extremes, it's important to be able to collect water during downpours for future non-potable uses such as watering the garden. Here are a few ways to collect and store that water in your city yard.

Installing a rain barrel

One of the simplest ways to collect water is by installing a rain barrel under a downspout of your gutters (see Figure 19-1). Newer technologies makes using a rain barrel safe, easy, and productive. For example, ½ inch of rain hitting a 1,000 square foot roof will yield more than 300 gallons of water. Commercial rain barrels are attractive, too. Some look like old whiskey barrels, while others are shaped like giant urns. They can be nice additions to your yard. Here's what you'll need to get started:

- ✔ **Gutters.** It's clear you'll need gutters on part of your roof to collect the rain water hitting it. Although a cost investment at first, they will pay for themselves in water savings later on. Ideally, place the downspout so that it connects to the gutters on that side of the roof closest to the garden.

- ✔ **Barrels and cisterns.** While a simple 60-gallon rain barrel is great for collecting water, as I mentioned earlier, at times you can collect hundreds of gallons of water in a day. It's hard to just let that water go to waste, especially if you're gardening in a dry climate. You can connect a few barrels together to save more water or use a cistern. Cisterns are large above or below ground vessels that hold hundreds of gallons of water. They may not be practical for the average urban homeowner, but are something to consider when building or buying a home in a dry climate.

- ✔ **Screens.** Water coming off the roof collects leaves, pine needles, and other debris. Place a heavy-duty, removable screen at the end of the downspout to catch these materials before they enter the barrel. This will prevent clogging the outflow spigots in the rain barrel. Clean them out periodically to allow the water to flow through.

- ✔ **Hoses.** Once you have all the pieces in place, you'll need a way to get the water to the garden. You could simply dip your watering can in the barrel and hand water. Also, many commercial rain barrels have spigots where you can attach a hose and run it to the garden. As long as the barrel is higher than the garden, gravity will feed the water through the hose and onto your plants.

Utilizing gray water

Another way to collect water for use in the garden is to create systems to reuse water from inside your house to water plants in your landscape. *Gray water* is the term to describe water generated by activities such as laundry, dishwashing, and bathing that does not contain human waste and is suitable for certain kinds of reuse. This technique takes a little more research, though. Start by checking with your local water municipality for restrictions and guidance on using gray water in your landscape. You'll have to be careful about the presence in the water of chemicals in products like soaps, detergents, and bleach that can harm your plants.

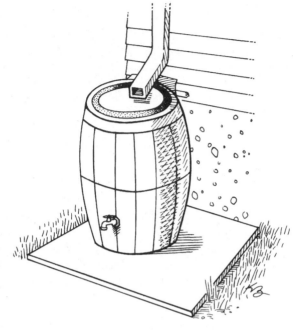

Figure 19-1:
A rain
barrel.

Illustration by Kathryn Born.

Probably some of the safest types of gray water to use on plants would be leftover cooled water from boiling pasta or eggs, or from buckets placed in a shower to catch extra shower water. Always use plant-safe soaps and detergents.

Creating a rain garden

While collecting water to bring to your plants is good idea, you can also divert the water directly to where the plants are growing. In many localities, rain gardens are being built to water plants and reduce the amount of storm water runoff going into municipal waste water systems. Rain gardens are perennial flower or shrub plantings that can grow in an area with occasional flooding. They are grown in a sunken garden created in your yard. Water is then channeled into the rain garden from roofs, driveways, and sidewalks. The benefits are a beautiful garden, habitat for wildlife, replenishment of the ground water since the water soaks into the ground in the rain garden, and filtering of chemicals out of the water by soil microorganisms. Most importantly, a rain garden catches and contains storm water before it becomes runoff. Runoff picks up pollutants as it makes its way to local waterways and often overwhelms city waste water systems, especially during summer thunderstorms. The untreated water then ends up in lakes and streams, adding to the pollution. A rain garden is a good way to harness that rain water for a better use.

Follow these steps to make a rain garden:

1. **Find a good spot.**

   Often your urban yard will have a low spot or a place where rain water naturally collects during wet periods. That would be the best spot for a rain garden as long as the water drains well there. If not, locate your rain garden down slope from a gutter downspout, but at least 15 feet away from the building and upslope from any municipal storm drains.

2. **Once you find your site, test the water drainage.**

   You'll want an area that not only collects water, but also allows it to drain into the soil. Water should only stand in the garden for a few hours after a rain. You can also amend the soil with compost, sand, and topsoil to increase the water drainage.

3. **Dig your garden.**

   The shape and size of the rain garden is up to you and your free space. It's important to have the garden gently slope down, at least 6 inches below the native soil line. The center should be deeper than the edges and the bottom should be fairly level so the water is distributed equally throughout the garden.

4. **Choose your plants.**

   Check out the light levels in your rain garden area and choose plants adapted to shade or sun, depending on your conditions. Some good rain garden plants that can withstand occasional flooding include aster, columbine, goldenrod, Joe-Pye weed, holly, dogwood shrubs, and elderberry.

5. **Plant and mulch.**

   Place water lovers in the deepest spot where more water will collect and other plants that tolerate less drenching on the edges. Work in a 1-foot-deep layer of compost and topsoil for the plants to grow in. Build an additional 6-inch-tall berm around the garden with mulch or soil to keep the water in the garden during heavy rains.

For more information on building a rain garden, go to www.raingardens.org.

Delivering Water to Your Plants

Whether you are using water from a tap or a barrel, you have to have a delivery system to get that water to the plants. Most urban gardens are small, so creating an extensive watering system may not be necessary. But, many urbanites are busy people, and spending lots of time watering may not be an option. Having the right watering system in place can help save money, water, and time. In this section, we look at some of the options.

Hoses and cans

For a small container garden or raised bed garden, a watering can may be all you need. Plastic cans are lighter in weight and more fashionable than the durable galvanized metal ones. Some plastic watering cans come in bright colors so they are easy to spot and not lose in the yard. Select a can with a removable nozzle or *rose*. This will make it much easier to clean out any leaves and debris that clog the flow of water out of the can. Also, for watering seeds, seedlings, and transplants, select a rose with small holes for a gentle spray of water that doesn't overwhelm your young plants or seeds.

Although not the most efficient way to water, hoses are probably the devices that most gardeners use to deliver water to their plants. Purchasing a hose with the right length is critical to being able to water all parts of your yard. Different types of hoses have advantages and disadvantages.

- ✓ **Vinyl hoses:** These are the lightest in weight, easy to carry, but may kink easily.
- ✓ **Rubber hoses:** These are heavy weight, more durable than vinyl, and more kink proof.
- ✓ **Reinforced hoses:** These are rubber/vinyl blends with thick layers that are reinforced to withstand higher water pressure.

When watering trees, shrubs, perennial flowers, and large vegetables such as tomatoes, it's best to create a basin around the drip line of the plant by building a low berm from soil or mulch around the outside circumference of the root zone. Fill the basin with water from your hose and let it sink into the subsoil. This will help you avoid wasting water on areas between plants.

Watering wands

The device you put on the end of your hose helps determine how efficient and effective your watering will be. Probably the best attachment for your hose is a watering wand. Watering wands have short or long metal necks with a small-holed rose at the end. The spray is gentle for plants, directed to where you want it to go, and easy to use. The long-necked versions allow you to stand upright and direct the water around the base of flowers, trees, shrubs, and containers easily. They also come in bright metallic colors so you're less likely to lose the wand or accidently run it over with the mower.

If you purchase a watering wand, spend a little extra to get one with an on/off switch. The switch allows you to turn off the water flow and save water when moving the hose from place to place.

Trigger nozzles

Trigger nozzles are another option for watering. These are the familiar handheld nozzles available in most home stores and garden centers that screw onto hose couplings. Some have multiple spray pattern options to deliver everything from a gentle flow to a highly pressurized stream of water. Trigger nozzles are helpful because they can fulfill many garden tasks. Use the gentle spray pattern when watering newly planted seedlings. Use the direct stream when blasting insects, such as aphids, off plant leaves.

Always turn off the water at the faucet when not watering the garden. Although it's tempting to leave it on, especially if you have a good seal on your couplings between the nozzle and hose, chances are it will still leak and waste water.

Soaker hoses

A more efficient way to water is to use a soaker hose. A soaker hose is a non-clogging, porous, rubber or plastic hose with small holes all along its length. Attach it to another hose and lay it out in your garden. It's best to use soaker hoses in annual gardens. Run the hose along a row of vegetables or annual flowers. Turn on the water faucet and water weeps through the small holes delivering moisture to the soil around the plant roots. You can snake the hose up and down rows. Although it is more efficient at delivering water to plant roots than a garden hose and nozzle, it does have some limitations. Soaker hoses will waste water in between plants because the holes run the length of the hose. Also, it works best on flat ground and may deliver water unevenly on bumpy or hilly terrain. The holes may clog over time, too.

Soaker hoses are best used in lengths of 50 feet or less. Hoses longer than 50 feet tend to lose water pressure, and the end of the hose doesn't deliver water evenly.

Watering from the kitchen faucet

Many city gardeners don't have an option of an outdoor faucet to attach their hose to. Or some will be living in apartments or condos and need to water plants on a balcony. A simple solution is to use your kitchen faucet. You can directly attach your garden hose to some kitchen faucets, but most will need an adaptor. A simple adaptor allows you to attach any garden hose to your kitchen faucet and run it to your outdoor balcony or patio to water your containers and gardens. Here's how. At a hardware store purchase a faucet adaptor that will screw onto your existing kitchen faucet. Unscrew and remove the existing faucet tip fitting, being careful not to lose any of the gaskets or washers. Set it aside. Make sure your female hose end has a gasket to prevent leaks, and screw this end onto the male end of the kitchen faucet adaptor. Hand tighten and run the hose to your garden to water. It's best to look for lightweight, slim hoses to run through your apartment or house to the garden. These are easier to use and store than traditional garden hoses. When finished watering, replace the garden hose coupler with the original faucet fitting and hand tighten.

Drip irrigation

Probably the most sophisticated and efficient way to water your garden plants is with a drip irrigation system (shown in Figure 19-2). Drip irrigation systems use plastic pipes to deliver water through holes or *emitters* spaced along the pipe. Some drip irrigation systems have main delivery pipes and then flexible lines running off those pipes with emitters at the end of the lines. These are particularly useful for watering containers.

Discovering the pros of drip irrigation

The beauty of a drip irrigation system is you're delivering water exactly where you want it in the garden. The emitters can be placed right under a tree, shrub, flower, or vegetable planting so the water drips in the soil where the roots can use it. There is no wasting water in between plants and in pathways.

Unlike soaker hoses, drip irrigation works well on slopes, delivering a uniform amount of water from all the emitters.

While drip irrigation systems are the best for delivering water efficiently, they also are the most costly. Also, they are more involved to set up and take down than other watering options. If you live in an area where the ground freezes, you'll have to drain the water, roll up the pipes, and remove the drip system each fall and reassemble it in spring. But, if you're into technology and really need to watch your water use, drip irrigation may be the best way to go for you. Drip irrigation is an excellent way to water a rooftop garden, since you'll be directing the water to exactly where it's needed. You won't waste water or create any problems with water leaking through the roof.

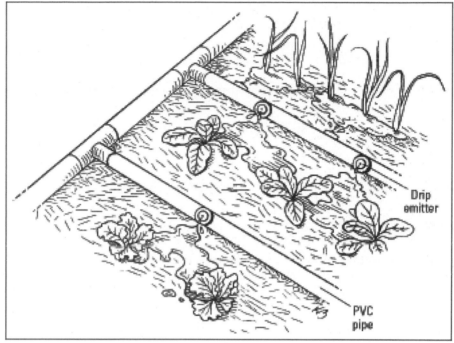

Figure 19-2:
A drip irriga-
tion system
delivers
water to the
right spot in
the garden.

Although emitters are the most common way to deliver water with a drip irrigation system, you can also purchase *microsprinklers*. These are tiny sprinklers that hook up to the drip irrigation pipes. They are attached to small stakes and emit a fine overhead spray. They are probably best used on germinating seeds and young plants.

Most garden centers sell drip irrigation systems, or you can purchase them through the mail. If you really want to get sophisticated you can include pressure-compensating emitters that guarantee an equal flow of water out of each emitter regardless of the water pressure.

Setting up a drip irrigation system

To set up your drip irrigation system in your garden, follow these steps:

1. **Decide on the size of the drip irrigation system you need.**

   Consider getting a slightly larger system to allow for future expansion of your garden.

2. **Lay the pipe on top of the soil or mulch over it. Run the pipe along the garden plantings.**

   Keep the pipes on the soil surface to more easily check for leaks and clogs. If you don't like the look of the pipe, bury it with a few inches of soil or mulch.

3. **Use flexible emitter lines to run water to shrubs, flowers, and trees spaced further apart.**

   Keep the emitters near the base of these plants to deliver water to the roots.

4. **Turn on the drip irrigation system for a few hours each day. After running the system, dig in the soil to see how deeply the moisture has penetrated.** If it hasn't gone at least 6 inches deep, run the system longer. Adjust the run time based on the temperature and amount of rainfall you receive.

Timers can really be lifesavers in the urban garden. These devices attach to your outdoor faucet and can be set to run your drip irrigation, soaker hoses, or sprinklers at set times during the day. There are even timers with moisture sensors that can sense if the ground is dry and turn themselves on automatically or turn the system off if it begins to rain. For a busy city dweller or someone who easily forgets to water, the timer will run the system based on your programming, ensuring water is delivered to your plants. Check out the various timer systems at your local garden center and in the appendix.

Sprinklers

Right behind the hose in popularity is the lawn sprinkler. A fixture on many suburban lawns, for urban gardeners with larger yards you may be tempted to use an overhead sprinkler to water not only your lawn but annual gardens.

Overhead sprinklers are best used on flat areas and on low-growing plants such as lawns, vegetable gardens, annual flowers, and low perennials. If you have plants that are more than a few feet tall, it's best to use another watering method. The overhead sprinkler will not evenly water your garden and may even injure some leaves as the spray hits them.

We placed overhead sprinklers last on our list of watering devices for a good reason. Overhead sprinklers easily waste the most water of any of the watering devices we've mentioned. If you use one with a fixed spray pattern, many times the water falls on places that don't need it. How many times have you seen portable overhead sprinklers watering a lawn — and a driveway and a sidewalk? Also, some of the water evaporates into the air before reaching plants, further wasting this resource.

However, overhead sprinklers are a quick way to deliver water to a large lawn area or big garden, especially if you set them on timers and can walk away while they work. And there are newer designs with adjustable water spray patterns and more water-efficient nozzles.

Overhead sprinklers come in two types; portable devices that you can move around the yard (see Figure 19-3) or in-ground pop-up sprinklers. The in-ground, pop-up sprinklers are the most expensive and require professional installation. Often used on golf courses and large yards, these systems have underground pipes linking to a sprinkler that literally pops out of the ground when turned on to spray water over a designated area. When set on a timer, you don't even have to think about your watering as the sprinklers disappear into the lawn when turned off.

Figure 19-3:
A portable overhead sprinkler.

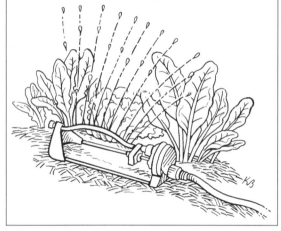

Illustration by Kathryn Born.

More gardeners use a portable overhead sprinkler. These sprinklers attach to a garden hose and come in many different shapes and sizes. Some rotate to spray a 360-degree water pattern, while others oscillate back and forth. These deliver water quickly to a large area, but they require you to drag hoses around the yard to move the sprinklers periodically or you may inundate your plants with water and spike your water bill.

We mention earlier in this chapter that watering is best done in the morning. Well, it's particularly important with overhead sprinklers. Since you're wetting the foliage with your sprinkler, the plants need time for leaves to dry before evening to avoid encouraging leaf diseases to take hold.

A few other watering methods to try

You may be a little intimidated with all these watering options for your city garden. Don't be. There are plenty of easy, lower cost ways to water, using simple devices and homemade products. Here are a few ideas to try:

- ✔ **Water jugs**. For the cost conscious, try this watering trick. Take an empty 1- or 2-liter plastic water or milk jug. Cut off the bottom and secure the cap. Poke 4 small holes in the top of the jug near the cap with a drill bit or knife. Dig a hole near some larger plants, such as tomatoes, and bury the jug, cap side down, one-third of the way into the soil. Fill the jug with water and let it drip slowly into the soil, moistening the roots. You can place the jug so that it's hidden by the plant's foliage.

- ✔ **Watering spikes**. If you want to get a little more sophisticated with your jug watering system, try watering spikes. These plastic tapered spikes have a hollow center and holes in their walls. They are like a mini-drip irrigation system and couldn't be simpler to use. Take that same 1- or 2-liter water or milk jug, cut off the bottom, and attach the jug's spout to the threaded end of the spike. Push a water spike into the ground around a tomato, perennial flower, or even small shrub and fill the jug with water. The water slowly drips out of the holes into the surrounding ground just like a drip emitter. It delivers water more consistently than a water jug alone and, depending on the soil, can hold water for up to 4 hours. It's perfect for a small-space gardener with a few plants.

  Water spikes are great for houseplants, too. You can purchase decorative water spikes that are attractive and slowly deliver water to your plant.

- ✔ **Moisture-absorbing polymers**. You can add these small white crystals to container soil mixes to enable them to hold more water. The polymers absorb the water and swell into a jelly-like mass. Then they slowly release the water back into the soil mix as it dries out.

- ✔ **Gator Bags**. These bags are perfect for keeping newly planted trees watered. Each double-layered, heavy-duty plastic bag has a sleeve that can be filled with water. At the bottom is a hole where the water slowly drips out, watering your tree. We talk more about Gator Bags in Chapter 6.

Chapter 20

Controlling Urban Garden Pests

. . . .

In This Chapter

▶ Attracting beneficial insects, birds, and butterflies to your garden

▶ Determining the steps to identifying plant damage

▶ Distinguishing good insects from bad insects

▶ Handling common diseases you'll find in your garden

▶ Sleuthing out animal damage and safe controls

. . . .

*N*o matter how well you garden and how carefully you care for your prized plants, sooner or later pests will become a concern. It's always amazing that even in the concrete jungles of many urban environments, insects, diseases, and animal pests can find a small garden tucked away between buildings. But pests are clever and they want to survive. If you plant it, they will come.

You can look at pest control as a type of warfare, where you are trying to kill pests once they arrive. But we like to take a more holistic approach. If you build a healthy garden, grow the right plants in the right places, create diversity within your landscape, and encourage nature to be your guardian, you'll be amazed at how little pest control you really have to do.

In this chapter, we show you how to encourage the beneficial insects in your garden that fight the bad guys. We help you determine the cause of the damage you see and whether you need to do anything at all to control it. We cover common insect, disease, and animal pests and give you strategies for preventing damage, and show you safe and effective ways to control pests when necessary.

Don't let pests get you down. Coexistence with the insect, microbe, and animal kingdoms in the garden is possible!

Knowing the Good Guys

Not all insects, microbes, and animals are pests. In fact, most of the fauna that's active in your yard and garden is either beneficial to plants or neutral. It's just a small percentage of these critters that can cause damage, and an even smaller percentage of those that create enough damage to warrant action.

The first step is to figure out who's who in your yard. Knowing who to look out for and who to encourage will help you create a habitat that is good for flora and fauna alike. Some of the most obvious "good guys" are bees, other beneficial insects, and birds. Encouraging them to visit your garden will do far more good than harm.

Bringing in beneficial insects

Many insects either prey on or parasitize other more harmful insects in your garden. For the city gardener, here are the top five insects you should entice to hang around. You can create a habitat to encourage them or buy these beneficial insects to spread in your garden.

- **Beneficial nematodes.** These microscopic, worm-like creatures love to parasitize many soil-borne insects that are a hazard to your garden such as Japanese beetles, grubs, and cutworms. Unlike other nematode species that attack plants, beneficial nematodes only are interested in meat. Apply these nematodes in the evening with temperatures between 60 and 90 degrees F and water the area well after applying. They will go on a search and destroy mission to clear your soil of the bad guys.

- **Braconid wasp.** These tiny wasps parasitize aphids, cabbageworms, and other caterpillars. Plant parsley family herbs, such as carrots and parsley, around to attract these beneficial insects to your garden.

- **Lacewings.** These delicate, transparent winged insects with green or brown bodies feed on a wide range of soft-bodied insects such as aphids, thrips, caterpillars, and mealybugs. Release lacewings into your garden and, believe it or not, leave some weeds nearby to entice them to stay.

- **Ladybugs.** Probably the best-known predator insect, ladybugs or lady beetles are small orange or red beetles with black spots that feed on a wide range of insects including mealybugs and spider mites. They are easy to purchase and release, but they like to fly away if they don't have a food source, so consider placing a small bowl of a sugar and water solution in the garden to keep them around to lay eggs and have multiple generations in the garden.

✔ **Trichogramma wasp.** These tiny beneficial wasps lay their eggs inside other insects, such as cabbageworms, cutworms, and codling moths. The eggs hatch and parasitize the insect.

 To lure and keep beneficial insects around your garden, make sure you grow a diversity of flowers, trees, and shrubs in your yard, just as you would to attract bees and birds. Consider planting parsley and sunflower family herbs and flowers, such as aster, cilantro, daisy, dill, marigold, and zinnia, to attract these beneficial insects, and have a water source nearby for them to drink from. Avoid using insecticides in the garden that can harm beneficial insects.

Attracting birds to your yard

Birds do a number of great things for your garden. They eat harmful insects such as aphids and mosquitoes. For example, just one baby robin can eat 1,000 insects in one day! Some birds, such as hummingbirds, pollinate flowers and vegetables and others, such as finches, eat weed seeds so they don't spread. Plus, in cities where there isn't a lot of nature happening, birds bring us back to our rural roots and provide endless hours of entertainment and stress relief.

Yes, birds can sometimes eat newly planted seeds and ripening strawberries, blueberries, and tomatoes, but there are simple ways to prevent this kind of damage. Let birds thrive in your garden and you will get more benefits than problems from their presence.

Here are some ways to encourage bird life in your yard:

✔ **Grow food birds like.** Grow a diversity of trees, shrubs, flowers, and vegetables that produce food that attract birds to your yard. Grow fruiting trees and shrubs such as crabapples and hollies. Consider setting up bird feeding stations by using different feeders for various species of birds.

✔ **Provide bird shelter.** Birds need places to nest and hide as much as they need food and water. Grow some evergreens, hedges, and clumps of native plants close to your garden to provide the best hiding places for your feathered friends.

✔ **Give them water.** Birds need a place to get a drink, especially in cities where natural ponds are scarce. Set up birdbaths or small artificial ponds for them to sip from.

✔ **House a bird.** Consider building and putting up bird houses to provide a safe place for your birds to nest and build their populations.

Beneficial bats and toads? You betcha!

When most people think of bats, they associate them with vampires and flying into your hair. However, bats are beneficial, too. Bats eat hundreds of insects including moths, mosquitoes, and beetles. So, when building houses for birds, erect a few bat houses, too. They can be purchased locally or through some of the resources listed in the "Resource" section.

Speaking of unusual beneficial creatures, encourage toads and frogs in your garden, as well. They eat hundreds of insects a night and make those great sounds that you often miss living in a city. Have a water spot nearby and provide shelter by turning broken clay pots upside down in the garden to make them a home.

Encouraging bees to stick around

Since you're bringing nature into your garden, don't forget about bees and butterflies. Honeybees are responsible for pollinating one-third of the food we eat. They are critical to our food supply and critical to your vegetables and fruits. Even in the city, honeybees, bumblebees, and native bees can thrive given the right conditions. For example, in Chicago, Beeline Urban Apiaries (www.sweetbeginningsllc.com) produce honey products from locally raised bees. Urban youth and adults help care for the hives and make honey-related products from what they produce.

Butterflies for a little beauty

Butterflies are another kind of insect that make your garden a lively place. Butterflies don't prevent other insects from attacking your plants, and the larval or caterpillar stage of some will eat the foliage of some of your herbs and vegetables. But butterflies are simply a pleasure to watch. Monarch, swallowtail, and sulfur butterflies are just some of the species that may adorn your garden. As with bees, plant

a diversity of annual and perennial flowers to attract butterflies to your yard. Don't spray pesticides on the plants that butterflies love, and you'll be rewarded with these beauties gracing your garden. Some good butterfly-attracting plants to grow in your garden include butterfly weed (*Asclepias*), butterfly bush (*Buddleia)*, lantana, cosmos, zinnia, marigold, coneflower, and rudbeckia.

Bees don't prevent other insects from attacking your plants, but they do pollinate the blossoms in your flower and vegetable gardens, making them more productive. While you might not be up for tending your own honeybee hives, it's easy to create a habitat that bees love. With native bee populations declining across the country, creating healthy places for bees, even in cities, is more critical than ever. Here are some ways to help bees be at home in your yard:

✔ **Grow a diversity of flowers.** Different bees love different flower shapes, patterns, and nectar. Grow a wide range of annual and perennial flowers, with some flowers in bloom from spring until fall. Umbrella-shaped flowers such as dill, fennel, and cilantro are particularly popular with many bee species.

✔ **Make a bee home.** While buying hives for bees may be more than you want to tackle, creating nesting places for native bees is less daunting. Here are a few ideas:

• Place mason bee houses around your yard.

• Make your own bee houses by bundling partially rotten, hollow stemmed plants such as raspberry canes together. Place them in a protected spot, such as under a balcony. Solitary bees in particular will find the stems and make use of them as a home.

• Use clay flower pots to attract bumble bees as well. Partially bury the pot upside down in an out of the way place. The bees will use the bottom drainage hole as an entrance and build a nest inside.

Being Proactive to Control the Bad Guys

Besides encouraging the arsenal of good guys to help you out, there are some other things you can do in your garden to fend off harmful insect attacks and make it less likely that you'll have to resort to using pesticides. Proper garden design techniques and good garden sanitation can go a long way toward preventing problems from occurring. It's also important to identify just what's causing the problem on your plant and determine if it's serious enough to warrant action on your part. Sometimes the damage you see is not enough to threaten the plant's health or your harvest and can just be ignored.

Designing your garden to prevent problems

How you lay out your garden can help deter insect attacks. Plants grown in the most suitable conditions of sun, soil, and wind exposure will be healthy and less likely to get attacked by insects and disease than weak plants struggling to survive. Just like in the animal kingdom, predators can sense when their prey is weak and will go after it with a vengeance. Keeping your garden healthy is the first step in preventing insects' attacks. Insects can actually pick up chemical clues from stressed plants that will lead them to their prey.

You can also make plants more vulnerable to some insects by giving them too much fertilizer. For example, aphids love young succulent growth on plants. If you apply too much nitrogen fertilizer, which encourages all that new growth, your plant is more likely to suffer an aphid infestation.

How you lay out your annual garden each year will also influence the likelihood of some insects and disease problems. Rotating crops by not planting the same family of crops in the same location for three years is a way to prevent certain insects and disease-causing organisms from building up in the soil and attacking your plants. If you plant a row of all one type of plant, it's like a giant calling card for insects. Mixing flowers, herbs, and vegetables together in the garden can confuse harmful insects.

Deciding whether you really have a problem

Once you find some damage, you'll then have to decide what caused it and if it warrants action. Not all damage to your plants is related to insects, diseases, or animals. Environmental factors such as hail, heavy rain, heat stress, high winds, or physical contact with humans, dogs, and other animals can all cause damage. For example, excessive heat and drought can cause leaf scorch (shown in Figure 20-1). You may see holes in leaves, browning of leaf edges, broken stems, and torn flowers. In the city, smog, excessive heat, and drought may harm your plants, causing yellowing or leaf dieback. We talk about these conditions later in the chapter. Identifying what's causing the problem is the first step to deciding what to do about it.

If you decide that the problem is being caused by insects, diseases, or animals, then you'll have to figure out if it's worth remedying. Try to accurately identify the insect or disease that's causing the damage. If you're not sure, take a sample insect or a plant part showing symptoms (or photos of the problem) to a Master Gardener or County Extension agent to have it properly identified.

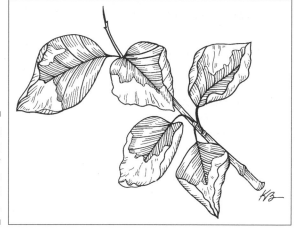

Figure 20-1:
Leaf scorch
caused by
excessive
heat and
drought.

Illustration by Kathryn Born

Check to see if you have just a few of harmful pests around or if they are crawling all over your plants. A few pests are actually a good thing because they will lure beneficial insects in by giving them something to feed on. As long as there's a meal available, the good guys will stay in your garden.

Decide if your problem plant is an important crop, one that can be replaced easily, or one you didn't care for too much anyway. Are all the plants infested with the same insect? If so, it may warrant action. If only a few plants are infested, perhaps you can pull out those plants or wait and let the good guys come in. Some damage to plants may be mostly cosmetic and not actually that harmful to the plant. For example, spittlebugs are small insects that feed on the sap of annual flower, herb, and vegetable stems. They create a frothy "spit" to protect themselves. If you just have a few here and there, they aren't worth controlling.

Think about your reasons for gardening. If you can tolerate some damage — a few spots on rose leaves, some brown patches on apples, or a scattering of aphids on lettuce — then you may not have to act at all. It may be more important to you to have a chemical free garden or yard than one producing perfect-looking, blemish-free plants.

Dealing with Insect Pests in Your Garden

Insect pests can be local problems or generalized across the country. Certainly, there are many insect pests and some may be very specific to your area. Consult your local Master Gardeners or County Extension agent with insect pest problems that are unique or baffling to figure out.

Know your bug

Here are some of the most common insect pests to watch out for on your vegetables, fruits, trees, shrubs, flowers, and lawns.

- ✔ **Ants**: Ants are actually okay in the garden and yard. They are mostly harmless to plants, unless you're talking about fire ants. However, their tunneling and nest building can cause plant roots to dry out. To remove a nuisance nest, use a commercial sugar and boric acid bait and place it near the ant nest. The ants will be drawn to the container, take the mixture back to the nest, and share it. The boric acid will kill the ants. This is also effective on cockroaches.

- ✔ **Aphids**: These small, soft-bodied, pear-shaped insects (see Figure 20-2) come in green, red, black, or translucent colors. They congregate on the undersides of leaves and new buds and new growth, sucking the plant juices. If severe, their feeding will cause yellow leaves and stunt a plant's growth. Aphids exude a sticky sap called *honeydew* as they feed. It makes leaves sticky and can drip on the ground or whatever else is below, making a sticky mess. The honeydew may turn black if a fungus called sooty mold starts growing in it. Avoid applying excessive nitrogen fertilizer, which creates the new growth that aphids love. Blast aphids off the leaves with water from a hose to manage minor infestations or spray with insecticidal soap to control them.

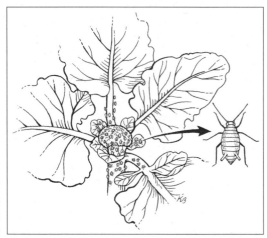

Figure 20-2:
Aphids.

Illustration by Kathryn Born.

- ✔ **Apple maggot**: These housefly-sized insects spend the winter in the soil and emerge to lay eggs on apples, crabapples, plums, and other fruits in June and July. The maggots tunnel into the fruit and ruin it. Clean up dropped fruit within a few day to reduce the number of over-wintering insects. Hang red balls coated with a sticky substance in June to trap the adults as they look for apples in which to lay their eggs. Hang two traps per young tree and six to eight per mature tree. Clean traps periodically and refresh with more sticky stuff. Although they won't completely eliminate apple maggots, they will reduce the population enough to allow you to enjoy the fruit.

✓ **Black Vine weevil**: This black beetle has a characteristic long snout. It hides in the soil and emerges to feed on the leaves of evergreens, such as rhododendrons, and fruit, such as strawberries. The larvae of the beetle live in the soil and feed on plant roots. Cover susceptible crops with a floating row cover and spray beneficial nematodes on the soil to kill the larvae.

✓ **Borers**: These are the larvae of certain beetles or caterpillars that burrow into plant stems, roots, and trunks, killing plant tissues and opening the way for diseases to enter. A wide variety of plants including raspberries, squash, roses, peaches, apples, dogwood, rhododendron, and irises are infected by various borers. When possible, plant borer-resistant selections, such as river birch instead of borer-susceptible white birch. Cover flowers and vegetables with a floating row cover to prevent adult insects from laying eggs. Wrap trees to prevent borers from entering bark. Once infested, slit soft stems of iris and squash to remove the larvae. Spray beneficial nematodes into active borer holes in woody plants.

✓ **Caterpillars**: There are many species of caterpillars that feed on leaves of a wide range of plants. The adult butterflies and moths may look beautiful and harmless, but the young can be devastating. Tent caterpillars, webworms, fruit moths, and gypsy moths are some of caterpillars that attack trees, while cabbageworms (see Figure 20-3), tomato hornworm, and corn earworm are some that attack vegetables. Luckily, a specific organic spray, *Bacillus thuriengensis* (Bt), kills these caterpillars safely and effectively.

✓ **Chinch bug**: These small, black insects suck the juice from grass blades in lawns, turning whole sections brown. They are particularly a problem on warm-season grasses in the South. Plant resistant varieties of grass and try spraying neem oil to control chinch bugs.

✓ **Colorado potato beetle**: This yellow-and-black striped beetle lays orange eggs in clusters under potato, nicotiana, and eggplant leaves primarily. The eggs hatch into soft, red larvae that can quickly defoliate a plant. Handpick adult beetles, crush the eggs, and spray Bt San Diego to kill the larvae.

✓ **Cucumber beetle**: These small yellow-and-black striped or spotted beetles love cucumbers, melons, and other squash family crops. Their feeding can do enough damage to kill young plants. Cucumber beetles also carry a bacterial wilt disease that infects cucumbers. Cover plants with a floating row cover to prevent damage. Spray spinosad or pyrethrin to control a severe infestation.

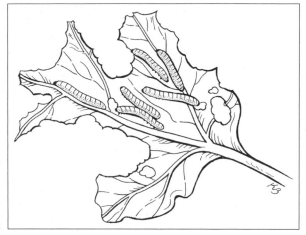

Figure 20-3:
Cabbage-
worms.

Illustration by Kathryn Born.

✔ **Cutworm:** Cutworms are soil-dwelling caterpillars that cut down tender young seedlings at ground level in spring. Control them by wrapping susceptible seedlings with strips of newspaper or an empty toilet paper cardboard roll to create a protective barrier around the stems. Remove the wrapping once the plants are big.

✔ **Flea beetles:** These small, black-shelled beetles hop when disturbed; hence their name. They attack young vegetable and flower seedlings, creating shotgun-like holes in the leaves. If damage is severe, the plant may die. Cover plants with a floating row cover to prevent damage and spray with neem oil to control a heavy infestation.

✔ **Fungus gnats:** These tiny black flies emerge from houseplant soils and fly around your house. Although not much of a threat to the plant, they are pesky in the house. Control them by repotting the plant, laying a layer of sand over the potting soil, hanging a yellow stick trap above the soil, and drenching the soil with Bti (*israelensis*).

✔ **Japanese beetle:** This metallic copper-and-black colored beetle is large and hungry. It feeds on a wide range of leaves and flowers including grapes, cherry, plum, hollyhocks, basil, and roses. The larval stage is a white, C-shaped grub (shown in Figure 20-4) found in the soil that feeds on the roots of lawn grasses and can cause severe damage. Control this pest by killing the grubs. Spray milky spore powder or beneficial nematodes on lawns in spring and late summer to kill the grubs. Handpick adult Japanese beetles, trap, or spray with neem oil to deter their feeding.

✔ **Leaf Miners and Sawflies:** These caterpillar-like pests are mainly leaf feeders. Sawfly larvae often feed on leaf undersides, while leaf miners tunnel within the leaves, leaving winding trails. These pests attack a variety of plants, including vegetables, such as beets, spinach, and Swiss chard, and trees and shrubs such as pines, birch, lilac, and holly. Rake up fallen leaves and destroy them. Spray spinosad to control leaf-feeding sawfly larvae on trees and shrubs. Once leaf miners are inside the leaf, they are protected from pesticide sprays. Prevent problems by covering susceptible vegetables with a floating row cover to prevent adult egg-laying.

✔ **Mealybugs:** These cottony, white insects are often found outdoors on citrus and other evergreens and indoors on houseplants. They suck the plant juices, causing leaves and stems to die. Like aphids, they leave honeydew behind that may develop sooty mold. Control mealybugs by spraying with horticultural oil. For small infestations dab individual insects with a cotton swab soaked in rubbing alcohol.

✔ **Root maggots:** These fly larvae are tiny but can cause damage on the roots of carrots, cabbage, onions, and radishes. The adult fly lays eggs on the roots at the soil line. The maggots tunnel into the root to feed, opening the way for diseases. Cover crops with a floating row cover to prevent damage.

✔ **Scale:** Looking like bumps along plant stems and leaf veins, these pests are either soft or hard shelled. Like mealybugs, they suck plant sap and create sticky honeydew. They attack a large number of shrubs and trees and are a common pest on houseplants. Spray horticultural oil to suffocate the scale insects or prune off infested limbs. To control small infestations, clean off scale with your thumbnail, flicking the insects into a pail of soapy water.

✔ **Snails and slugs:** These gastropods are slimy and slow moving. They love to feed on leaves of many plants, especially lettuce, hosta, and basil. They thrive during periods of cool, wet weather and mostly feed at night. To limit their damage, remove hiding places such as mulch, space plants further apart, and cultivate often to dry out the soil. Trap them with beer traps or boards. In the morning clean out beer traps and lift boards to remove the slugs and snails that have congregated there; toss them into a pail of soapy water. Try ringing container plants with copper strips to repel slugs. Spread non-toxic (to all but the slugs!) baits containing iron phosphate.

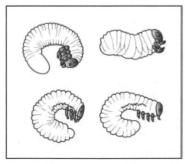

Figure 20-4:
Grubs.

Illustration by Ron Hildebrand.

- **Spider mites:** These tiny, spider-like pests are hardly noticed until their numbers are great and they create webbing on plant leaves and flowers. Their feeding causes leaves to yellow and die. If severe, their feeding can kill plants. Spider mites thrive during periods of dry, windy weather and attack a wide range of fruit trees, ornamental plants, flowers, roses, and houseplants. Mist plants often to keep the leaves humid and prevent spider mites from attacking. Spray with insecticidal soap or horticultural oil sprays.

- **Whiteflies:** If you see a cloud of small white flies take off when you brush against your tomatoes, flowers, or other bedding plants, then you have an infestation of whiteflies. These pests suck plant juices and, like mealybugs, leave sticky honeydew and yellowing leaves in their wake. Use yellow sticky traps to catch whiteflies and spray with insecticidal soap or horticultural oil.

Managing your pests without sprays

I know what you're thinking. You designed your garden well with lots of diversity, your plants are growing strong and are all placed in the right spots, you've set up places for beneficial insects, birds, and bees to roam, and you've been diligent about watching for pests. But there are still some of the previously listed insects and perhaps others in your garden. Now what?

As we mentioned earlier, if you identified an insect as a problem and it is spreading like the plague, then it's time to step into action. But the first order of business is not to spray. In fact, following the *integrated pest management* approach now used around the country, spraying is the last resort. This approach looks for the least toxic ways to thwart insects that might be or have become a problem. It's safe for you, pets, wildlife, and the environment while still being effective in solving the problem. Here are some of the techniques and products you can use to control your pests without sprays.

Exerting physical force

This may sound strange, but you can remove and control many insect pests with physical force. Handpicking beetles and dropping them into a pail of soapy water, blasting aphids off a plant leaf with a strong burst of water from a hose, and even sucking up flea beetles and leafhopper insects with a handheld vacuum cleaner are all examples of using force to stop bugs.

Blocking them out

Physical barriers are a good way to avoid having the pest problem in the first place. This takes a little forethought and planning, but these barriers are safe and effective. Here are a few examples of barriers to use on your plants.

✔ **Floating row covers** (see Figure 20-5) are made from white, translucent cheesecloth-like material that allows air, water, and light through but blocks insects and can protect plants from frost. The best types for summer pest control are lightweight row covers that don't trap too much heat. They can stop a wide variety of insects, such as leaf miners, cabbageworms, potato bugs, and cucumber beetles. They also help keep critters like rabbits away; we'll talk about those later. Get covers in place when plants are young and make sure the edges are secured to the ground so pests can't slip under. But check periodically under the row cover for any insects that might have sneaked inside. Remove row covers from vegetables that need pollination by bees, such as squash, when flowering begins.

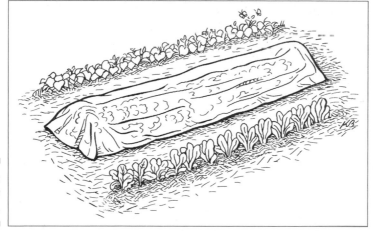

Figure 20-5:
Floating row cover.

Illustration by Kathryn Born.

✔ **Collars and mats** can be used to prevent insects from attacking roots or stems. Wrap layers of newspaper strips around stems or place empty toilet paper tubes around transplants, extending 1 inch below the soil and 3 inches above to keep cutworms from attacking young plant stems. A square piece of tar paper laid on the soil around cabbage, cauliflower, or broccoli transplants will prevent root maggot flies from laying their eggs.

✔ **Copper strips or mesh** wrapped around raised beds or containers prevent slugs and snails from crossing. When the slimy slugs come in contact with the copper, a chemical reaction causes a shock that repels them. Make sure the slugs and snails are totally removed from the container or bed because this trick only works when they try to cross the barrier.

✔ **Irritating materials** such as sharp sand, wood ashes, and crushed sea and egg shells all will repel certain pests. Spread these materials around plants slugs love to deter them, and place in the holes when planting bulbs to thwart mice and voles.

✔ **Tree wraps and plastic protectors** (see Figure 20-6) help young trees withstand attacks by mice, voles, and rabbits in winter. These rodents love to eat tree bark, and their damage can girdle a tree and kill it. See Chapter 16 for more on these products. Tree wraps also can stop borers from tunneling into peach, apple, and other fruit trees.

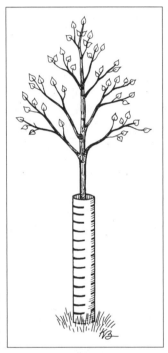

Figure 20-6:
Tree guards.

Illustration by Kathryn Born.

Trapping them

There are a number of new technologies using traps to lure insects to their death. These traps use a bug's attraction to color or mates to bring them in.

✔ **Japanese beetle traps** have a sex lure that attracts the beetle to the trap. The key is to place the traps away from prized plants or the beetles will have a snack on the way to the trap. It's best if your neighbors trap the beetles also or you'll have all the beetles from the community in your yard. There are similar traps for codling moths on apples.

✔ **Yellow sticky traps** are plastic squares coated with a sticky substance called *tanglefoot*. Whiteflies, aphids, fungus gnats, and cucumber beetles are attracted to the color yellow and fly onto the trap and get stuck. Place these traps right above the infested plants.

✔ **Apple maggot traps** use the adult apple maggot fly's love of the color red to trick it on to this sticky ball to lay its eggs. The female fly thinks she's landing on a red apple to lay her eggs. Once stuck on the trap, she dies. This technique may not control all the maggots on an apple tree, but it will reduce the number of pests.

Using safe sprays

Sometimes all the prevention and trickery in the world isn't enough to save a flower, vegetable, tree, or shrub from attack. You may need to use sprays and dusts as a last resort.

First of all, always read the label completely before applying any pesticide; wear gloves, hat, goggles, a long-sleeved shirt, and any other protective gear that's recommended. Spray on calm, clear days, ideally in the early evening to have the least impact on bees. Be sure to cover the upper and lower surfaces of leaves.

Here are some of the safest and most common organic sprays and dusts available.

✔ **Diatomaceous earth:** This powdery dust is made from the skeletons of tiny ancient diatoms. Its sharp edges are lethal to slugs and aphids and the powder repels ants, flea beetles, and whiteflies.

Diatomaceous earth and any other pesticide powders can also harm your lungs. Whenever you use these powders, wear a mask to avoid breathing in the dust.

✔ **Horticultural oil:** This product is made from vegetable, herb, or petroleum oils. It works primarily by coating and suffocating the eggs, young, or adult insect. A heavier formulation called dormant oil is sprayed on deciduous trees and shrubs in winter before leaves emerge. Summer oil is a lightweight version that can be used on plants in summer. It kills aphids, spider mites, mealybugs, and scale. It can harm plants when sprayed during very hot or cold temperatures.

✔ **Insecticidal soap:** This simple product is refined liquid soap that's safe for most plants, yet kills a wide range of insects including Japanese beetles and slugs. It is mild acting but can harm certain plants such as peas, so read the label carefully.

✔ *Bacillus thuriengensis* **(Bt):** This bacterial pesticide kills a number of caterpillars such as cabbageworms and tent caterpillars without harming beneficial insects, pets, wildlife, or humans. There are strains to control Colorado potato beetles and fungus gnats as well. The bacteria is ingested by the insect and rots out the bug's gut. It may take a few days to see results after spraying.

Spinosad is another product made from bacteria that is effective against caterpillars and a number of other kinds of insects.

✔ **Neem oil:** The pesticide is derived from the oil of neem seeds. The oil doesn't necessarily kill insects but deters their feeding, disrupts egg laying, and inhibits their ability to grow. It's effective against a wide range of insects including caterpillars, beetles, and leafminers. Like Bt, it takes time to work. Neem oil is also effective as a fungicide against a variety of diseases we talk about soon.

✔ **Pyrethrin:** This organic spray is derived from a daisy-like flower. It is widely toxic to a number of good and bad insects and honey bees. It has a quick, knock-down effect on insects and should be used only as a last resort on hard-to-kill insect pests. Spray in the evening to avoid harming bees.

Spotting and Treating Diseases

You can certainly control many insect pests with the techniques we've mentioned and the organic sprays that are widely available. But with plant diseases, prevention is the name of the game. Once a disease has taken hold of your plant, it's often much more difficult to prevent its spread and control its damage.

The other issue with diseases is that the symptoms are often similar to weather stress, environmental stress, nutrient deficiencies, and some insect attacks. It's important to determine if it is a disease that attacked your plants and not just air pollution or ozone damage, mechanical damage from a string trimmer, heat or cold stress, or a lack of nutrients. Here are some tips to help you determine what's a disease and what's not.

Knowing whether you're really dealing with a disease

Air pollution is a common problem in many cities. One of the most common air pollutants is ozone. It can cause plant leaves to have a speckled white appearance. Another pollutant, sulfur dioxide, turns leaves yellow, especially between the veins. Some plants, such as beans, lettuce, pines, and English ivy, are more susceptible to this type of damage than others. Hellebore, hosta, lilac, and barberry are some of the plants more tolerant of common city air pollutants. Check out Chapter 16 for more information on pollution-tolerant trees and shrubs. If you are gardening in a heavy traffic area, consider pollution as a cause of leaf dieback before assuming a disease.

In northern areas, road salt is commonly used in winter to melt snow and ice. The salt sprays onto the foliage of trees and shrubs near roadways and can accumulate in the soil. Consider creating a physical barrier between the sidewalk and road and your garden to limit the road salt spray. Also, grow plants not adversely affected by road salt spray such as junipers, lilac, forsythia, potentilla, Russian sage, and spirea.

Heat stress and drought damage often show up as browning on the leaf edges. Keep plants healthy and well watered during hot periods to avoid this. Avoid planting trees especially susceptible to heat stress, such as maples.

Nutrient deficiencies can look like disease symptoms on the leaves. For example, iron deficiency in acid-loving plants such as blueberries and hollies will show up as a yellowing between the green veins of leaves. This may look similar to sulfur dioxide air pollution. The only way to know for sure if your plants have a nutrient deficiency is to do a soil test as described in Chapter 4.

Sometimes physical damage to a plant will show up as a disease-like injury. Mowers and string trimmers banging into tree trunks can cause wounds that open the door for diseases to get started. Although the symptoms later are certainly from a disease, the problem started because someone was careless using machinery around the trees. Mulching around trees and shrubs and using tree guards on trunks are ways to help prevent this kind of damage. See Chapter 18 for more on mulching and tree guards.

Even the weather may cause disease-like symptoms. A late frost can cause leaves that emerged earlier in spring to curl, yellow, and drop. Harsh winter weather can injure plants so they don't leaf out well in spring, or evergreens may have brown leaves or needles that drop. Growing the right plant for your location is important in preventing these problems.

Preventing damage in the first place

How you garden certainly can have an impact on how susceptible your plants will be to disease problems. As we said earlier, prevention is the key. Your attention to the details will help you avoid a problem. Here are some tips on how to be a good disease cop:

- ✔ **Start out right.** Select plants that are disease-resistant, such as 'Jacob Cline' bee balm that resists powdery mildew disease. Choosing plants adapted to your climate and the space you have to grow them, and spacing plants properly to promote good air circulation will help avoid many diseases in the first place.

✔ **Care for your plants well.** Watering plant roots and avoiding wetting foliage will help reduce the amount of fungal diseases on the leaves. Water in the morning, so the leaves are dry before night fall. Wet leaves at night may mean more diseases. Keep your yard clean by picking up diseased leaves, flowers, and fruits each fall and disposing of them properly. Mulch to keep plants healthy and avoid physical damage.

✔ **Keep watching your plants.** Inspect your plants often for any signs of diseases. Some diseases can be stopped in their tracks if caught early. Even if you can't stop the disease on that one plant, you may be able to prevent it from spreading to others in the garden.

✔ **Rotate.** Don't plant the same family of annual flower or vegetables in the same location year after year. Diseases can build up in the soil and more easily harm your plants. Rotate crops by not planting any of that family of plants in the same location for three years, if possible.

Being aware of some common diseases

While there are many diseases that can infect plants, here are some of the most common and most obvious ones that you may find in your city garden. Details on their controls are described later in this chapter.

✔ **Apple scab.** This fungus attacks apples and crabapple trees, especially during periods of cool, wet, and humid weather. The leaves have brown spots and eventually turn yellow and drop. Plant disease-resistant varieties, clean up the ground well in fall, and spray copper sulfate or Serenade sprays early in the season to limit the damage.

✔ **Black spot.** Found mostly on roses, this fungal disease causes black spots on leaves (see Figure 20-7). The leaves eventually turn yellow and drop. It spreads quickly during periods of wet weather. Grow resistant varieties, clean up the dropped leaves and flowers well, and spray Neem oil, Serenade, or a baking soda solution as a preventive spray. Mix 1 tablespoon of baking soda in 1 gallon of water with a dash of liquid soap and spray leaves weekly or after a rain.

✔ **Botrytis blight.** Another fungal disease that likes humid weather, botrytis blight causes leaves and fruits to have fuzzy white and gray patches, brown up, and drop. It's found on flowers such as geraniums, peonies, and begonias and fruits such as strawberries and raspberries. Remove infected plant parts when you see them and space plants properly to avoid the disease.

✔ **Damping off.** See Chapter 6 for more on this fungal disease of seedlings.

✔ **Mildew.** Powdery mildew (see Figure 20-8) and downy mildew are two of the most common forms of this fungal disease. Both cause white, powdery coating on leaves that eventually die. It's found on a wide range of plants including lilac, garden phlox, bee balm, roses, and zinnias. Powdery mildew likes warm days and cool, dewy night. Downy mildew prefers cool, wet weather. Plant resistant varieties, clean up the area well of infected plant parts, and use Serenade as a preventive spray on susceptible plants.

Figure 20-7:
Black spot
on roses.

Illustration by Kathryn Born.

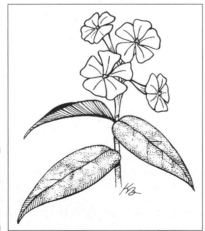

Figure 20-8:
Powdery
mildew on
leaves.

Illustration by Kathryn Born.

✔ **Root rots.** These diseases are caused by a number of kinds of fungi and bacteria. They attack a wide variety of plants such as rhododendron and roses, causing branches to die off and may eventually kill the entire plant. The keys to preventing root rot are building a healthy soil before planting, planting the right plant for your location, and keeping the soil well drained. Cool, wet soils are perfect for many root rot diseases to get started.

✔ **Virus.** Viruses, such as the tobacco mosaic, infect a broad spectrum of edible plants, flowers, shrubs, and trees. These incurable diseases cause mottled and curling leaves, stunted plants, and fruits that ripen unevenly. Prevention starts with using disease-free stock when planting, removing infected cultivated and wild plants nearby, and controlling insects that spread the viruses, such as aphids.

✔ **Wilt.** *Verticillium* and *fusarium* are the two most common fungal wilts. They attack a wide range of plants including tomatoes, peppers, melons, cabbages, strawberries, roses, and cherries. Often the leaves will curl and wilt even though the plant is well watered. The leaves eventually drop and the whole plant may die. Choose resistant varieties, keep the plants healthy, and rotate crops to avoid wilt disease problems in your yard.

Finding the safest sprays for diseases

There are many sprays on the market to stop diseases from spreading. However, as we said with insects, the best controls are cultural, mechanical, and preventative. Here are a few organic sprays that may be helpful in getting a newly started disease under control or preventing one from spreading.

✔ **Baking soda.** It's thought that baking soda changes the pH of the leaf surface, causing it to be unfriendly to disease spores. You can mix your own solutions of baking soda and water to spray or buy a commercial product such as Remedy. Avoid repeated sprays because they may burn the leaves.

✔ **Copper.** Copper sulfate is a powerful spray, killing a broad range of fungi and bacteria. Unfortunately, it also is toxic to mammals and fish, so only should be used as a last resort.

✔ **Neem oil.** Used as an insecticide on a broad range of pests, it also is an effective fungicide on roses and perennials. Use neem oil, not extract, to get the highest potency product.

✔ **Serenade.** This product contains bacteria (*Bacillus subtilis*) that have been found to prevent and slow down the spread of a number of fungal diseases such as black spot and powdery mildew. It's safe for wildlife, beneficial insects, pets, and humans, so should be one of the first sprays you try.

✔ **Sulfur.** This is one of the oldest fungicides used by mankind. Dust or spray it on a variety of diseased plants. Don't use it when temperatures are above 80 degrees F, or it may cause damage to leaves.

Critters in the Bean Patch

It's bad enough having a whole array of insects and diseases that can attack your prized plants, but there are some hungry critters out there that would love to visit your garden as well. Even though you may be in the city, many two- and four-legged animals will frequent your garden, especially those that have adapted to living in urban settings. Because there are slim pickings for animals in the city and you're creating an Eden of greenery, these animals will sooner or later find your garden.

Identifying animal damage

First, you have to know if animals are causing the damage on your prized plants. The easiest identification is to catch them in the act of eating, but many of these critters are most active at night, so you'll need to look for other signs of their visits.

- ✔ **Tracks.** Look for animal tracks in moist, freshly turned soil. If you see a damaged plant and animal tracks nearby, you're one step closer to identifying the culprit.

- ✔ **Sudden damage.** Look closely at the damage. Animals such as rabbits can mow down an entire row of carrots in a few hours. If the damage is sudden and extensive and the weather isn't to blame, chances are it's an animal.

- ✔ **Telltale signs.** Some animals, such as rodents, leave telltale teeth marks in the bark of your trees and shrubs. Moles don't feed on plants, but leave tunnels that voles and mice also use to cause damage. Know your critter and the habitat they like, and you can figure out who's eating your garden.

Homemade repellent sprays

There are many commercial repellent sprays on the market featuring rotten eggs and animal urine as their active ingredients. You certainly can try these as well as homemade products using human hair, garlic, and hot pepper flakes.

The key to using any repellent spray it to rotate between three or four different sprays so the animal never gets used to just one. Also, spray after a rain or after a flush of new growth.

Figuring out which common city animals to watch for

Here area a few of the more common city animals that may be enjoying your garden as much as you are.

- ✔ **Birds.** We waxed poetic earlier in this chapter about attracting birds to your garden, but they can cause problems, too. Birds will dig up newly planted corn or sunflower seeds or peck at ripening tomatoes, blueberries, or strawberries. The best control is to cover seed beds with floating row covers until plants are established and cover berry bushes with bird netting. Scare devices such as plastic owls, reflective tape, and scare eye balloons may work for a short period of time but birds usually get used to them fairly quickly.

- ✔ **Cats.** Roaming cats love to dig up freshly turned soil and use it as a litter box. Kitty poop is not good to use in the garden, so they need to be stopped. Cover newly planted beds with a floating row cover or spread shredded lemon or grapefruit peels around the bed. Cats don't like the smell. Place sharp rose or bramble canes on the bed. The thorns irritate their tender paws.

- ✔ **Dogs.** City folks love their dogs. You'll often see one person walking four or five dogs at a time. Unfortunately, dogs love to mark their territory. Dog urine can burn the leaves of plants and cause them to die. If your garden is near the sidewalk, place a fence between it and the walkway. If you own a dog, take it elsewhere to relieve itself.

- ✔ **Moles, voles, and mice.** Moles make tunnels in garden beds and lawns looking for earthworms and other critters to eat. They often get blamed for damage to bulbs and plant roots because voles and mice will use the tunnels to feed. Voles and mice love bulbs and flower roots. Prevent mole, vole, and mouse damage by spraying castor oil on your garden. These rodents hate the smell and they quickly go away. Stop mice and voles from girdling young trees and shrubs in winter by placing a tree guard around the tree in fall.

- ✔ **Rabbits.** Bunnies seem to have adapted well to city living. All they need is a green patch and a burrow for a home and they'll be happy to help you eat carrot tops, beans, lettuce, and many other plants. A good fence will keep rabbits away. Build it so it extends 1 foot underground, bent away from the garden at a right angle so the bunny can't dig under it, and about 4 feet above ground. Use fencing with small enough mesh that even baby bunnies can't squeeze through it.

- ✔ **Squirrels.** Here's an animal that has adapted very well to living with humans. Squirrels nest in trees, attics, and other buildings. They love to gather and store food for winter. Unfortunately, they also are curious and will pluck tulip flowers, ripening tomatoes, peaches, and plums at will. Protect individual plants with a floating row cover and try repellent sprays to confuse them long enough for you to get a good crop.

Part VI
The Part of Tens

The 5th Wave   By Rich Tennant

I don't think they actually believe it, but they wouldn't be as inspired to work in the garden if they knew it was rutabaga and turnips.

CHEWY BARS   CREME COOKIES   DONUTS   CUP CAKES   BROWNIES

In this part. . .

From the top ten essential garden tools to ten kid-friendly ways to garden in the city, in this part, we provide an assortment of helpful and creative urban gardening solutions. In addition, we provide a chapter on ten ways to develop a *sustainable* urban garden, including how to involve your community and collaborate with others.

Chapter 21

Ten Tools for Urban Gardeners

In This Chapter

▶ Identifying the best tools for urban gardening

▶ Using the right tool for the job

Creating the perfect urban garden is one thing. Keeping it looking great and producing food is another. Maintenance is a critical part of a successful gardening. Hopefully, you've gotten tips by reading our chapters on soil building, watering, weeding, and pest control. But to actually do the work, you need the right tools. The right tool makes or breaks a gardening job. Using a hoe to dig a hole for planting a tree is like eating soup with a fork. It's just not the right tool for the task.

A gardener can buy many different tools. Some are critical to your success, while others are more about show and fun. In this chapter, we focus on ten essential tools you need for gardening in the city.

While you certainly can go to garden centers and home centers and buy all the tools we talk about here, there are other ways to score a good tool. Garage sales or tag sales are our favorites. Often old tools are for sale for next to nothing. They can be cleaned up and used for many years to come. Keep this list of essential garden tools with you as you travel around the city and be on the lookout for purchasing opportunities.

Tools for the city should all have one aspect in common. They should be small enough to work in your space. For each tool, we suggest the right types to be easy to use, functional, and simple to store in a space-starved city home.

Keeping your garden tools clean not only keeps them looking good, it extends their life. After working in the garden, wash your tools clean of soil, let them dry, and store them properly. Periodically sharpen the edge of shovels and hoes so they cut through the soil more easily. Oil wooden-handled tools annually with linseed oil to preserve them.

Hand Trowels and Cultivators

Hand tools are perfect for gardening in raised beds, containers, and window boxes. A hand trowel has a plastic, wooden, or metal handle and a curved metal or plastic blade that comes to a point at the end so you can scoop soil and dig small holes. You can also use it to dig out weeds or even transplant small perennial flowers. Metal is more durable than plastic, but plastic is lightweight and comes in bright colors that make it easier to find when you set it down in the garden.

Hand cultivators (see Figure 21-1) are my favorite. They also have plastic, wooden, or metal handles, but the head is made of three prongs of metal that act like teeth in the soil. Hand cultivators are great for a variety of uses, and I consider it the most essential tool for a small-space gardener. You can dig small holes, create planting furrows, weed, work in fertilizer, and floss your teeth (just kidding) with this tool.

When you buy a hand trowel or cultivator, try a few different types to find one that fits best in your hand. There are even ergonomic versions of hand trowels and cultivators that have a forearm extension so you use the muscles in your arm more than those in your wrist. This is good for gardeners with carpal tunnel or wrist problems.

Figure 21-1:
Hand culti-
vators are
essential
small-space
gardening
tools.

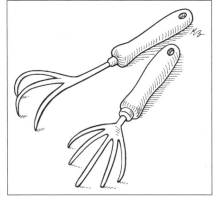

Illustration by Kathryn Born

Shovels

Shovels and spades are two important tools for the garden. A spade has a flat blade that's best for digging holes, while a shovel has a round one that's best for digging and moving soil, mulch, and fertilizer. If you have to choose one, get a shovel. It's still functional as a digging tool, but allows you to scoop and spread other materials better than a spade. There are two versions of shovels to consider — long- and short-handled types. Long-handled shovels give you more leverage when digging holes, while a short-handled shovel is easy to work with in tight places. You probably can guess which one we think is best for an urban garden. Select a short-handled shovel with a D-shaped grip for easier handling and use. Metal-handled shovels are more durable than wooden-handled ones.

Hoes

There's a lot you can do with a good hoe. Hoes can help you build raised beds, create furrows for planting, dig holes, weed, and hill potatoes. There are many different types of hoes available to choose from. Some, such as the oscillating hoe, are specific for weeding, while others, such as the swan neck hoe, have a curved handle that allows you to stand more upright and have less stress on your back.

We like the small-bladed collinear hoe. This hoe has a 1- to 2-inch-high, 3-to 4-inch-long blade on a long handle made of wood or metal. While the common garden hoe has a bigger blade that allows you to move more soil with each stroke, the small-bladed version is better for tight spaces in urban areas.

Hand Pruners

If you're growing trees, shrubs, roses, or perennial flowers, a good pair of hand pruners are essential. Hand pruners cut the small stems and branches of these plants. Getting the one that fits your hand well is key. There are hand pruners for left-handed folks, right-handed people, small hands and large hands. It's best to "try a few on" before purchasing one. Hand pruners come in two types. Anvil hand pruners cut by pressing a sharp blade into a soft metal anvil in the bottom. These are least expensive and are best used for soft, woody branches like raspberries. Bypass pruners feature two blades that cut like a scissors. These are more expensive than anvil pruners, but will cut larger branches on roses, shrubs, and small trees more easily. If you maintain your hand pruners well by cleaning, oiling, and sharpening them annually, they should last many years.

Garden Clothes

Most urbanites love fashion, and they want to look good in the garden, too. But garden clothing should be as much about functionality as fashion. Sure, you can buy the latest Gucci mud boots and color coordinate it with your designer hat, but gardeners need to be practical, too. Here are some things that should be in your gardening wardrobe.

- ✔ **Gloves.** A good pair of gloves keeps your hands clean and blister-free. Although cotton gloves are the cheapest, look for higher quality leather gloves that offer more protection and last longer.

- ✔ **Hat.** The summer sun can be brutal on a gardener. Always wear a hat in the garden. It's best to wear a wide-brim hat with good air ventilation to keep the sun off your neck and head.

- ✔ **Footwear.** You can buy the latest Martha Stewart–inspired designer boots, but mostly you want a waterproof pair that fit properly. Another popular type of garden footwear is clogs. They are made of rubber and are easy to slip on and off as you go in and out of the house. And yes, you can get them in designer colors.

Buckets and Baskets

A city gardener needs a practical device to carry tools, plants, soil, compost, and seeds around in. The simpler the better, we say. A simple, colorful rubber garden tub (shown in Figure 21-2) is lightweight, durable, flexible, and easy to use in the garden. More chic wicker baskets are great for cutting flowers and herbs. There are metal wire baskets that are great for harvesting vegetables. You can simply wash off the soil from your produce right in the basket. When in doubt, there's always the 5-gallon plastic pail. They are sometimes free and as versatile as your imagination.

Figure 21-2:
A flexible garden tub is a simple way to haul materials around in the garden.

Illustration by Kathryn Born

Watering Hoses and Wands

It's essential to be able to water your plants on a regular basis. Having a watering system that's easy to use, convenient, and close by is important. Vinyl or plastic hoses are the cheapest way to go, but if you're having issues with hoses kinking, use a more expensive rubber hose. They are heavier, but worth it in convenience. Get a hose that's long enough to reach to all parts of your garden.

It's also important to get a good watering wand. Watering wands differ from watering nozzles in that they emit a gentle spray of water onto your plants. Some more sophisticated nozzles have multi-spray head options that include a gentle spray option. Use watering wands and the gentle spray option on the nozzle for tender seedlings, small flowers, and young plants. It is easier on the plants and less water is wasted and soil eroded.

Even if you have a good length of hose, a simple watering can is nice to have for tending individual containers or plants. A plastic one is lightweight and probably the best for a small-space garden. Metal cans are more durable, but much heavier.

Wheelbarrow

Although most city gardeners may not have the need to move large quantities of soil, compost, fertilizer, and mulch around, in bigger yards a wheelbarrow may be essential. We prefer a wheelbarrow to a garden cart because wheelbarrows can easily maneuver in tight spaces. The one-wheeled types fit into close quarters, making delivering heavy materials much easier. Garden carts have two wheels and are better balanced but need more room to maneuver.

As with many other tools, carts and wheelbarrows come in metal and plastic versions. For longevity, invest in a metal wheelbarrow. It will be your friend for many years in the garden.

Composter

We talked a lot about making your own compost in Chapter 5. It's clear that in a small-space urban lot having a commercial composter offers many advantages. It's compact, built to last, and most importantly, looks good in the landscape and hides your compost. As we said, composting is messy business. You want a unit that will keep out rats and other city critters, be functional, and look good.

There are two types of composters: *free standing and tumblers*. Free standing composters are basically boxes with doors at the top and bottom. You put the raw ingredients in the top and the finished compost comes out at the bottom. Tumblers are barrel-shaped, and they have a door for adding ingredients. Turn the tumblers daily to mix the ingredients. Keep them well watered.

Freestanding composters are less expensive but are fixed parts of your landscape. Unless you empty them out completely, they can't be moved. Compost tumblers produce finished compost sooner, can be moved around the property even with compost in them, but are more expensive.

Garden Shed

This is really stretching the tool list, but realistically, where are you going to store all these essential tools we've talked about? Many city dwellings are short on storage space to start with. A simple garden shed offers a weather-proof, safe place to store not only tools but fertilizers, pesticides, hoses, and pots. You can build your own shed if you're handy or buy a pre-fab one at the local lumber yard.

Don't consider a shed a necessary, unattractive evil. You can hang window boxes on it, grow vines up it, and paint and decorate it to become part of the landscape.

Chapter 22

Ten Kid-Friendly Ways
to Garden in the City

In This Chapter

▶ Discovering kid-friendly places to garden

▶ Finding fun gardening projects

*M*ost of this book has been devoted to helping you become a better
city gardener, but let's not forget the kids. Children's gardening has
become huge all across the country. Many educators, parents, and public
officials see gardening as a way to reconnect kids with nature, get them outside
for some healthy exercise, and teach them about healthy eating habits.

You don't have to sign your kids up in an official gardening program to get
them involved in a little patch of heaven. You can find many ways to encourage
and entice your children to be involved in the garden at home. Actually, if it's
not seen as a chore, kids love to garden. They often are amazed at the great
taste of home-grown vegetables, fruits, and herbs; look in wonder at insects,
butterflies, and birds; and develop a sense of belonging and responsibility for
their prized plants.

So include your child, grandchild, or neighbor's child in your gardening
plans. This chapter shares ten ways to gets kids growing (gardens, that is).

Garden at School

Thousands of schools in all 50 states now have some form of school gardening
program. Many of these schools are in cities, where they have gotten creative
about where to garden. Often these programs are combined with health
education, exercise, and environmental studies classes. Educators have seen
many benefits from involving school kids in a hands-on gardening program.
Evidence shows that students who participate in school gardening programs
score significantly higher on standardized science achievement tests.
Teachers have also noted that kids involved in school gardening programs

exhibit better cooperation with other students, demonstrate a higher level of responsibility toward others, and show fewer behavioral problems.

If your local school doesn't have a school garden program, you can become involved in the PTO and form a group to encourage teachers to offer them. For more information on how to start a school garden program, go to www. kidsgardening.org.

Garden at a Community Garden

Many urban dwellers would love to garden but don't have the room. Luckily, there are more than 18,000 community gardens in cities and towns across the United States and Canada. We talk about being involved in and starting a community garden in Chapter 12.

Planting a community garden with your child is a great way to initiate them into the fun of gardening. Community gardening isn't just about growing food and flowers on your small parcel of land. It's also a way for you and your child to get to know neighbors and make new friends. It will help them, and you, feel more a part of your community. Involve your child in the plant selection, lay out, and planting of the garden. Depending on his age, let your child help decorate the garden, make plant labels, and add personal touches. It might look a bit messy and chaotic, but your child will be more invested in the garden if she knows she had a hand in its creation.

For old kids, a number of the community gardens now offer kids' gardens as part of their plots. You can rent a small garden for your child and instead of working together with you, he will have his own plot to plant and care for.

To find a community garden in your city, go to the American Community Gardening Association (www.communitygarden.org).

Garden at a Local Botanic Garden

Botanical gardens are local treasures. They are beautifully landscaped with a variety of plant collections, often from around the world. They are education centers and places of peace in a busy urban environment. Many of the more than 1,700 botanic gardens around the world are located in or close to an urban setting.

While botanic gardens are great places to go and relax, get some exercise, and learn about plants, many offer educational programs for members and the general public. These programs often include kids' gardening. Some gardens have plots available on the grounds for kids to use as part of a summer program to teach children about growing food and flowers. Check out the local botanic gardens in your area to see if they have a kids' gardening program or summer camp. For more information on botanic gardens in the United States, go to the American Public Gardens Association (`www.public gardens.org`).

Grow a Sunflower House

Kids love hiding places in the garden. One way to build a hiding place without having to resort to building a structure is to grow a sunflower house (see Figure 22-1). Sunflowers grow tall and by creating a hiding place in the middle of planting, kids feel like they have their own room to play.

To create a sunflower house, grow a 6- to 10-foot-diameter ring of tall sunflowers in the garden (the diameter will depend on your garden's size). Leave a space for an entrance. As these quick-growing annuals grow and eventually start to flower, tie the tops of the sunflowers heads together to create the roof of the house. Wait until the flower heads form before tying the heads together. The heads don't need to be closely tied together, just enough to create the effect of a ceiling. Have your kids decorate the inside room any way they like with small chairs, tables, toys, signs, and anything else that will foster a sense of excitement for their house.

Figure 22-1: A sunflower house is a fun structure to grow in your kids' garden.

Illustration by Kathryn Born.

Select tall varieties of sunflowers to create the house. 'Mammoth Russian' is a particularly good variety because it grows 8 to 10 feet tall and produces 1- to 2-foot-diameter yellow flower heads, but any tall variety will do.

Plant the sunflowers on a raised bed, clearly marking where they are growing. This will help your kids know where the path is and where the sunflowers will be popping up. Sow seeds after all danger of frost has passed in your area.

When the sunflowers mature, teach kids how to harvest and roast the seeds, or let birds, like finches, enjoy the harvest.

Let Kids Decorate the Garden

In order to make a garden their own, kids will often want to help "decorate" it with toys, containers, and personal items. Unless you are in a community garden where these items may disappear, let your kids put their stamp on the garden. They will be more likely to visit and play in the garden if they have familiar objects in there. Once in the garden, it's more likely your child will help with watering, weeding, and harvesting. The garden should be a fun place to learn and live.

You may have to censor some of the objects your child wants to play with outdoors. Stuffed pets, special blankets, or breakable games may not be good items for outside, especially if they are forgotten during a rainstorm. It might be devastating for a child if her favorite stuffed pet is ruined in the rain. Encourage children to use waterproof objects like plastic animals and plastic signs to decorate the garden.

Create a Child's Window Box Garden

Windowsills are great places to grow small, kid-sized gardens. If you have a south, east, or west-facing window, consider building a window box to hang from the sill. Work with your children to pick out the best plants for their window box. Select medium-sized or cascading annual plants. They can pick out annual flowers by favorite colors, shapes, or their names. They may love growing flowers with names such as clown flower, money flower, and fan flower.

Work with your children to design, buy plants, and plant the window box. Encourage them to keep up with watering and fertilizing the plants. Let them give their flower names and suggest making up stories about their flowers. There are so many ways to engage your children in a fantasy world using a small window box garden.

For more on container gardening go to Chapter 8.

Create a Windowsill Herb Garden

If you can't attach a window box on your building's exterior, consider an indoor windowsill garden. Have a specific windowsill dedicated to your child. Work with her to select herbs that will grow best in that window. In most areas, it would be ideal if the window is facing south to get the most light. However, even a west or east-facing window will be able to support some herbs.

Some of the best herbs to grow in pots on a windowsill include chives, parsley, oregano, thyme, and rosemary. Work with your child to pick out the seeds or plants and pots. Have your child paint the pots and give the plants names. Help him water and care for the herbs and come up with specific recipes to use them. Have an herb garden party using the herbs in a meal with family and friends. We talk about growing plants indoors in Chapter 11.

Grow a Terrarium Garden

Winter doesn't have to mean the end of the garden. There are other ways to grow plants with your kids indoors in winter. One of the easiest and most fun is to grow a terrarium garden. Here's how.

1. **Use a fishbowl or a glass jar of almost any size with a large mouth as the growing container. Wash it with soapy water and let it dry.**

2. **Create a 1-inch-deep layer of crushed stones, a 1-half-inch layer of horticultural charcoal (available at garden centers) on top of the stones, and a 2-inch-thick layer of potting soil as the top layer of your growing medium.**

3. **Select plants that will grow well in low light, humid environments such as begonia, fern, mini-orchid, moss, and African violet.**

   Select small-sized plants that will fit well in the container and have room to grow. Make small holes in the soil medium and gently place and tuck in the new plants.

4. **Decorate the terrarium also with small rocks, sticks, and even your child's plastic toys.**

   Keep the soil moist, but not too wet and grow your terrarium in a room with indirect light. Prune plants as needed so no one plant grows large and takes over.

Grow a Potato Barrel

If you have space for a garbage can in your yard, you can grow potatoes in a barrel. It's fun, and kids will get a big kick out of the results.

Use a 5-gallon pot, an old garbage can, or a wooden barrel. Make sure it has adequate drainage holes in the bottom. Place 6 to 8 inches of potting soil on the bottom and two to three seed potatoes on top of the soil. Cover the spuds with more potting soil and water well. As the spuds grow, keep covering them with soil until you reach the top of the container. Keep the potatoes well watered all summer, and once the vines yellow and die, turn over the container with your kids and let them hunt for all the potatoes in the soil.

Grow Plants from Store Produce

Another fun way to get kids interested in gardening and growing food is to grow plants from vegetables and fruits you buy in the store. You may not be able to eat all the plants you create, but it fascinates kids that you can create new plants from produce in the grocery store. Here are some popular vegetables and fruits to grow:

- **Avocado.** Let an avocado pit dry out for a day or two, then plant it, pointed end up, in a 6-inch-diameter plastic pot filled with moistened potting soil. Leave the tip of the pit exposed to air. A fun way to sprout avocadoes is to suspend a pit over a glass of water. Poke three toothpicks around the middle of a pit and rest the toothpicks on the rim of the glass. Add water until it just touches the bottom of the pit. Kids can watch the roots and sprout emerge. It can take a month or two for roots to appear. If you're using the glass method, plant the pit in potting soil once a sprout emerges.

- **Carrots and beets.** Slice off the head end along with 1 to 2 inches of root and place it in a saucer filled with pebbles for support and water. In a week or so new greens should appear from the top. Then snug the root into a container filled with potting soil for a carrot or beet houseplant.

- **Pineapple.** The same technique used for carrots and beets can be used for pineapples. They take longer to regrow, but sure look cool.

- **Potatoes.** Take an old, shriveled potato. Prop up the potato with toothpicks (like an avocado pit) with its bottom end in a water-filled glass or place a potato piece with one to two eyes in a container of moistened potting soil. Within a week a new sprout will emerge.

Chapter 23

Ten Tips to Manage a Sustainable Urban Garden

• •

In This Chapter

▶ Defining sustainability for the urban gardener

▶ Discovering some important tips to maintaining a sustainable urban garden

▶ Remembering to involve your community and collaborate locally

• •

*S*ustainability involves three practices that ensure the wise use of water, materials, and other resources to make sure they last from one generation to the next and in harmony with nature. What are the responsible practices for the urban gardener (see Figure 23-1)? Sustainability boils down to the following three questions:

✔ Am I being environmentally responsible?

✔ Is what I want to do economically feasible?

✔ Can I have my community involved?

Figure 23-1: A sustainable urban gardening diagram.

Illustration by Paul Simon.

To make it easier on you, in this chapter, we've provided you with ten tips to help you maintain a sustainable garden.

Know Your Soil Conditions

Many urban gardeners are correct in thinking they have poor soil. The urban garden area is likely to be compacted and poor in structure and quality.

Once you have selected a garden area, test the soil to determine the soil type, pH, organic matter content, and available phosphate and potash. You can buy soil-testing kits at garden centers or send a soil sample to a soil-testing laboratory. See Chapter 4 for all the steps involved in analyzing your city soil conditions.

The key to improving the soil is to do it before you begin any planting. If you incorporate the proper amounts of organic matter and soil amendments, your soil will provide nutrients and make air and water more available to plants.

Compost Is Key

Aside from the conservation aspect of reducing our waste and not filling up our landfills, compost is a valuable *key* soil amendment and an effective mulch.

Compost improves soil structure, promotes plant growth, and helps soil store nutrients to keep them available for plants. Research shows that plants mulched with compost are more disease-resistant and sturdier than plants grown without compost.

Compost also improves all aspects and types of soil. What organic matter you use depends on local availability and personal preference. If you have enough homemade compost, use that. Otherwise, check garden centers or the Yellow Pages for companies that produce compost in bulk. Visually check the compost for weeds, insects, and foreign material. See Chapter 5 for more on adding compost to your urban garden.

Conserve Water and Harvest Your Rain

Clean water is a very precious commodity and in some regions of the world a scarce resource, especially in our urban communities.

A sustainable urban gardener will employ numerous methods and strategies to conserve water. From installing rain barrels and rain gardens to simply adjusting your mowing height, there are several easy steps to reduce your water use at home and employ sustainable conservation strategies. For more details see Chapter 19.

Use Organic Fertilizers

Being a sustainable urban gardener requires you to be environmentally responsible. Organic urban gardeners avoid using chemical fertilizers. Chemical fertilizers are carried into the soil via salts, and this part of their chemistry threatens the living creatures that work every day to build your soil.

You may think of chemical fertilizers as fast food. The plants respond rapidly to it, but because the salts dehydrate essential bacteria and fungi in the soil, its impact is short-lived and so must be repeated often to get the same effect.

Organic fertilizers add to the ecology in the soil because they are not carried by salts and have both short- and long-term impacts. Going with organic fertilizers is one simple choice that you can make to manage your garden's sustainably. See Chapter 5 for more on using organic fertilizers.

Preserve Existing Agriculture and Natural Resources

You may have heard the term *sustainable agriculture*, but what does it mean? In essence, it means putting as much back into the land as you take away, so that the land can continue producing indefinitely. Techniques include cover-cropping to add nutrients back to the soil to replace those harvested in crops, recycling nutrients by applying farm animals' manure to crop fields, and minimizing off-farm inputs. It also means minimizing the use of nonrenewable resources, because by definition these resources are finite and their use cannot be sustained indefinitely.

Advocates of sustainable farming — and sustainable living in general — feel that our mainstream consumer culture is not sustainable: We are using up our nonrenewable resources, especially fossil fuels. We are living on borrowed time, until the day that the earth's resources can no longer support us. Only by adopting more sustainable lifestyles can we conserve these nonrenewable resources and expect our children, grandchildren, and great-grandchildren to enjoy our high standard of living.

Urban gardeners can employ sustainable management practices to help gather community support and preserve remaining open lands available in our cities for continued agricultural and urban farming uses for the next generation.

Know Your Microclimate Conditions

We learned extensively in Chapter 3 about the urban microclimate. The urban climate is influenced by a variety of factors including solar radiation, surrounding air temperatures, air movement, sun orientation, humidity, topographical location, proximity to lakes or waterfront exposure, paved surfaces such as roads and parking lots, buildings, and existing rooftop conditions.

Understanding how to appropriately develop your landscape to mitigate the impacts of light and wind can help you create a microclimate that is beneficial to the urban environment and your wallet.

Being sustainable requires you to be economically responsibly as well! These green design initiatives can help reduce summer cooling costs and lower your winter heating bills. What a great incentive to be a sustainable urban gardener!

Select "the Right" Plants for Your Area

"The right" plants are well adapted to your urban environment and require little to no maintenance whatsoever. Native plants are pretty good candidates since they have evolved and adapted to local conditions. Natives are vigorous and hardy, able to withstand local weather patterns including winter's cold and summer's heat.

Once established, native plantings require no irrigation or fertilization. They're resistant to most pests and diseases. All these traits mean native plants suit the sustainable needs of today's urban gardener.

Besides natives, lots of hardy varieties of trees, shrubs, and perennials are available, many of which are also low maintenance and good sustainable choices. Chapter 16 discusses in detail how you can select "the right" planting varieties for your urban garden.

Consider Hydroponic and Aquaponic Gardening

Hydroponics involves growing plants without soil, however hydroponics, in its simplest form, is growing plants by supplying all necessary nutrients in the plants' water supply in a nutrient solution rather than through the soil. Growing plants hydroponically helps gardeners and farmers grow more food more rapidly in smaller areas (greenhouses, living rooms, classrooms, and rooftops, for instance) and to produce food in parts of the world where space, good soil, and/or water are limited.

In order for the plants to grow successfully, the nutrient solution must contain several elements, including nitrogen, potassium, phosphorus, iron, manganese, and sulfur.

In *Aquaponics*, the nutrient solution is water containing fish excrement. Aquaponics is the integration of hydroponics and aquaculture (the cultivation of the natural produce — like fish or shellfish — of water). Live fish are raised in a traditional fish tank. The fish excrete their waste into the surrounding water, which is used to supply nutrients to the growing plants positioned above the tank. Bacteria living in the water and on the growth medium eat the fish wastes and unlock nutrients for the plants. The plants absorb the nutrients, and the filtered water is returned to the fish tank.

Because hydroponic and aquaponic gardening can be done in small spaces, they are great options for urban gardeners.

Minimize the Costs

In order to meet the goals of being sustainable, you need to keep your costs low, and develop eco-friendly products that are financially reasonable so that the community as a whole can afford to take the steps they need to be sustainable urban gardeners.

Lighting is a good example: When energy efficient rated lighting products were first delivered to the market years ago they were generally too high in cost; However years later these prices have drastically fallen and today, many people are now purchasing and using energy efficient light bulbs in their homes. They are doing better for themselves and the environment because they can afford to do so.

Of course saving energy helps you save money on utility bills and helps protect the environment by reducing greenhouse gas emissions in the continued fight against climate change. But cost is a huge consideration for most of us and as stated at the beginning of this chapter, we need to ask ourselves: *"Is what I want to do economically feasible?"*

As our urban gardening products continue to become economically feasible, you will definitely see increased community interest to grow locally in urban centers.

Involve Your Community

Whether up on the rooftop or between buildings in a vacant lot, opportunities abound in your city to grow together with your community.

Urban gardening is about growing — growing flowers, growing vegetables and fruits, and growing a community of people who can share their love of gardening while taking good care of the earth.

Community gardens provide a place to meet new friends and to share gardening experiences. In fact, many community gardens offer workshops to help gardeners learn about seeds, crop rotation, companion planting, and organic pest control solutions to help keep the soil and their plants healthy.

Sometimes gardeners have their own plot, and sometimes the work and the harvest are shared by all the gardeners together. Some community gardens encourage other gardeners to grow a row for neighborhood food banks, kitchens, or local urban shelters.

Each community garden has its own personality, its own flavor, and its own pace, but all the gardens share the same general focus. Urban gardens are places where families can come together to produce their own food, help one another by sharing their experiences and enthusiasm for gardening, and beautify their neighborhoods in the process.

 Sustainability is not an outcome, it's a process of responsible maintenance. In order to manage your urban gardening practices well, you must succeed in all three areas, including environmental, economic, and community involvement. A collaborative effort and responsible management of the city landscape will grant you a successful and beautiful urban garden now and into the next generation!

Index

• **N** •

• **O** •